MW01122750

Humber College Library
3199 Lakeshore Blvd. West
Toronto, ON   M8V 1K8

MARKETING PUBLIC POLICY

Policy analysts and policy planners should start from the premise that obstacles, uncertainties and surprises are important features of policy-making. All public policies should be treated as complex problems, from the outset. Complexity theorists start from the premise that complex policies are ill-defined and ambiguous. There is often little consensus about what the problem is, let alone how to resolve it. Into the complexity of the wicked problem fray, *Marketing Public Policy* introduces the role of communication scholars and practitioners whose models and practices focus on people, processes, opinions and behaviour as causes of organisational complexity. Communication practice's role is to provide ideas on how to navigate, diagnose and interpret issues with a view to persuading the public to change its behaviour or opinions.

From the case studies presented in this book, we see that despite rationally excellent macro- and micro-planning of policies to win the hearts and minds of citizens, public policies still deteriorate into hurts and minefields. The case studies are drawn from China, Indonesia, India, the USA, the UK and Europe to show that policy-making is always a complex issue in any country, whatever the political structure, whether democracy or communism.

Basskaran Nair is an Adjunct Associate Professor at the Lee Kuan Yew School of Public Policy, Singapore, and the author of the books, *Primer in Public Relations in Singapore* and *From Main Street to Cyber Street: Changes in the Practice of Communication*. His research interests cover marketing communication, investor relations, media relations and issues management.

MARKETING PUBLIC POLICY

Complexity, Hurts and Minefields

Basskaran Nair

HUMBER LIBRARIES LAKESHORE CAMPUS
3199 Lakeshore Blvd West
TORONTO, ON.   M8V 1K8

Routledge
Taylor & Francis Group

LONDON AND NEW YORK

First published 2018
by Routledge
2 Park Square, Milton Park, Abingdon, Oxon OX14 4RN

and by Routledge
711 Third Avenue, New York, NY 10017

Routledge is an imprint of the Taylor & Francis Group, an informa business

© 2018 Basskaran Nair

The right of Basskaran Nair to be identified as author of this work has been asserted by him in accordance with sections 77 and 78 of the Copyright, Designs and Patents Act 1988.

All rights reserved. No part of this book may be reprinted or reproduced or utilised in any form or by any electronic, mechanical, or other means, now known or hereafter invented, including photocopying and recording, or in any information storage or retrieval system, without permission in writing from the publishers.

Trademark notice: Product or corporate names may be trademarks or registered trademarks, and are used only for identification and explanation without intent to infringe.

British Library Cataloguing-in-Publication Data
A catalogue record for this book is available from the British Library

Library of Congress Cataloguing-in-Publication Data
Names: Nair, Basskaran, author.
Title: Marketing public policy : complexity, hurts and minefields /
by Basskaran Nair.
Description: Abingdon, Oxon ; New York, NY : Routledge, 2018.
Identifiers: LCCN 2017047092| ISBN 9781138559967 (hbk) |
ISBN 9781138559974 (pbk) | ISBN 9780203712177 (ebk)
Subjects: LCSH: Policy sciences—Case studies. | Public policy—Case studies. |
Communication in politics—Case studies. | Advocacy advertising—Case
studies. | Persuasion (Psychology)—Case studies.
Classification: LCC H97 .N35 2018 | DDC 320.6–dc23
LC record available at https://lccn.loc.gov/2017047092

ISBN: 978-1-138-55996-7 (hbk)
ISBN: 978-1-138-55997-4 (pbk)
ISBN: 978-0-203-71217-7 (ebk)

Typeset in Bembo
by Wearset Ltd, Boldon, Tyne and Wear

To Chor Eng

CONTENTS

INTRODUCTION

The marketing of public policy

The premise in this book, *Marketing Public Policy: Complexity, Hurts and Minefields*, is that public policy execution is often not a neat sequential flow of actions. It is not a linear flow from the *identification* of policy problems, *agenda setting*, *formulation* of policy proposals, *legitimation* of policies through political actions and interest groups, to *implementation* of policies through the activities of executive agencies. And *evaluation* of policies by government agencies, the press, and the public is performed throughout the policy process. In the real world, these processes often happen simultaneously, each one collapsing into the others; an overlap, not a straight line. Public policy process is complex, volatile, uncertain, and ambiguous, minefields blowing the minds, hurting rather than winning the hearts of the public. For example, emotive opinions are often expressed even before the policies are correctly identified and the policy agendas properly framed. This book brings together complexity theories and communication (marketing) principles and applies them in order to understand and manage complex public policies.

Managing policy perception and understanding the hearts and minds of the public from initiation to implementation are often the missing elements in the public policy process. Consequently, a well-thought-out population paper on the hopes and aspirations for the people and the future of Singapore falls on hard and harsh grounds of public opinion. A thoughtful, detailed and experienced leader, Hillary Clinton, is defeated by an off-the-cuff, tweet-happy Donald Trump in the 2016 US presidential elections. The majority of UK voters opt to 'Leave the EU', falling prey to unaddressed, deep-seated anger leading to the resignation of the British Prime Minister, David Cameron; similar demagoguery has affected the 2017 European elections in several European nations.

In contrast, unpopular, complex and polarising policies are planned and implemented, resonating with the hearts and minds of the people. In the Philippines, President Rodrigo Duterte runs a kill-all-drug-pushers campaign and an anti-US foreign policy while his people are pro-America. He wins the presidency and continues to be popular with the people, despite human rights accusations and a foreign policy favouring China, when the people distrust China, because the people perceive law and order are being restored in a 'lawless' nation. In India, the Prime Minister Narendra Modi embarks on a highly disruptive demonetisation policy that leaves millions of people without cash, forcing rural folks in particular to queue at banks, and leading to a drop in the GDP. And yet he is still highly regarded as a strong leader doing a good job for them and for the nation in his anti-corruption drive. In China, President Xi Jinping adopts a long-drawn-out, painfully deep corruption drive that takes down ministers, top officials and thousands of government officials. It is carried out in the midst of economic and financial rollercoaster policies and with a high level of censorship, and still the majority of people look upon him as the leader doing the right thing.

For complex policy issues, this book takes as its reference the complexity theorists, Horst Rittel and Melvin Webber, Louis W. Koenig, James Horn, and more recently Jeff Conklin, Graham Room, Reimut Zohlnhofer, Friedbert Rub and others in the same field. The original thinkers on this subject are Rittel and Webber, two professors at the University of California, who wrote an article, 'Dilemmas in a general theory of planning' (1973). They define a wicked problem or a complex social problem:

> The search for scientific bases for confronting problems of social policy is bound to fail, because of the nature of these problems. They are 'wicked' problems, whereas science has developed to deal with 'tame' problems. Policy problems or social problems cannot be definitively described.[1]

Communication models and practice by Harold Lasswell, Wilbur Schramm, Carl Hovland, David Berlo and Leon Festinger share similar approaches to complexity theorists. For example, the policy process in the communication model entails viewing events and relationships as ever-changing without beginnings, ends, or any fixed sequence of events, and with all factors affecting one another. However, the aim of communication models and practices is to persuade, to change opinions and behaviour with the view to finding solutions, no matter how complex the policy problem, how uncertain the situation, and how polarising the stakeholders confronted with the problem. Communications practice is to deal with hearts and minds issues facing complex public policies, as described by complexity theories.

Structure of this book

The book is divided into three parts. Part I, 'Complexity and communication theories', contains Chapters 1–3 on complexity issues in relation to public policy and introduces the importance of institutions in the policy-making process. Part II, 'Communication practice', contains Chapters 4–7, focusing on communication-related issues, and the application of communication strategies to manage complex public policies. Part III, 'Issues management', contains the concluding chapter that wraps up the themes of the book, with case studies related to a deeper analysis of complexity and communication issues in the context of policy trade-offs.

Chapter 1 Public policy dynamics: it's communication in a complex world

In Chapter 1, policy dynamics are explored by looking at a range of conceptual policy models. Concepts express the fact that policies are often produced through patterned, path-dependent activity among a variety of policy actors. Various theoretical models are discussed that capture the significance of individuals, interest groups and institutions, how they interact, and how issues in the public domain find their way to become public policies. Some theories focus on the bottom-up flow of issues to become public policies (for example, claims making theory), while others focus on the top-down approach (for example, elite model and polyarchy theories). The next section examines a range of complexity theories described as critical junctures, 'wicked problems' or a 'social mess', all terms to describe the policy dynamics. The third section looks at communication models and practices mandated to pursue opinion and behaviour change as the key measurement of successful implementation. The final section is a case study, the Singapore White Paper on Population and Land Use; how the well-researched and well-thought-out policy paper to win the hearts and minds of the people became a 'hurts and minefield' policy outcome.

Chapter 2 Wicked problems and their application: it's hearts and minds communication

In Chapter 2, we will examine two cases of complex or wicked problems, namely, the US Affordable Healthcare Bill, eventually passed in 2012, commonly called ObamaCare, and the 2016 UK Referendum to Leave or Remain in the European Union, commonly called Brexit, when the Leave vote won. Both policies are classic cases of wicked problems, based on the definition of wicked problems by complexity theorists. Both policies were plagued by controversies at the time of policy implementation and execution. And realistically they will continue to be public policy case studies on volatility, uncertainty, complexity and ambiguity over the next decade. The discussion in this chapter takes Rittel and Webber's ten-point guidelines on what constitutes complex policies. Each case study is discussed in the light of these guidelines. The final section is on how a messy or complex policy can be addressed by marketing communication challenges. Communication models and theories share common grounds with complexity theories and are effectively geared to address the concerns of the receivers of public policies.

Chapter 3 Institutions and political structures: it's the source and channel of communication

In Chapter 3, we will look broadly at the key aspects of institutions, namely, people power, policy elites, core institutions, media, markets and global institutions. Each section, for example, people power, elite networks and so on, is not assumed to exist in a silo. They all intersect and are sometimes indistinguishable as distinct processes. For example, media are interlinked with people power and the elite network. Policy leaders have cited interfering forces that limit their ability to govern: factions within their parties, uncooperative legislators, the aggressive agents of global capital markets, international regulators, multilateral institutions, investigative journalists and social media campaigners and the micropowers of activists. The next two sections examine the role of these institutions in two vastly different forms of political structure: democracies, with a focus on the USA, and a communist structure, namely, China, where institutions exist for the good of the nation and its publics but without the democratic credentials. The final section is a further discussion of institutions and complexity, reflecting what complexity theorist Jeff Conklin calls fragmentation.

Chapter 4 Agenda setting, framing and priming: it's about managing your message

Chapter 4 examines the core concepts of agenda setting, framing and priming, followed by three case studies: (1) Indian Prime Minister Narendra Modi's unique effort to remove corruption; (2) Indonesian President Jokowi Widodo's management of ethnic and religious tensions; and (3) Chinese President Xi's strengthening of the Communist Party's control on domestic matters. Within the agenda framing-priming continuum, there are additional communication strategies. For instance, the best way for policy analysts to discover the real problems, in a complicated issue of many unknowns, is not by asking directly 'What's the problem?' but rather asking 'What's the story?' behind the issue. Policy narratives are structured storytelling to explain the complex policy dynamics for better public consumption. Persuasion tactics are also treated as priming the change in behaviour and opinions as part of the policy implementation and are planned around three elements: media, message and source. In recent years, social media have aggravated policy complexity; the final section discusses the role of social media, Facebook and Twitter, in the agenda framing and priming context.

Chapter 5 Social marketing: it's about managing your public's behaviour

Chapter 5 examines the use of social marketing to manage complex or wicked problems. The first section discusses social marketing and its development as a communication tool. Next is a detailed examination of barriers to action, based on a list of policy complexities faced by social marketers. One overriding question for social marketers is 'Why can't we sell human rights like we sell soap?' The next section examines how nudging principles based on the (2009) book *Nudge* by Richard Thaler and Cass Sunstein. They describe how neuroscience, social psychology and behavioural economics can help policy-makers influence people's behaviour, make their lives longer, healthier and better, while remaining free to do what they like. Nudging incorporates many social marketing principles to bring about opinion and behavioural changes. Subsequent sections highlight two distinct social marketing approaches. One states that behavioural change takes time as citizens move from ignorance or indifference before policy acceptance. The second is the appreciation of sense-making and segmentation to better influence behavioural and opinion change.

Chapter 6 Activism, advocacy and public opinion: it's about managing social movements

Chapter 6 discusses concepts related to advocacy and activism, making a distinction between three types of activism, namely, single issue mobilisation (SIM), volcanic events and social movements. This is followed by a discussion of activism in three countries where single issues and volcanic issues have become social movements. The three case studies are: (1) the Egyptian Movement for Change (popularly known by the slogan *Kifaya*), and the discussion includes harassment and violence against women protestors; (2) France's Poujadists, related to industrialisation and loss of traditional ways of life, morphing into a nationalist social movement that has similarities to other European countries, the UK and the USA; and (3) China where despite total control by the communist regime, activism exists. Egypt represents the Middle East's so-called Arab Spring movements; France represents the western world's 'left behind' social movements; and China represents the human spirit seeking redress from social injustices, despite total government control. Finally, in this chapter, there is a discussion on communication strategies by activists.

Chapter 7 New media are mainstream: it's a new channel for communication

Chapter 7 looks at complexity in the age of the Internet, exploring its impact and influence on policy formulation and execution. The Internet has created a global village where technology companies are almost nation states in their own rights. People are empowered by technology, and emboldened by living anonymously in a global village without leaving their nation states. The next section is the application of cyber communication to social marketing, social activism, and the agenda-framing–priming strategy. The third section examines a unique phenomenon in western democracies, namely, alternative or fake news, adopting strategies similar to rumour-mongering and propaganda. The final section examines challenges as nations and governments grapple with their citizens as netizens in a post-fact global village. The policy politics issue is governance in a new media age.

Chapter 8 National issues and trade-offs: it's communicating what is the best option

In Chapter 8, complexity in trade-offs is examined in several contexts. Trade-off, for example, takes place in a policy-making environment where most policy-makers do not know what their people want. Multiple changes and severe disruptions create trade-offs, and policy-makers cannot attend to each piece of the policy in isolation. Trade-off is linked closely to the marketplace and global trade. The next two sections are case studies on trade-offs. One is on migration, identity and assimilation with an overarching question: 'Why can't we sell human rights (migration) the way we sell soap?' Migration is a significant global issue. The other case study is on the South and East China Seas and the various claimants' trade-off positions and postures, with China as the chief protagonist in the trade-off discussion. The final section looks at communication practices applicable in trade-offs. Policy leaders are required to rally the stakeholders and persuade them to appreciate the policy vision and the policy challenges.

Note

1 Horst W. Rittel and Melvin M. Webber, 'Dilemmas in a general theory of planning', *Policy Sciences*, 4 (1973): 155–169.

PART I

Complexity and communication theories

1

PUBLIC POLICY DYNAMICS

It's communication in a complex world

To appreciate policy dynamics is to look at it from the perspective of 'objective' policy analysts: Policy issues are thrown up by the conflicts and tensions of human wants; policy politics dominate contemporary societies, as policy planners face counter-policies of activists and special interests groups; and these politicised wants take place in a world undergoing cataclysmic change, such as deglobalisation, technological change and nativism sentiments. Policy analysis is itself a form of cognitive mapping; policy-makers and their publics cannot be free of their own cognitive filters and prior preferences and bias. Complexity theories highlight the VUCA – volatile, uncertain, complex and ambiguous – world of politically motivated policy planning and execution. Any discussion on public policy dynamics, from incubation to implementation, uses as its reference a wide range of complexity theorists, primarily Horst W. Rittel and Melvin M. Webber,[1] James Horn,[2] and Jeff Conklin,[3] and, in addition, Louis W. Koenig,[4] Euel Elliott and L. Douglas Kiel,[5] Mark Mason,[6] Graham Room,[7] and Reimut Zohlnhofer and Friedbert W. Rub.[8]

In this chapter, policy dynamics are explored by looking at a range of conceptual policy models. Mark Considine advocates that we need to appreciate concepts which express the fact that policy is often produced through patterned, path-dependent activity among a complex of actors.[9] In the first section, the theoretical models capture the significance of individuals, interest groups and institutions, how they interact and how issues in the public domain find their way to become public policies. Some theories focus on the bottom-up flow of issues to become public policies while others focus on the top-down approach. The next section examines a range of complexity theories described as either critical junctures, 'wicked problems' or a 'social mess'. The third section looks at communication models and practices mandated to pursue opinion and behavioural change as the key measurement of successful implementation. The final section is a case study, the Singapore White Paper on Population and Land Use; how the well-researched and well-thought-out policy paper to win the hearts and minds of the people became a 'hurts and minefield' policy outcome.

Understanding policy models

In policy dynamics, people's wants and demands become policies only when they are directed at policy-makers and public officials, who decide to take them up as part of the policy process. How these wants and demands are modified or merged with others' wants and demands are discussed in numerous, conceptual models about public policy and complexity. A few models are examined in this section. For instance, the bottom-up social science models such as the claims-making, interest groups and social learning theory models. The top-down policy-making models include incrementalism, the elites, and polyarchy models. These models are not competitive in the sense that none of them could be judged to be the 'best'. While each concept is a thumbnail presentation in a silo, in reality, it exists in a combination: for example, rational policies are discussed with emotional theories, or claims theories with interest groups theories, and policy analysts have to see the interplay and overlap of these theories in practice.

The *rational policy process* assumes a systematic flow from problem identification (publicising societal problems), agenda setting (deciding which issues to be addressed), formulation (developing proposals to resolve issues), legitimation (persuading the public of the right thing to do, enacting into law), implementation (executive structures, communication strategies) and evaluation (impact studies, review and feedback, proposing future changes). This public policy model maintains that policy planners' aim to achieve the maximum social gain to society, which is to the benefit of the people, should exceed the costs by the greatest amount.[10] Page and Shapiro, in their (1992) book, *The Rational Public*, maintain that collective public preferences pursued as rational policy display a greater degree of stability and cogency, far exceeding the typical individual level of preferences.[11] From the complexity perspective, there are many barriers to rational decisions. For example, rational policy decisions are often stonewalled by the almost irrational reactions of the citizen-publics. People generally have 'non-attitudes' and do not have meaningful beliefs even on issues that have been in the public domain for substantial periods of time.[12]

Emotional theories focus on the role that emotions play in shaping policies, guiding attention and modulating how actively citizens take actions or perform no actions at all. Policy planners pay attention to three common emotions: (1) enthusiasm causes people to take a greater interest in politics and policies; (2) fear causes citizens to pay greater attention to what is happening, seek out more information, reconsider their options in the light of available information, avoid risky courses of actions, and prefer public policies focused on prevention and protection; and (3) anger causes citizens to stick to their convictions, eschew promises, spend less time thinking things through, embrace risks more readily, and prefer aggressive and punitive public policies.[13] From the complexity perspective, emotions are extremely difficult to quantify. Often when the policy has been implemented, then the emotional outpouring, often as negative reactions to the public policy, appears.

Social learning theory, developed by behaviourists Albert Bandura[14] and B. F. Skinner[15] maintains that to bring about behaviour change, for example, safe sex or safe driving, there must be continuous reciprocal interaction and continuous feedback to the individuals. Individuals in other words have to practise behavioural changes personally, but are aided by continuous feedback from their environment, and rewarded for their efforts to accomplish the relevant task. The theory assumes that through communication of the accepted norms of behaviour, such as making the tasks easy to accomplish and encouragement, the individuals and the affected community of individuals will change. From the complexity perspective, it assumes self-discipline of the individual and the policy planners' capacity to provide 'continuous' environmental support. Behavioural change being determined by self-discipline and appreciation of the consequences is easier said than done.

Claims-making theory examines people and the interest groups representing them to make claims about social conditions; it does not matter whether the conditions exist; it matters only that people make claims about them.[16] Crime problems are social problems brought to public attention and to policy-makers through claims made by activists, public officials or the press. Claims-making attracts media coverage and that often results in receiving policy-makers' attention. People learn to cooperate after they assess whether or not other people will assist them; the potential cooperators will find that working together is usually more in their interests than being in dispute.[17] From the complexity perspective, policy planners cannot escape the constant bombarding of claims by citizens and the interest groups. Even if seemingly solved or satisfied, claims-making groups will return as all solutions are inherently subjective.

Interest groups theories: people come together for a common cause and generally have already developed strong emotions relating to the public policy. David Truman, in his (1954) book *The Government Process*,[18] states that individuals with common interests band together to press their demands on government. Interest groups become essentially the bridge between the individual and the government. Interest groups have organisational strength and persistence to bring about changes through bargaining, negotiation and compromise. From the complexity perspective, excessive activism by such interest groups impacts negatively on policy implementation, creating complexity, ambiguity and polarisation. Vested interest groups sometimes believe they are the public, confusing their own opinions with public opinion.

The *elite model* examines the preferences and values of governing elites, generally drawn disproportionately from the upper socio-economic strata of society. Given the vested interests of the elites, changes in public policy initiated by them will be incremental rather than revolutionary. Active elites are subject to relatively little direct influence from the masses who are regarded by the elites as apathetic, largely passive, and ill-informed. Communication between elites and the masses, most of the time, flows downwards.[19] From the complexity perspective, public policy does not reflect the demands of the masses but rather the prevailing values of the elites. However, when the masses feel deeply aggrieved at elite-driven policies that negate their livelihood, it engenders 'people power' activism.

Polyarchy theory is a variant of elite theory, influencing policy decisions. Charles E. Lindblom, an early writer on the polyarchy theory in policy and decision-making, notes the privileged position of business in the polyarchy model.[20] He introduced the concept of 'circularity', or 'controlled volitions' where the masses, even in democracies, are persuaded to ask from elites what elites wish to give them. There are similarities between polyarchy and elite theories. From the complexity perspective, any real public choices and competition are limited. In the polyarchy model, even with democratic governance, certain groups of elites – bankers, Wall Street investment community – gain crucial advantages, and collude with one another instead of competing.

The *incrementalism model* refers to incremental modifications to public policies in part due to imperfect information and the policy-makers playing it safe. Political scientist Charles E. Lindblom discussed this model, pointing out that the constraints of time, information and the costs of alternative policies prevent the identification of the full range of policy alternatives and the consequences. Incrementalism is conservative and tends to be politically expedient.[21] From the complexity perspective, the constraints of politics and the uncertainty concerning fresh policy alternatives preclude any radical change. Comfortable and often complacent elite policy leadership prefers to pursue incrementalism.

The *public choice model* recognises that governments perform certain functions related to providing the public good, such as national defence, which the market cannot provide. In public choice policy-making, the leadership is preoccupied with the future; it aspires to anticipate and even to prescribe what the future should be, despite imperfect knowledge and information, limited human ability to conceive all possibilities latent in a complex social problem.[22] All stakeholders – voters, politicians, bureaucrats, interest groups, elites, institutions – seek to maximise their personal benefits in politics as well as in the marketplace. While the stakeholders pursue self-interest, the public mutually benefits through this collective decision-making.[23] From the complexity perspective, politicians, especially during election campaigns, make policy promises to win elections, fail to offer clear policy alternatives, and after the elections do not feel compelled to pursue the policy promises.

The *institutional model* focuses on government and quasi-government institutions that enable public policy to be authoritatively determined, implemented, and enforced by these institutions. Institutions are the rules of the game in political systems. They are often formal in the sense they are binding upon participants, though they do not have to be.[24] The institutional grid that shapes public policy begins at the macro level, namely, the constitutions which establish formal relationships between the legislature, the executive and the judiciary. From the complexity perspective, it is a study of the complex interplay of the three main institutions, namely, the judiciary, the legislative and the executive branches and the Fourth

Estate, the media. Often the interaction of these institutions leads to the politics of decision-making as politics dominates the policy-making process.

Public opinion is embedded in all the above models and theories. Gallup Poll's question – *What is the most important issue facing the United States today?* – is a question all nations should ask of their people to understand the groundswell issues. The ebb and flow of social issues that emerge out of the polls raise important questions: What is the social problem? What affects the cycle of defining social problems? Who gets to define social problems and what to do about them? How do we discover information that shapes people's perception of social problems?[25] In practice, there are many factors that negate this perfect congruence between public policy and public opinion. The media, an active player, with political bias, often negates the 'idyllic' congruence. Whatever the theoretical or conceptual framework, policy leaders must treat all social issues as complex problems; not doing so attracts *faux pas*, particularly with public opinion going against well-meaning public policy.

Understanding complexity theories

Any discussion of public policy dynamics, from incubation to implementation, must take as its reference the complexity theorists, Rittel and Webber, Jeff Conklin, and James Horn. In this book there is a stronger focus on the perspectives of complexity from the original thinkers on this subject, Rittel and Webber, two professors at the University of California; presented in their Abstract to their article, 'Dilemmas in a general theory of planning'. The key points are that while science has developed to deal with 'tame' problems, this is not the case in the social science field. One cannot apply scientific bases to confront social policy problems. They describe the nature of these problems as 'wicked' problems, as there is no objective definition of social equity. It makes no sense to talk about 'optimal solutions' to social problems unless severe qualifications are imposed first. Even worse, there are no 'solutions' in the sense of definitive and objective answers.[26]

James Horn, in his (2008) book, *Human Research and Complexity Theory*, writes that the new sciences of complexity signal the emergence of a new scientific paradigm, challenging the core assumptions of positivism. Positivism states, like science, there is a positive solution to a problem. On the one hand, this requires a new kind of social science inquiry. One that demands both rigour and imagination in coming to understand the emergence and behaviour of social systems and the subsystems that comprise them. The language, concepts and principles of complexity are central to the development of a new science of qualities to complement the science of quantities that has shaped our understanding of the physical and social worlds.[27]

Most of the conceptual models and the literature on public policy focus on the policy-making and implementation processes. They are not adequately focused on the public or the receivers who are affected by the policy. Complexity theorists pay more attention to the 'restive clients'. Rittel and Webber talk about the restive clients, 'hearing their ever-louder protests' about public services. Few modern professionals seem to be immune to popular attack – whether they are social workers, educators, public health officials, policemen, city planners, highway engineers or physicians.

> Our restive clients have been telling us that they don't like the educational programs that schoolmen have been offering, the redevelopment projects urban renewal agencies have been proposing, the law-enforcement styles of the police, the administrative behavior of the welfare agencies, the locations of the highways, and so on. In the courts, the streets, and the political campaigns, we've been hearing ever-louder public protests against the professions' diagnoses of the clients' problems, against professionally designed governmental programs, against professionally certified standards for the public services.[28]

Jeff Conklin discusses tame problems as positivism, as the stagiest approaches. Tame problems have well-defined problem statements, a definite stopping point, i.e. we know when a solution has been reached, a solution which can be objectively evaluated, and they have solutions which can be tried and abandoned. In contrast, given the complex interdependences associated with public policies, wicked problems are often never solved but rather they keep recurring and morphing into other aspects of complexity. Wicked problems, or a 'social mess', are not well understood until after the formulation of a potential solution. The problem definition tends to change over time, and has different meanings and salience to different people. Moreover, there are so many factors and conditions, all embedded in a dynamic social context, that no two wicked problems are alike, and the solutions to them will always be custom-designed and fitted to their own coordinates. Over time, one acquires wisdom and experience about the approach to wicked problems, but one is always a beginner in the specifics of a new wicked problem.[29]

Louis Koenig, in his (1986) book, *An Introduction to Public Policy*, maintains that policy complexity or critical junctures, as he calls them, are seen at both the macro-policy and micro-policy levels. *Macro-policy* comprises an array of critical junctures stemming from the interactions of individuals and groups, public officials and government entities at major stages in policy-making. After the policy alternatives have been developed, policy-makers are engrossed in choosing between them. After adoption, the policies require implementation, which Koenig maintains is fraught with obstacles, uncertainties and surprises; implementation is a frequent provider of critical junctures. *Micro-policy* reflects the reality taking place in the minds of the individual participants: how do participants perceive the environment and its problems? How do they think about solutions? How do they act under conditions of incomplete information and under the pressures of personal motivation and political interest? Micro-policy is more granular: who decides, and by what criteria, which wants or issues are to be taken up and which are not? Do responses to these questions disclose patterns by which some groups enjoy far greater success then others in pushing their concerns onto agendas, indicating that the policy system is far from even-handed? Or is it that the system responds to issues pressed by a broad range of groups and the real question is not yes or no, acceptance or rejection, but compromise, often of some complexity, with roughly equitable sharing of results?[30]

In short, complex policies are ill-defined, ambiguous and associated with strong moral, political and professional public issues. They are strongly stakeholder-dependent, there is often little consensus about what the problem is, let alone how to resolve it.

Communication models track complexity

Communication models track many of the public policy conceptual models as they are also involved in knowing the policy planners, the publics, and the policy politics, and they highlight the role of the media in the policy process. One communication model is the *Source-Message-Channel and Receiver* (SMCR) model: Source is the policy planner/leader; Message is the policy context; Channel is the means of communication between policy leaders and the public; and Receiver is the citizens, communities, voters, and so on. In another communication model, *social marketing*, the social marketers spend a lot of time to understand people and communities when implementing their respective social or public policy campaigns. Social marketers calculate the cost-benefit in social programmes to achieve the maximum social gain and select the most efficient policy alternatives. In the case of claims-making theories of public policy, the media highlight, for example, the public issue of sexual abuse of minors by priests, sporting and TV personalities. The media spotlight reveals widespread social problems requiring urgent remedies by policy planners. Communication studies include issues and media management and content analysis. In the elite public policy model, we see the rise of movements like the Occupy Movement, as a result of elite dominance that has gone too far: the '1% dominating the 99%' slogan galvanised activism against elite power abuse.

Communication scholars like Wilbur Schramm[31] and Joseph T. Klapper[32] introduced the concept of communication as process. Communication models track the Behaviourists' School and fit closely with the traditional Newtonian view of process as chance, as flux.[33] They pay more attention to behaviour, which was defined relationally, and the basic unit of analysis is an individual behavioural act – a response. The behaviourist's primary assumption is that events are more serial than hierarchical. Process in the communication model entails viewing events and relationships as ever-changing without beginnings, ends, or any fixed sequence of events, and with all factors affecting one another. Communication is a process, sequences of communicative acts that are managed over time, and these acts mutually influence one another.[34] Wilbur Schramm, a communication guru, looked at innovation diffusion and adoption (from early to late adopters); policy adoption by the majority take much longer as it depends on motivations to accept policy changes.

Communication process was also made famous by Harold Lasswell, often quoted in the policy-making and political science literature, as the author of this dictum:

'*Who? Says what? To whom? In what channel? And with what effect?*'[35] Berlo and other communication theorists took this Lasswellian perspective and added that process suggests the time-dependent and sequential character of communication exchanges. Walter Lippmann, in his (1922) book, *Public Opinion*, on human communication, observed the contestation between man and his environment, which he called the 'pseudo-environment':

> To that pseudo-environment, his behavior is a response. But because it is behavior, the consequences, if they are acts, operate not in the pseudo-environment where the behavior is stimulated, but in the real environment where action eventuates ... besides 'not understanding the problem' shows up as different stakeholders who are certain that their version of the problem is correct. In severe cases, such as many political situations, each stakeholder's position about what the problem is reflects the mission and objectives of the organization (or region) they represent.[36]

Communication writers on persuasion approach the subject from the perspective of policy complexity: the need to proactively address public reactions, often negative, to public policies. They focus on the policy content as messages or narratives to be conveyed to the public. To be persuasive, a message has to present something of value to the target public. It must also be compatible with public's motives and sentiments, and the politics of the policy process. If the public has to make some adjustments to accept a new or different idea, the communication planner must provide a clear statement of that adjustment and the rationale for making it. This message management falls within Leon Festinger's theory of cognitive dissonance. That is, there is a tendency for individuals to seek consistency among their cognitions (i.e. beliefs, opinions). When there is an inconsistency between attitudes or behaviours (dissonance), something must change to eliminate the dissonance. In the case of a discrepancy between attitudes and behaviour, it is most likely that the attitude will change to accommodate the behaviour. Two factors affect the strength of the dissonance: the number of dissonant beliefs, and the importance attached to each belief. There are three ways to eliminate dissonance: (1) reduce the importance of the dissonant beliefs; (2) add more consonant beliefs that outweigh the dissonant beliefs; or (3) change the dissonant beliefs so that they are no longer inconsistent. Dissonance occurs most often in situations where an individual must choose between two incompatible beliefs or actions. The greatest dissonance is created when the two alternatives are equally attractive. Furthermore, attitude change is more likely in the direction of less incentive since this results in lower dissonance. In this respect, dissonance theory is contradictory to most behavioural theories which would predict greater attitude change with increased incentive (i.e. reinforcement).[37]

In discussing dissonance, the public's reaction to the policy implementation is usually the 'critical juncture' that defines the hearts and minds issues. There are at least three schools of thought on public opinion: (1) pessimists; (2) pragmatists; and (3) populists, or optimists. Sherry Devereaux Ferguson notes:

In conclusion, the first school of philosophers (pessimists) views citizen engagement as undesirable and unnecessary. The second school of thought (pragmatists) views citizen involvement as undesirable but necessary. The third group of philosophers (optimists) views citizen engagement as both desirable and necessary.[38]

The different schools have different beliefs:

- *Pessimists*: Converse's work (1964) has suggested that a large proportion of the electorates do not have meaningful beliefs, even on issues that have formed the basis of intense political controversy among elites for substantial periods of time. His argument was based on an analysis of the stability of people's opinions on political issues. It turned out that some people easily change their opinions about certain issues even though exactly the same question is asked, while others do not change their opinions at all. This change was interpreted as indicating a lack of a strong opinion on these issues, which Converse referred to as non-attitudes.[39]

- *Populists*: They advocate full participation in matters of government, arguing that decisions made without the knowledge of public opinion will not represent the opinion, often influenced by lobby or special interest groups. They certainly do not believe that governments should check daily public opinion polls or referenda to decide their agendas. Pessimists would disagree and argue that when leaders look to public opinion (as manifested in surveys, focus groups, the press, and Internet news groups), they become followers rather than leaders. For the populist's supporters, in a modern democracy, the government is elected to facilitate public participation in the management of the nation, while the media are included within the structure to 'serve as an institution that, in structural terms, mediates between the state and society'.[40]

- *Pragmatists*: They maintain that public consent is a prerequisite to the formation of government but it should not extend to much more. Pragmatists see that activists – elites within society – occupy this platform, guiding opinions by working on the people's expectations, oxygenating them with a wide and varied array of information that dovetails with social cues, current conditions and the anticipation of events and outcomes to favour their agenda.

Enter the Internet age and in communication practices and models, social media are turning communication theories on their head. The public, the citizens are both the source controlling the message and the medium – for example, with the smartphone – to manage the communication. In addition, exceptional speed is now the norm. John Tomlinson, in *The Culture of Speed* (2007), writes that speed has preoccupied the cultural imagination of modern societies and that the experience of speed and immediacy has been reflected in the inherent economic unevenness and the inequality of capitalist globalisation.[41] The incredible shrinking news cycle has forced governments and politicians to be on the alert every minute to respond to an opponent, respond to a news story, or simply respond to an errant tweet.

When complex is treated as a neat problem

John Authers, a *Financial Times* correspondent, writes that the greatest dangers to us are not things we perceive to be high risk, because we generally treat them carefully.[42] Trouble arises from that which we perceive to be low risk. Authers was referring to the 2008 financial crisis when rating agencies gave securities firms (stock-broking firms) Triple-A ratings when it would have been more prudent to have alerted the investors that these firms' ratings were 'Speculative'. His remark is pertinent to public policy management. It is better for policy planners, elites or leaders to rate or approach public policies, from the incubation through implementation, not as low risk or neat issues with positive assessment but as high risk or complex or 'wicked' or a social mess.

It is the nature of policy politics that makes public policies inherently 'wicked'. It involves people who live in pluralistic societies with a pluralistic perspective. Planners talk about solutions but in reality solutions are a moving target and are never definitive. One must avoid being caught in a 'decision trap', typically producing sub-optimal decisions. Horn warns of challenges to the core assumptions of positivism and asks that planners develop a new kind of social science that demands both rigour and imagination.

Case study 1.1: the Singapore White Paper on population

Singapore's White Paper on population, *A Sustainable Population for a Dynamic Singapore*,[43] is an example of a complex policy executed as a neat problem. It fits in with Jeff Conklin's definition of a tame problem, namely, a relatively well-defined and stable problem statement; has a definite stopping point, i.e. we know when a solution is reached; the solution can be objectively evaluated as being right or wrong; and it has solutions which can be tried and abandoned. It did not factor 'wickedness' as strongly as it should have if treated as a complex problem. Cognitive dissonance among stakeholders seemed irrelevant and did not take into consideration the complex interdependences when an issue is treated as a problem. It was executed with complacent confidence by both the bureaucratic and political leadership.

A neat social problem: the hearts, home and hope narrative

The Singapore government has a well-deserved reputation for its long-term, forward-looking approach to land use planning. Over the years, it had earned high praise for planning and execution. It successfully transformed the island-state from a chaotic 'Third World' country without adequate housing, basic sanitation and infrastructure in the 1960s, to the gleaming, efficient, well-run country it is today. In recent years, however, Singapore has experienced rapid population growth, largely due to immigration. The heightened increase in the numbers of foreigners introduced unfamiliar friction into Singapore's societal and political fabric. Public dissatisfaction grew. In response to growing public concerns over the long-term viability of its population policies and the liveability of the island, the Singapore government formulated and released a White Paper on Population.[44] The White Paper was produced by the National Population and Talent Division, charting how the citizen population would change under various social scenarios, and it proposed a major shift in the light of a significant slowdown in the growth rate of the work-force and the resident population. In addition, it addressed complex policy issues related to an ageing population and elderly citizens, the poor and those left behind, discussing health care with a strong focus on medical costs, education, and foreign workers and immigrants, based on a year-long public engagement effort to gather the views and suggestions of Singaporeans.

Since immigration issues featured prominently as a public concern, the White Paper's key suggestions pertained to the immigration issue. Options included: set tighter controls on the inflow of new immigrants; set more stringent criteria to ensure quality and the commitment of immigrants; greater differentiation in bene-fits for Singaporeans, commensurate with National Service obligations; and provide more information on the immigration framework and criteria. It elegantly placed issues and solutions against the backdrop of the home, heart and hope narrative for Singapore residents. In the summary, the White Paper stated that the government would plan and invest in infrastructure ahead of demand, create high quality urban spaces and ensure that the infrastructure could support a range of population tra-jectories, with a total population of about 5.8–6.0 million in 2020, and 6.5–6.9 million in 2030. The White Paper had a supplementary paper on the Land Use Plan, which was issued a day after the White Paper. Moreover, it was presented to the public that the government under Prime Minister Lee Hsien Loong's steward-ship would not leave the controversial population issue to his successor.

Public reaction: hurts and minefields

This thoughtful, well-researched, neatly prepared and efficiently presented major public policy paper was badly received by the public. The government did not expect such a negative reaction. It came as a big surprise. Prime Minister Lee himself acknowledged that the government could have done better in presenting the White Paper on Population to the public. Writing on the subject, *Straits Times* columnist Rachel Cheng said:

> In the wake of the parliamentary debate on the Population White Paper, People's Action Party (PAP) politicians probably feel like they have been hit by a truck. Some think that they had actually anticipated the national furore

and therefore scheduled the White Paper for the Monday after the Punggol East bye-election. But the chain of events was so unfortunate that it is unlikely that it unfolded by design. It is hard to imagine any senior politician wanting to be caught on the back foot, clarifying that the paper contained a 'worst-case scenario' and beseeching the people to trust them.[45]

Coming in the midst of the year-long National Conversation in which citizens' views were sought on national issues, the White Paper turned out to be a major public relations gaffe.

It triggered a passionate and lively week-long debate in Parliament on the document. Criticism online and offline honed in, sometimes in a xenophobic manner, on the projected population of up to 6.9 million in 2030. At least 42 Members of Parliament (MPs), including all ten from the opposition, raised residents' concerns about overcrowding, the cost of living, and competition for jobs and university places by foreigners. Party affiliation mattered little as even ruling party MPs spoke up strongly against it. Not only did the White Paper elicit the normal grumblings that Singaporeans are well known for, but it also sparked online protests and real ones at Hong Lim Park, (a Speaker's Corner) where the rallying cry was 'Singapore for Singaporeans'.

What happened? First, the public reaction was a classic 'hurts and minefield', a case study of policy leadership treating a complex 'wicked' policy as a neat one. Policy leaders focused on the rationale argument, rationally presented. In the years leading up to the 2011 General Elections (GE 2011), there had been heated debates on public issues related to the elderly, the poor, healthcare, education, and foreign workers and immigrants, the overcrowded transport system and housing. Strong negative public sentiments had built up against the government. The outcome of the GE 2011 elections is that the ruling governing party lost almost 40 per cent of the votes. It shook the government sufficiently to address these public issues. For example, on housing, the challenge was to fine-tune policies to meet the aspirations of the different sectors more closely. The housing segmented categories included the first-time flat seeker; the sandwich middle class; the singles; and the marginalised groups like single mothers and divorcees with children. In other areas such as in the transport sector, commuters were challenged by overcrowded trains and buses. There was intense competition for road space among cars, buses, taxis, bicycles and pedestrians. Vehicle owners were frustrated with the Certificate of Entitlements (COEs), which is a permit to buy a vehicle. The supply of COEs depended on market forces, the growth of the car population, and government policies regulating demand. Public anger was compounded when the transport public listed companies reported profits, while overcrowding, rail breakdowns and delayed buses were the norm. The government addressed these complex problems expeditiously, including the following policies: segmenting the public; being relevant; and implementing policies with focused attention and in quick succession to resonate with the target publics.[46]

Second, the government's timing and management of the White Paper presentation created considerable uncertainty, and ambiguity. It gave very little time from the release of the White Paper to the parliamentary and public debate on it. Questions were raised on the haste to push the policy through, even though it was a proposal that is going to have a 'huge impact on every one of us, our children and our grandchildren'. It cannot be rushed through in one week. Academics, economists and sociologists were left puzzled over the scholarship behind the White Paper's research, with some calling its trade-offs between population, workforce growth and economic dynamism 'overly mechanistic, economically simplistic and astonishingly sociologically and politically naïve'.[47] In the haste to push it out, there were glaring mistakes. A section that classified 'nursing' as a low-skilled occupation triggered an apology from the Prime Minister.

The ruling party's own MPs felt the White Paper came across as too 'hard', in that it was all about numbers. They wanted more clarity on the assumptions to highlight the Singaporean core, and to clarify the numbers. The projection of a total population of about 5.8–6.0 million in 2020 and 6.5–6.9 million in 2030 was not accepted. There were differing views. Former urban planner Liu Thai Ker said Singapore should plan for population growth, both local and foreign, as slow a pace as possible, should look at the land use and they need not be confined to only 6.9 million but should think in terms of 10 million.[48] It seemed like the policy intent was perfectly sound but the policy execution was poorly conceived.

Third, as indicated, the communication planning process was badly handled. For example, the media were briefed before the MPs were informed!! MPs were given the whole report to digest and communicate to their constituents and other interest groups within a time span of only 24 hours. The media asked the MPs for their views and the MPs were stumped as the media had received the report before they did. And the Land Use White Paper came out one day after, when it contained critical support data on how the government could accommodate 6.9 million people. In recent years, on its own admission, infrastructure growth has not been able to catch up, the planning system has been 'thrown out of gear', creating an unprecedented infrastructural crunch.[49] In the Mass Rapid Transit (MRT) stations, dense crowds would gather on the train platforms during peak hours, unable to squeeze on to the overcrowded train carriages. The framing of the White Paper section on transport was wordy and maybe too rational. As one blogger noted, in an age of social media, nobody shares a 41-page White Paper full of jargon and pie charts, and suggested that the government should adopt a better and more succinct headline presentation.

Fourth, the interconnecting complexity of the issues raised were a problem. For example, the ageing population and healthcare services for the elderly were negatively framed. There was a request from women's movements and related organisations for more transformational thinking to mobilise the elderly population to continue contributing to society and to view them in the context of the silver-hair economy. This 'positive ageing' concept ran counter to the worries expressed in the White Paper regarding the ageing population. The White Paper focused on the increase in the dependency ratio (number of ageing adults to a working young adult), and whether the ageing population would raise the tax burden of the workforce.

Also, people do not think about the future population shrinking when daily they encounter the present big squeeze in the trains, on the roads and common areas, together with the prices of homes, food and cost of living escalating with heightened demand. The people wanted short-term issues to be solved before addressing the longer-term challenges of including how to support an ageing population. Consequently, the positive tone in the Population White Paper was in sharp contrast to the excessive negativity among the media and netizens who framed the projected population of up to 6.9 million by 2030 as a disaster scenario for Singapore's well-being.

And, finally, given the public backlash, there were contradictory comments from the government leadership. The political leadership started reframing the issue, fudging on the 6.9 million population projection. Two days after the public backlash, the National Development Minister Khaw Boon Wan reframed the 6.9 million figure as a 'worst-case scenario'. Deputy Prime Minister Teo Chee Hean took yet another approach. He presented three scenarios in Parliament – of unbridled, moderate and zero growth. He emphasised that the government proposed to take the middle path.[50] The Prime Minister posted on his Facebook page that 6.9 million is not a target but an aggressive scenario and that the government must prepare and build infrastructure far ahead of demand. If that was the case, the better option would have been to release the Land Use White Paper first, and then issue the Population White Paper one or two days later and put population projections in the context of urban planning and land use.

As a complex problem, this White Paper falls well within Horn's list of what constitutes the classic 'wicked' problem. Most of the criticism weighed in on the White Paper's projection that Singapore's population could hit 6.9 million by 2030. The Prime Minister acknowledged that it was a very complicated and emotional issue. Political observers say this marked a big shift in position, with some saying the government had to backtrack and effectively set aside its highly controversial projection of 6.9 million. The shifting population targets given by ministers hinted at confusion within the Cabinet. There were unfortunate, unintended consequences: people used this complex issue to engage in destructive discourse, which was neither responsible nor reasoned, and front-line civil service officers had to endure abuse and threats as anti-establishment sentiments swelled. A key message that the Ministry of National Development tried to get across was that dense cities are not the same as unliveable ones. Government planners were confident that they could, through innovative urban solutions and more efficient use of land, cater comfortably to a population much larger than Singapore's current size.

Aftermath of the Population White Paper

One outcome is that, while the Prime Minister, after being praised for not leaving the controversial issue to his successor, did leave it to his successor when he promised that the government would not decide on a population size beyond 2020. Another outcome was a different tack taken regarding the ageing population. It recognised their past contributions and the government set aside S$8 billion as a Pioneer Package, to help senior citizens above the age of 65 till their demise with medical and other subsidies. The narrative that followed was more on positive ageing and the government encouraging greater collaboration with several advocacy groups.

Four years later, the key assumptions in the White Paper have not changed. Productivity growth in Singapore has been uneven and uncertain. The White Paper had projected that in order to achieve an average of 3–5 per cent GDP growth by 2020, Singapore would need 2–3 per cent productivity growth. Singapore citizens' continued displeasure at the immigration problem has been reflected on a global scale – a backlash against seemingly uncontrolled immigration led to Brexit and the election of an anti-immigrant US president. Similar nationalism and a nativism backlash have been recorded in several European nations. The ruling party paid a political price not because the reasoning behind its immigration policies was wrong, but because it messed up the execution. One cannot expect the people to support a policy with no immediate benefits to their daily lives, while enduring daily infrastructure deficiencies in the present.[51]

Conclusion: complexity, hurts and minefields

Policy analysis is cognitive mapping, and policy analysts and policy planners should start from the premise that obstacles, uncertainties and surprises are important features of policy-making. All public policies should be treated as complex problems, from the outset. Complexity theorists start from the premise that complex policies are ill-defined and ambiguous and there is often little consensus about what the problem is, let alone how to resolve it.

Into the complexity of the wicked problem fray, this book introduces the role of communication scholars and practitioners whose models and practices have focused on processes, opinions and behaviour as causes of organisational complexity. Communication models and practice use relationships, individual behaviour, and not discrete events, as the unit of analysis. They take into consideration public sentiments which, for instance, under the theory of cognitive dissonance means that the policies people are persuaded to accept collides with what they think they should do. In practice, people resolve the conflict by justifying their actions, rationalising their behaviour and modifying their opinion.

Communication practice is to provide ideas on how to navigate, diagnose, and interpret issues with a view to persuading the public to change its behaviour or opinions. Governments, policy planners and leaders must pay more attention to the public communication of complex issues at the macro-policy level where there is an array of critical junctures (or complexity). From the case study of the Singapore White Paper on Population, and other case studies in subsequent chapters, we can see that despite rationally excellent macro- and micro-planning of a policy to win the hearts and minds of its citizens, public policies deteriorate into hurts and minefields.

Notes

1 Horst W. Rittel and Melvin M. Webber, 'Dilemmas in a general theory of planning', *Policy Sciences*, 4 (1973): 155–169.
2 James Horn, *Human Research and Complexity Theory* (Chichester: John Wiley & Sons, 2008).
3 Jeff Conklin, 'Paper on wicked problems and social complexity', available at: www. cognexus.org, 2010.
4 Louis Koenig, *An Introduction to Public Policy* (Englewood Cliffs, NJ: Prentice Hall, 1986).
5 Euel Elliott and L. Douglas Kiel, *Non-Linear Dynamics, Complexity and Public Policy* (New York: Nova Science Publishers, 1999).
6 Mark Mason (ed.), *Complexity Theory and Philosophy of Education* (Chichester: Wiley-Blackwell, 2008).
7 Graham Room, *Complexity, Institutions and Public Policy: Agile Decision-making in a Turbulent World* (Cheltenham: Edward Elgar, 2011).
8 Reimut Zohlnhofer and Friedbert W. Rub (eds), *Decision-Making under Ambiguity and Time-Constraints: Assessing the Multiple Streams Framework* (Colchester: ECPR Press, 2016).
9 Mark Considine, *Making Public Policy: Institutions, Actors, Strategies* (Cambridge: Polity Press, 2005), p. 47.
10 Thomas R. Dye, *Understanding Public Policy*, 11th edn (Englewood Cliffs, NJ: Pearson Prentice Hall, 2008), p. 15.
11 Benjamin I. Page and Robert Y. Shapiro, *The Rational Public: Fifty Years of Trends in American's Policy Preferences* (Chicago: University of Chicago Press, 1992), p. 14.
12 Philip Converse, 'The nature of belief systems in mass publics', in David E. Apter (ed.), *Ideology and Discontent* (New York: Free Press, 1964), p. 245.
13 Ted Brader, *Campaigning for Hearts and Minds* (Chicago: University of Chicago Press, 2006), p. 211.
14 Albert Bandura, *Social Foundation of Thought and Action* (Englewood Cliffs, NJ: Prentice Hall, 1986).
15 B. F. Skinner, *Beyond Freedom and Dignity* (New York: Knopf, 1971).
16 Joel Best (ed.), *Images of Issues: Typifying Contemporary Social Problems* (New York: Aldine De Gruyter, 1995).
17 Robert Axelrod, *The Evolution of Cooperation* (New York: Basic Books, 1984).
18 David B. Truman, *The Government Process* (New York: Knopf, 1954).
19 Dye, *Understanding Public Policy*, p. 24.
20 Charles E. Lindblom, 'The science of muddling through', *Public Administration Review*, 19(Spring) (1959): 79–88.
21 Charles E. Lindblom, *The Intelligence of Democracy* (New York: The Free Press, 1965), p. 70.
22 Koenig, *Introduction to Public Policy*.
23 James Buchanan and Gordon Tullock, *The Calculus of Consent* (Ann Arbor, MI: University of Michigan Press, 1962).
24 Peter John, *Making Public Policy* (London: Routledge, 2011).
25 Kenneth J. Neubeck, Mary Alice Neubeck and Davita Sifen Glasberg, *Social Problems*, 5th edn (New York: McGraw-Hill, 2007).
26 Rittel and Webber, 'Dilemmas'.
27 Horn, *Human Research*.
28 Rittel and Webber, 'Dilemmas'.
29 Jeff Conklin, *Dialogue Mapping: Building Shared Understanding of Wicked Problems* (Chichester: John Wiley & Sons, Ltd, 2005). See also CogNexus Institute, available at: www. cognexus.org. © 2001–2008 CogNexus Institute.
30 Koenig, *Introduction to Public Policy*, p. 93.
31 Wilbur Schramm (ed.), *The Process and Effects of Mass Communication* (Urbana, IL: University of Illinois Press, 1955).

32 Joseph T. Klapper, *The Effects of Mass Communication* (New York: Free Press).
33 David K. Berlo, *The Process of Communication* (New York: Holt, Rinehart and Winston, 1960).
34 Joseph N. Cappella, 'Research methodology in communications: review and commentary', in Brent Rubin (ed.), *Communication Yearbook 1* (New Brunswick, NJ: Transaction Books, 1977), p. 43.
35 Harold D. Lasswell, 'The structure and function of communication in society', in Lyman Bryson (ed.), *The Communication of Ideas* (New York: Institute for Religious and Social Studies, 1948).
36 Walter Lippmann, *Public Opinion* (New York: Free Press, 1922), p. 15.
37 Leon Festinger, 'The theory of cognitive dissonance', in Wilbur Schramm (ed.), *The Science of Human Communications* (New York: Basic Books, 1963), pp. 17–27.
38 Sherry Devereaux Ferguson, *Researching the Public Opinion Environment: Theories and Methods* (Thousand Oaks, CA: SAGE, 2000).
39 Philip Converse, 'The nature of belief system in mass publics', in David E. Apter (ed.), *Ideology and Discontent* (New York: Free Press, 1964).
40 Robert J. Spitzer, *Media and Public Policy* (New York: Praeger Publishers, 1993), p. 6.
41 John Tomlinson. *The Culture of Speed: The Coming of Immediacy* (London: SAGE, 2007).
42 John Authers, 'Unnatural calm sparks visions of a "Minsky Moment"', *Financial Times* Weekend, 31 Dec./1 Jan. 2017.
43 Singapore Government White Paper, 'A sustainable population for a dynamic Singapore', available at: https://lkyspp.nus.edu.sg/wp-content/uploads/2013/12/LKYSPP-Case-Study_-Landuse-Case.pdf.
44 Tan Shin Bin and Donald Low, 'Long-term land use and planning in Singapore', Lee Kuan Yew School of Public Policy case study, 2013, available at: LKYSPP-Case-Study_-Landuse-Case.pdf.
45 Rachel Cheng, 'Why 6.9m was too much information: major policy shifts eclipsed by uproar over population projection', *Straits Times*, 16 Feb. 2013.
46 Basskaran Nair, 'Transport lessons from Govt's housing policies', *Straits Times*, 19 May 2014.
47 Jeanette Tan, 'Population White Paper triggers nationwide debate', Yahoo News, Year in Review, 27 November 2013, available at: sg.yahoo.com/-yir2013 – population-white-paper-triggers-nationwide-debate-10 …
48 Denyse Yeo, 'Dr Liu Thai Ker: Singapore needs to plan for 10 million population', *The Peak*, 7 October 2014.
49 Teo Chee Hean, 'Opening speech at the parliamentary debate on Population White Paper', 20 February 2013.
50 Ibid.
51 Calvin Cheng, 'The Population White Paper: time to revisit an unpopular policy?' *Straits Times*, 9 January 2017.

0134147613135

HUMBER LIBRARIES

2

WICKED PROBLEMS AND THEIR APPLICATION

It's hearts and minds communication

In the abstract to their article 'Dilemmas in a general theory of planning', Horst Rittel and Melvin Webber write that there is a distinction between neat and wicked problems. In 'hard' science, the researcher is allowed to make hypotheses that are later refuted. One is not penalised for making hypotheses that turn out to be wrong; science has been developed to deal with neat or 'tame' problems. Not so in the world of social sciences and human communication where no such immunity is tolerated. Here the aim is not to find the truth, but to improve some characteristic of the world where people live. Planners are liable for the consequences of the actions they generate. The authors maintain that the search for scientific bases to confront problems of social policy is bound to fail, because of the nature of these problems. Even worse, there are no solutions, in the sense of definitive and objective answers.[1]

In the world of complexity theorists, there is no 'science' of policy-making or execution. This premise is reflected by other complexity theorists like Louis Koenig,[2] Euel Elliott and L. Douglas Kiel,[3] James Horn,[4] Mark Mason,[5] and Jeff Conklin[6] Graham Room,[7] and Reimut Zohlnhofer and Friedbert W. Rub.[8] Louis Koenig describes complexity as critical junctures; Jeff Conklin as fragmentation; while Deborah Stone uses policy paradox. In her (2002) book, *Policy Paradox*, Deborah Stone notes that policy politics looks messy, foolish, erratic and inexplicable and that events, actions, and ideas seem to leap outside the categories that logic and rationality offer.[9] Philip Ball in his (2004) book, *Critical Mass*, maintains that complexity analysis can be applied to a wide range of policy issues, including markets, social networks, urban development, traffic management, or racial zoning in cities; others have applied complexity analysis to broad subjects like education, economics, environment, behavioural science, engineering and nautical sciences.[10]

In this chapter, we will examine two cases of complex or wicked problems,[11] namely, the US Affordable Healthcare Bill, eventually passed in 2012 (commonly called ObamaCare), and the UK Referendum to Leave or Remain in the European

Union (EU), commonly called Brexit, when the Leave vote won by 52 per cent in June 2016. Both policies are classic cases of wicked problems, based on the definition of wicked problems by complexity theorists. Both policies were plagued by controversies at the time of policy implementation and execution. And realistically they will continue to be public policy case studies on volatility, uncertainty, complexity and ambiguity, over the next decade. The discussion in this chapter takes Rittel and Webber's ten-point guidelines on what constitutes complex policies. Each case study is discussed in the light of these guidelines. The final section is on how a messy or complex policy can be addressed by marketing communication challenges. Communication models and theories share common grounds with complexity theories and are effectively geared to address the concerns of the receivers of public policies.

Characteristics of wicked problems

Rittel and Webber list ten characteristics of wicked problems as:

1 There is no definitive formulation of a wicked problem.
2 Wicked problems have no stopping rule.
3 Solutions to wicked problems are not true-or-false, but better or worse.
4 There is no immediate and no ultimate test of a solution to a wicked problem.
5 Every solution to a wicked problem is a 'one-shot operation'; because there is no opportunity to learn by trial-and-error, every attempt counts significantly.
6 Wicked problems do not have an enumerable (or an exhaustively describable) set of potential solutions, nor is there a well-described set of permissible operations that may be incorporated into the plan.
7 Every wicked problem is essentially unique.
8 Every wicked problem can be considered to be a symptom of another problem.
9 The existence of a discrepancy representing a wicked problem can be explained in numerous ways. The choice of explanation determines the nature of the problem's resolution.
10 The planner has no right to be wrong (planners are liable for the consequences of the actions they generate).

The questions are re-categorised into four broad areas for the convenience of discussion of the two case studies: the US Affordable Healthcare Bill or ObamaCare, and the UK Referendum to 'Leave', called Brexit.

No definite formulation of a wicked problem

There is no definite formulation of a wicked problem. Every wicked problem is essentially unique. The causes of a wicked problem can be explained in numerous ways. The choice of explanation determines the nature of the problem's resolution. Every solution that is offered exposes new aspects of the problem, requiring further adjustments of the potential solutions. Indeed, there is no definitive statement of 'the problem'. The problem is ill-structured, an evolving set of interlocking issues and constraints. As Rittel and Webber said, 'One cannot understand the problem without knowing about its context; one cannot meaningfully search for information without the orientation of a solution concept; one cannot first understand, then solve.'[12]

There is no rule or procedure to determine the 'correct' explanation or combination of explanations for a wicked problem. Adrian Kay, in his (2006) book, *The Dynamics of Public Policy*, writes that it is only by virtue of hindsight and the analysis of the conjunction of different processes that we can make any sense of which process is dominant, which structures and constraints may have been operating and the direction of their net effect.[13] Deborah Stone advocates that the essence of policy-making in political communities is the struggle over ideas. Ideas are the medium of exchange and a mode of influence and shared meanings motivate people to action and mould individual striving into collective action.[14]

Wicked problems have no stopping rules

Wicked problems are inherently dynamic and one should accept the fact that one cannot 'come to a "final", "complete" or "fully correct" solution'. The best approach is to define the complex problem from the outset as discrete, measurable goals and at the same time be realistic that the problem will be continually evolving and mutating. Communication practice and complexity theorists share the view that in order to describe a wicked problem in sufficient detail, it is imperative to develop an exhaustive inventory for all the conceivable solutions ahead of time, recognising that causes and effects of the problem are extremely difficult to identify and model, and that from the outset on should define discrete, measurable goals and be realistic that the problem will be continually evolving and mutating. It is a constant solution adapting to a changing position.[15]

Adrian Kay notes that policy messages or policy narratives embrace the complexity of different processes of different speeds and at different levels coexisting in the policy path; indeed it is the aim of the narrative to weave these together into coherent whole. The narratives are assessed in a social context in which many parties are equally equipped, interested, and/or entitled to judge them. And these judgements are likely to vary widely and depend on the stakeholder's independent values and goals.[16]

No ultimate test of a solution to a wicked problem

Solutions to wicked problems are not true-or-false, but better or worse. Every solution to a wicked problem is a 'one-shot operation'. There is no opportunity to learn by trial and error, every attempt counts significantly. Wicked problems do not have an enumerable set of potential solutions, nor is there a well-described set of permissible operations that may be incorporated into the plan. As Rittel and Webber maintain, 'One cannot build a freeway to see how it works.'[17] This is the 'Catch-22' dilemma with wicked problems: you cannot learn about the problem without trying solutions, but every solution is expensive, with unintended consequences, which are likely to spawn new wicked problems. It is a matter of creativity to devise potential solutions, and a matter of judgement to determine which one should be pursued and implemented. These criteria are more descriptive than definitional. One takes note of the complex theorist view that:

> There are no criteria which enable one to prove that all the solutions to a wicked problem have been identified and considered. It may happen that no solution is found, owing to logical inconsistencies in the 'picture' of the problem.[18]

Every wicked problem is a symptom of another problem

Every wicked problem can be considered to be a symptom of another wicked problem. Many of these unintended consequences of inter-linkages of wicked problems have been covered in the social sciences literature. Wicked problems are characterised as having high uncertainty associated with multiple stakeholders' viewpoints on the desirability of alternative outcomes. Any solution, after being implemented, will generate waves of consequences over an extended – virtually an unbounded – period of time. The immediate consequences of the solution may yield utterly undesirable repercussions, which outweigh the intended advantages or the advantages accomplished. By their nature, wicked problems cannot be easily categorised into separate disciplinary boxes nor can they be divided into more manageable parts under the assumption that there are clear and known casual paths.[19]

Case study 2.1: ObamaCare

No definite formulation of a wicked problem

During President Barack Obama's first term in office (2009–2013), the 2010 Patient Protection and Affordable Care Act, popularly called ObamaCare, was passed, with the federal government offering to pay states 100 per cent of the cost of expanding Medicaid for three years beginning in 2014, declining to 90 per cent in subsequent years. It was a highly controversial Act that had all the classic features of a social mess. The US healthcare issue was first defined as a national issue by the Republicans. Democrat President Bill Clinton pursued the healthcare Bill but most Republicans opposed it. The Heritage Foundation then advocated a universal healthcare insurance programme as an alternative to 'Hillarycare', which was a failed reform advocated by Hillary Clinton, then the First Lady. The Heritage Plan then became 'Romneycare' enacted in 2006 by then Massachusetts Governor Mitt Romney.[20] It was imposed at the state level not at the federal level. However, within the Republican Party there was opposition, some arguing on the grounds that universal healthcare was government intrusion into private decision-making. Then Obama became president. Obama in his 9 September 2009 Presidential Address to Congress said:

> I am not the first President to take up this cause, but I am determined to be the last. It has now been nearly a century since Theodore Roosevelt first called for healthcare reform. And ever since, nearly every President and Congress, whether Democrat or Republican, has attempted to meet this challenge in some way.[21]

After winning the 2008 elections, President Obama decided to focus on health as a priority to bring about change; his healthcare campaign started early in 2009. He framed his Affordable Care reform (popularly called ObamaCare) as insuring the uninsured, controlling runaway health spending, and improving the quality of care. The Bill would be revenue-neutral. The controversy, arousing highly political issues, was focused on three points: (1) what the reform would cost; (2) how it would be paid for; and, especially, (3) what role a new public insurance plan might play.[22] Since it was first mooted, the policy leaders have never agreed which type of solution to apply to healthcare policy. They muddled through numerous definitions to accommodate changes to win political support.

The definitions, in the course of implementation, were framed within highly political terms and often along partisan lines. Republicans stridently sought to repeal the measures, saying that the reforms, signed into law in March 2010, would increase costs, would cause insurance premiums to rise, and would hurt the quality of healthcare, and they vowed to repeal it. In the public debates, data was often hijacked and the true picture of the issues was distorted. The core policy value of healthcare was not in dispute. Virtually every expert, the politicians and the people agreed that the root of the runaway health inflation was the fee-for-service system. Every visit, test and exam is money in the bank for a doctor, hospital and test centre, so there is an incentive to do more of them. That is how doctors get paid – and also get protection from lawsuits.[23] In practice, however, it did not matter. Whichever Party came to power, politics was favoured ahead of policy imperatives.

Wicked problems have no stopping rules

When the Patient Protection and Affordable Care Act or ObamaCare was passed in March 2010, as the most comprehensive reform, it continued to be an inherently dynamic problem, one that cannot come to a final, complete or fully correct solution. When it was finally approved, it faced endless execution problems, including multiple computer-related problems. The implementation process was messy, as the responsibilities passed to the governors and health departments of the nation's 50 states. Two years after ObamaCare was signed, most of its provisos had yet to be implemented. Twenty states filed legal challenges, and the Supreme Courts had to hear arguments about its constitutionality. The Obama administration postponed the enforcement of the Affordable Care Act by one year to eliminate redundancy and streamline paperwork burdens. The execution problems continued as insurers, insured and doctors left the scheme.

With Donald Trump as President, the healthcare Act has been revisited. He signed an executive order to repeal ObamaCare without a solution in place. His broad-brush rejection of ObamaCare resonated with a large number of his voters during the 2016 presidential race. Republicans have had enough votes in the Senate to repeal parts of ObamaCare through budget reconciliation. However, in the main, the Republicans were still not united in their approach to repeal and replace the healthcare Bill. Complexity for the Republicans is repealing a popular provision in ObamaCare, namely, not to deny coverage to the people with medical histories. President Trump wanted to keep this pre-existence provision in place. Republican House Speaker, Paul Ryan had included this in his 'A Better Way' report to replace ObamaCare.[24] However, the more conservative elements in the Republican Party rejected the 'A Better Way' report as they want to wind down financial expansion of the healthcare Act and curtail Medicaid spending. After further adjustments, the new healthcare Bill was passed among the Republicans. President Trump told the Republicans they should not be viewed as attacking Americans from low-cost households and advocated more robust tax credits to buy insurance on the individual market.[25]

No ultimate test of a solution to a wicked problem

With wicked problems, the determination of the quality of a solution is not objective and the solutions are assessed by many parties equally equipped and entitled to judge the solution. We see this in the Affordable Care Act, in terms of attitude and behaviour. Republicans who objected cited that it is unfair for people to get a 'free ride' – to skip coverage to save money – knowing if they get sick, they will be able to throw themselves on the mercy of society. Others framed this point in emotive words, like Republican Michele Bachmann, calling it 'social engineering playground of the Left'. Meetings across the country positioned ObamaCare as 'death panels', focusing on the public insurance panel that decides whether seriously ill Medicare patients would continue to receive treatment.[26] Media supporting the partisan perspective charged that if the famed scientist Stephen Hawking lived in America, that the health insurance would not save his life. Hawking, 67, suffers from Lou Gehrig type motor neuron disease, is a British subject and receives lifelong care from Britain's national health system. He was one of 16 recipients of the Medal of Freedom from Obama in the course of the acrimonious debate on the insurance programme. Danielle Vinson notes that the language used by congressional members are often 'crafted words' – words and phrases that have been tested in public opinion polls and focus groups – to frame debates. The language used has the potential to move public opinion on the issue.[27]

Complexity of execution impacts on people's attitude and action on whether it is better or worse. For the Affordable Care Act to be implemented, a state law had to be passed establishing an exchange with a computer for citizens to shop for insurance online. There is cost and coordination. The computer system, costing millions of dollars, must be connected seamlessly to both the state's Medicaid system and the federal government's system. It required bringing together people from government, consumer groups and the industry to advise the Board that oversees the exchange. In the USA, the connection between employment and healthcare is not only inefficient but also is a huge burden on American business. American companies pay tens of billions to provide healthcare for their employees and former employees, while their German, Canadian, Japanese and British counterparts do not have such a burden on their balance sheet. Moreover, in the US healthcare programme, insurance brokers in the early implementation of ObamaCare worried that the state exchanges, which had enlisted 'navigators' to help steer uninsured people to the right plan, would siphon off their customers. By 2016, many insurers had exited from the exchanges, leaving citizens with usually one insurer to choose.

And the complexity deepens with Donald Trump as President. In his first few days in office President Trump signed an executive order to end ObamaCare. Republicans are divided into two major schools of thought: 'Repeal and delay' and 'Repeal and replace'. For Republicans, the complexity is that they will soon face the Congressional mid-term elections in 2018. Consumers will not want to lose the coverage, that is, they will want to keep the pre-existing provision. Republicans fear political fallout in the mid-term elections. In his speech to a joint session of both Houses, President Donald Trump conceded: 'I have to tell you, it's an unbelievably complex subject. Nobody knew that healthcare could be so complicated.' During his address to Congress, after his executive action to repeal ObamaCare, he vowed to make healthcare accessible through tax credits and said governors should get the resources they need with Medicaid 'to make sure no one is left out'. After the speech, the Republican Party members were still not united. 'He didn't say "refundable tax credit". He said "tax credit",' said Republican Mark Sanford of South Carolina, a member of the conservative Freedom Caucus. 'There's a world of difference between the two.'[28]

Every wicked problem is a symptom of another problem

The Patient Protection and Affordable Care Act is a classic problem connected to other problems. For example, on the constitutional powers of the president, Republicans in the House of Representatives continuously threatened to sue President Obama for exceeding his constitutional powers in the way he enforced the 2010 healthcare law. They accused him of flouting the law, breaking a solemn constitutional oath and going too far in selectively enforcing parts of the healthcare overhaul, such as delaying the requirement that employers provide health insurance for their workers. There are perpetual multiple conflicts, for example, controlling costs by denying expensive treatments, squeezing suppliers' incomes, and taxpayers and employers being asked to pay the cost for violation. There were widespread complaints from businesses and their lobbyists about reporting requirements for employers with 50 or more full-time workers. Companies had to pay the Internal Revenue Service US$2,000 for each full-time employee who did not get health coverage when the Affordable Care Act came into full effect.

In the Trump presidency, there are plans to deal with the insurers. Insurers are contractually committed to the plans; carriers are allowed to exit the market if they do not receive payments from the government that reduce insurance costs for lower-income consumers. The danger is that the US Treasury does not make such payments to carriers. In such a scenario, insurers would leave so as not to lose money; however, their departure would cause 'chaos' in the insurance market. Market turmoil could mean life or death for certain consumers – say, certain patients in the middle of cancer treatment – and Republicans know this. While this worst-case scenario is unlikely, some say it cannot be completely discounted, given the unpredictable political climate.[29] Moreover, the 'Repeal and replace' decision and the cuts in social programmes are related to releasing more funds for the infrastructure development and tax cuts, both are part of the policy agenda. The Trump administration has a US$1 trillion infrastructure plan to modernise US roads, bridges, airports, electricity grids and water systems, and it needs to raise funds. Conservative Republicans would prefer to cut Medicaid and other social and healthcare programmes to help fund the infrastructure projects. The big conservative superpacs (election funding groups) will unleash a lot of campaign money in repayment for the tax cut. Republicans will be banking on this to shield them from the voter backlash.[30]

Case study 2.2: Brexit, the UK to leave the EU

No definite formulation of a wicked problem

What is Brexit? It is a term used to describe an event when the majority of the voters in the United Kingdom (52 per cent) decided to vote to leave the European Union (the EU) on 23 June 2016. This happened when British Prime Minister, David Cameron called for a Remain in or Leave the European Union Referendum. To understand it as a wicked problem or social mess, one has to look at the historical flow of events that led to Brexit.

When the EU enlargement took place between 2004 and 2007 to include the former communist countries of Central and Eastern Europe, it brought into the bloc at least 12 new nations, most of them far poorer than the Western European average. EU regulations granted a seven-year grace period to control immigration inflow. However, at that time, the then Prime Minister Tony Blair confidently announced that Britain, rather than take the seven-year grace period, would lead the way in Europe and open its frontiers immediately for all newcomers from

Eastern Europe. Taking this generous policy position was political: Blair wanted to define Britain as a more enlightened country than Germany or France, which kept their immigration controls on East Europeans for the full seven years. It was a foolish act of chutzpah as that policy position soon led to a massive inflow of unskilled Eastern European labour migrating into the UK. Gordon Brown, who succeeded Blair as Prime Minister, continued the catastrophic policy miscalculation.

Hundreds of thousands of East Europeans started arriving each year. By the end of 2016, at least 3.5 million people, mostly from Eastern Europe, had settled in the UK. Without proper guidance and with poor action plans by the political leadership in power, public discontent among the locals kept pouring from all directions. The pressure on housing became acute. Schools could not cope with the demand for spaces and daily wages in some sectors like construction fell by a whopping 50 per cent, as cheap immigrant labour far outstripped local needs.[31] Policy leaders were aware of the problem. At every UK election, campaigners appealed for the re-imposition of border controls and the promotion of jobs for locals. It was possible to do so but policy leaders ruled that option out since it signified an embarrassing admission of defeat. The local authorities were told to manage as best as they could.[32]

Besides the migration labour issue, there was a long-standing 'democratic deficit', the gap between perceptions and reality regarding the EU, which was, in the eyes of the UK's Eurosceptics, a bureaucratic monster capable of almost every chicanery.[33] And one dangerous element in the battle for hearts and minds was mainstream media, such as the ones owned by Rupert Murdoch, who ironically had first supported the UK joining Europe in the 1975 Referendum. His group of newspapers was firmly anti-Europe. For instance, when Jacques Delors, President of the European Commission, spoke at the annual British Trade Union Congress, inviting the trade unions to join the EU to construct Europe, Murdoch's *Sun* newspaper attacked Delors. The *Sun* front page was filled with headlines attacking the President of the European Commission with personalised anti-Delors hate campaigns, including T-shirts bearing anti-Delors slogans. Similarly, the *Daily Telegraph* and the *Spectator*, the biggest circulating political weekly in Britain, were anti-European. The papers' owner, Conrad Black, had earlier appointed Boris Johnson as editor of the *Spectator* magazine to ensure that a very clever anti-European propagandist was at the centre of the London press hostility against the EU. Boris Johnson, who had ended his term as Mayor of London and was the potential Prime Minister candidate to succeed David Cameron, campaigned vigorously to Leave the EU.[34]

During the 2016 Referendum campaign, the explanations on the issues facing the country were highly polarised and aggravated with lies. The Remain campaigners had businessmen, chambers of commerce leaders, policy analysts and other experienced experts explaining the wide range of economic, political, security, social and defence downsides, explaining with numbers and scenarios what would happen if the people voted to leave. The Leave campaigners dismissed 'experts' as self-serving, as boring and always wrong. They assured the electorate with simple not-so-truthful explanations, for example, that the UK could reclaim a supposed £350 million that Brussels takes from the UK each week. They promised to spend

£111 billion on the National Health Service, cut the value added tax (VAT) and council tax, make higher pensions, a better transport system and replace the EU subsidies to the arts, science, farmers and deprived regions. The false formulation of a complex policy worked. Nick Clegg, in his (2016) book, *Politics: Between the Extremes*, noted that the outcome of the referendum is one of the greatest acts of self-immolation which in the long term will probably lead to the break-up of the UK, the possible disintegration of the EU itself and possibly the end of Britain's role as a major world force.[35]

Wicked problems have no stopping rules

Brexit was defined as an immigration issue from the outset, and continued to be an inherently dynamic problem. When Prime Minister Cameron resigned and addressed his European colleagues, he warned them that the issue they would face, as Britain had faced in Brexit, in their respective upcoming elections would be the issue of immigration.[36] Brexit was a classic case of different strokes for different folks. For those living in the cities, the arrival of migrants from Eastern Europe boosted prosperity: Improved services, increased consumption and sustained rising property prices. In contrast, in the heartlands, for millions stuck in the decaying, old industrial towns of the North of England, immigration was an economic disaster. Before EU enlargement and free movement of immigrants, the heartlanders had to compete for work in a domestic market of just 64 million; after EU enlargement, they were competing for work in a labour market almost ten times bigger. Yet the leadership ignored this glaring, ongoing social cost imposed by immigration.

One event after another unfolded as the UK government grappled with the Brexit issue. After the referendum, it was challenged by an interest group as illegal unless reviewed by the British courts and sent to Parliament for approval. Given the tough negotiation ahead with 27 EU nations, Prime Minister Theresa May then decided, to the surprise of everyone, to seek a stronger negotiating hand by calling for an early general election. She failed miserably, losing her party's parliamentary majority, had to form a coalition with the DUP to stay in power, and entered into negotiation with the EU members from a weaker negotiating position.

In March 2017, Tony Blair, the former Labour Party Prime Minister, addressed the complexity issue of Brexit as a private citizen. While acknowledging the will of the people that Brexit should prevail, he maintained that people voted on Brexit without knowledge of the full terms. He warned Brexit would starve other public priorities in the UK, like the health service and that it would imperil the EU too. He argued that voters can change their views; it is right to do so; it is up to the politicians, if they think the country is making a terrible mistake, to make the case.[37]

No ultimate test of a solution to a wicked problem

Literally every one of the British Prime Ministers made a 'one-shot' political judgement on dealing with the EU and failed. Tony Blair, besides showing off that

Britain was a more enlightened country, was also influenced by a study provided by his own civil servants, which estimated that only 13,000 East Europeans would arrive each year after Britain's borders are open. Prime Minster Gordon Brown, who succeeded Blair, continued the policies, and neither the prime ministers nor any other British ministers asked how the figures were arrived at. And no civil servant volunteered that information either. As Eurosceptics grew in Parliament, among both Labour and Conservative MPs, Prime Minister David Cameron called for the Leave or Remain Referendum. PM Theresa May called for an early election and that fell flat as Conservatives lost their majority. The complexity saga has not stopped yet; the centre of gravity for policy politics has shifted from the UK-domestic to UK-Europe at large.

Every wicked problem is a symptom of another problem

Immediately after Brexit, however, there were other important interlinked issues. For example, within a month, the Cabinet deferred the approval of Hinkley Point C – a proposed 3,200 MW nuclear power station financed by Électricité de France and China General Nuclear Power Group. That decision (which was approved two months later) was interlinked with concerns for national security. That in turn was interlinked to potentially jeopardising several economic issues such as London's emerging position as a major overseas yuan trading centre and China's plans to invest in British infrastructure over the next decade. Other interrelated policy positions would include unilaterally eliminating all tariffs and relying on the World Trade Organisation Framework or becoming a low-tax, minimal-regulation investment hub to cut an extremely favourable contrast with heavily regulated continental European economies.

Besides, Brexit potentially set a precedent for other complaining EU members where political opportunists played up negative emotions in promoting their nationalistic ideologies. A new politics started taking place in western democracies, one that has become a confrontation between establishment and anti-system parties. There are already anti-system parties in other western democracies: Italy's Five Star Movement, France's National Front, Spain's Podemos and the Alternative for Germany. Described as far-right and some as far-left, they almost all share a claim, namely, the system is 'rigged' and that ordinary people are being trampled by elites. In foreign policy, they even tend to be pro-Russian.[38]

Marketing complex policies

President Obama did a better job at defining and explaining the healthcare programme than Prime Minister David Cameron did with the Leave or Remain in the EU Referendum. President Obama focused on the benefits to the communities and citizens, and the times scale of the benefits to be derived: immediate, medium-term or long-term. People must feel, perceive or experience (hearts and minds) that the outcome of policy governance and initiative is in their welfare. President

Obama defined the issues as multi-sector and multi-faceted. In such a long-drawn-out campaign, what 'the problem' is depends on who you ask – different stake-holders have different views about what is the problem, the time taken to solve the problem, and what constitutes an acceptable solution.

On wicked problems having no stopping rules, ObamaCare's focus should have been implemented by the states, and in stages – fixing the computer systems and understanding execution among key stakeholders like the insurers. Social marketers address the complexity conundrum by looking at public campaign issues, such as healthcare, from the viewpoint of high involvement of target publics, and the seg-mentation of the target public, or micro-targeting. A behaviour modification model describes policy initiation to implementation as undergoing five stages, namely: (1) pre-contemplation; (2) contemplation; (3) preparation; (4) action; and (5) main-tenance/confirmation.[39] President Obama's healthcare campaign, suffering from the polarising of the citizens along party lines and its implementation fraught with problems, floundered at the 'action and maintenance' level. He himself did not keep the sustained pace of persuasion required at the maintenance/confirmation level because of other national priorities, such as the global financial crisis that engulfed the world.

This deep partisan dichotomy over healthcare is succinctly noted by Danielle Vinson, who states that the debate is a public relations battle. Democrats claim a necessary extension of healthcare to millions of uninsured people, while the Repub-licans claim a step towards socialised medicines and a violation of the Constitution; it has raged for nearly two years with no indication yet that the public has been completely convinced of either interpretation.[40] The polarised partisanship con-tinues. Nonetheless, it is a credit to the ObamaCare campaign that 20 million Americans who would never have been insured were insured and that insurers cannot deny coverage to those people with medical histories. As the Republicans attempt to repeal and replace ObamaCare, they are also faced with a policy conun-drum and political backlash as 20-odd million Americans will be without any healthcare and many of those affected are also Trump supporters, who want to replace ObamaCare but not at the expense of their healthcare coverage.

For Brexit, the leadership should have addressed the immigration issues in the heartlands from the outset, and not let it fester to this extent. After he had set a date for the referendum, an overconfident Cameron did not run a sustained robust activism campaign. The Leave campaigners, led by Boris Johnson, former Mayor of London, were in the activism mode; a campaign based on emotionally charged messages but often using lies, half-truths and misinformation. These emotional messages clouded hearts and minds about what is at stake for the future. On the other hand the Remain campaigners ran a lukewarm initiative: the EU vision was not vigorously 'marketed' and the narrative that Britain was an active and enthusi-astic member significantly benefiting from being part of the EU lacked an emo-tional punch. PM Cameron relied on experts, businesses and the markets to use rational and logical arguments to win the voters. The Remain message resonated within the major cities like London, where skilled migrants were making positive contributions, but not among the heartlanders who experienced the negative fallout of Eastern European labour. He and his team should have applied activism strategies, particularly among the heartlanders, for example, to oxygenate the public with a regular flow of information through various methods and channels, and demonstrably improving goods and services among the local citizens hard hit by arrival of the migrant workers. Quantity and quality of information and strong policy action play a big role in the public opinion dynamics.

The Economist magazine suggested that Tony Blair should develop an activism communication strategy to end the 'Brexit is Brexit' narrative and should revisit the Referendum issue to change the minds of Leave voters to Remain in the EU and drop the idea of Brexit. It suggested three campaign options for Tony Blair: Option one, he could let another figure take up his narrative for voters to rise up against the costs and dislocations of Brexit; or alternatively as Option two he becomes the lead figure – clamber into the trenches and become a full participant in Britain's domestic politics once more; re-engage and build the case for a change of course on Brexit, week-by-week, battle-by-battle, going head-to-head with his critics, appearing on the influential TV programme *Question Time*, hosting radio phone-ins, shooting from the hip in television interviews, appearing at town hall events, travelling around the country meeting people who voted for Brexit; in short, reset his relationship with the British public for the sake of the UK remaining in the EU. The third option is a compromise between the two options in that he chooses public figures to do the battle on the ground but he is active in financial support, arranging stage-managed events, creating a political institute, writing ops-eds for broadsheets and endorsing an appropriate candidate.[41]

Option two is also an activism strategy that could be adopted by Prime Minister Theresa May to get into the trenches and to press forward her 'Brexit is Brexit' narrative. Unfortunately she entered the wrong trenches by calling for an early election. With a weakened bargaining position after losing her parliamentary majority, she has to soften her policy position from hard Brexit to a softer one. Meanwhile the EU negotiators have laid down the communication strategy – they have developed policy position papers in advance, made known their requirements and that every step of the negotiation is communicated clearly to their respective domestic publics. Michel Barnier, the EU's chief negotiator, said he wanted press conferences at the beginning and end of each round of negotiation, noting that if you have somebody who cannot commit or cannot sell to the public, that is a real risk.[42]

There are triangular relationships in understanding the 'picture' of the problem. There could be more than one relationship and each has their own bias and 'pictures' of self-interest.[43] We see this in the two case studies. ObamaCare faced endless bickering among competing interest groups, for example, consumer groups wanted insurers to lower premiums. Communication practitioners have also addressed wicked problems as inter-related and therefore there is always a need for a planned and sustained activism campaign. In his road shows, as part of his activism campaign to market the healthcare message, Obama and his team hammered home a simplified message, emphasising the benefits of the proposal to insured and older Americans, whose support is critical for the plan – with its promise of expanding the pool of insured people. Obama personalised the debate by referencing his own grandmother. 'I know what it's like to watch somebody you love who is aging deteriorate, and struggle with that', he said, his voice rising. 'Pulling the plug on grandma? When you start making arguments like that, it's simply dishonest.'[44] For both ObamaCare and Brexit, the real uncertainty is that activists as players debate and disagree, representing vested organisational positions to polarise the public.

Understanding the groundswell and micro-targeting are important communication initiatives. For Brexit, the policy leadership should have continued to do their homework on knowing their own domestic groundswell. After the general election debacle, Nick Timothy, co-Chief of Staff to PM Theresa May, said that modern campaign techniques require ever-narrower targeting of specific voters.[45] The core issues are related to migrant problems and grassroots attitude towards Brussels (the agenda). There are emotive aspects during the campaign, such as the EU's excessive bureaucracy and the stakeholders' deep mistrust of their political bureaucrats and elites (framing). Post-election, the decision is to market the soft Brexit option. The UK retains some form of access to the single market by maintaining the free movement of people but it will be hard put to end the immigration status quo. The most pragmatic option would probably be moving from full EU membership into a relationship similar to that of Norway, remaining in the single market and customs union as a rule-taker. This could hold until the UK has free trade deals and the systems in place to cope with a decisive break.[46]

Conclusion: complexity, hurts and minds

This chapter explores complexity and communication theorists' respective models and how they work in practice. It is examined through two classic complexity case studies: the US Affordable Care Act (ObamaCare) and the UK's Brexit plan. Communication theorists maintain that if the policy planners can find those causal forces which produce the behavioural response, one can also explain as well as predict the behaviour – one can deduce the theoretic prediction. Like the behaviourist's primary assumption, communication practice looks at events such as ObamaCare and Brexit as more serial than hierarchical.

In most western democracies, lobbyists, special interest groups, and activists work closely with the policy planning team and politicians to manage the intricacies and implications of complex policies. How do you move complex policies from the margins to the mainstream? How do you ensure political understanding and acceptance of these complex policies? Further discussion on the communication perspective for managing wicked problems is pursued in the next four chapters: Chapter 4 is on the agenda setting, framing and priming continuum, a favourite management and persuasion strategy among lobbying groups; Chapter 5 is on social marketing, favoured by professional campaign strategists for policy issues; while, in Chapter 6, activism is the tool for cause-driven individuals and institutions actively pursuing social issues. In Chapter 7, the growth of social media as mainstream media is examined in the context of affecting and aggravating complexity in the execution of public or social policies.

The bottom line for communication is often effects and effectiveness – to win the hearts and minds of the targeted public. As Rittel and Webber said, it is a matter of creativity to devise potential solutions, and a matter of judgement to determine which are valid, and which should be pursued and implemented. These criteria are more descriptive than definitional. The point is not so much to be able to determine if a given problem is wicked or not as to have a sense of what contributes to the 'wickedness' of a problem.

Notes

1 Horst W. Rittel and Melvin M. Webber, 'Dilemmas in a general theory of planning', *Policy Sciences*, 4 (1973): 155–169.
2 Louis Koenig, *An Introduction to Public Policy* (Englewood Cliffs, NJ: Prentice Hall, 1986).
3 Euel Elliott and L. Douglas Kiel, *Non-Linear Dynamics, Complexity and Public Policy* (New York: Nova Science Publishers, 1999).
4 James Horn, *Human Research and Complexity Theory* (Chichester: John Wiley & Sons, Ltd, 2008).
5 Mark Mason (ed.), *Complexity Theory and Philosophy of Education* (Chichester: Wiley-Blackwell, 2008).
6 Jeff Conklin, 'Paper on wicked problems and social complexity', available at: www.cognexus.org, 2010.
7 Graham Room, *Complexity, Institutions and Public Policy: Agile Decision-making in a Turbulent World* (Cheltenham: Edward Elgar, 2011).
8 Reimut Zohlnhofer and Friedbert W. Rub (eds), *Decision-making under Ambiguity and Time-Constraints: Assessing the Multiple Streams Framework* (Colchester: ECPR Press, 2016).
9 Deborah Stone, *Policy Paradox: The Art of Political Decision Making* (New York: W. W. Norton & Company, 2002).
10 Philip Ball, *Critical Mass: How One Thing Leads to Another* (London: Heinemann, 2004).
11 The terms 'complexity', 'social mess' and 'wicked problem' are used interchangeably.
12 Rittel and Webber, 'Dilemmas', p. 164.
13 Adrian Kay, *The Dynamics of Public Policy* (Cheltenham: Edward Elgar, 2006).
14 Stone, *Policy Paradox*.
15 John Kingdon, *Agendas, Alternatives and Public Policy* (Boston: Little Brown, 1984), p. 181.
16 Kay, *Dynamics*.
17 Rittel and Webber, 'Dilemmas', p. 163.
18 Ibid., p.164.
19 Edward P. Webber and Anne M. Khademian, 'Wicked problems, knowledge challenges and collaborative capacity builders in network settings', *Public Administration Review*, 68(2) (2008): 334–349.
20 Edward Luce, 'On life support', *Financial Times*, FT Big Read: US Healthcare, 11 July 2017.
21 President Barack Obama's Address to Congress, 9 September 2009, available at: https://web.archive.org/web/20100919222243/http://c-span.org/Transcripts/SOTU-2009-0909.aspx.
22 Albert R. Hunt, 'Obama wins traction for health plan', *International Herald Tribune*, 17 August 2009.

23 Clive Cook, 'The Republican healthcare paradox', *Financial Times*, 3 August 2009.
24 Elizabeth O'Brien, 'ObamaCare repeal: what you need to know right now', *Time*, 17 January 2017.
25 Burgess Everett, Jennifer Haberkorn and Josh Dawsy, 'Trump knocks House health care bill as too harsh', Politico.com, 13 June 2017, available at: www.politico.com/story/2017/06/01/trump-urge-gop-senate-repeal-obamacare-239504
26 Cook, 'The Republican healthcare paradox'.
27 C. Danielle Vinson, 'Congress and the media: who has the upper hand?', in Travis N. Ridout (ed.), *New Directions in Media and Politics* (New York: Routledge, 2013), p. 150.
28 Sam Frizell, 'President Trump's toughest sales pitch was to his own party', *Time*, 1 March 2017.
29 O'Brien, 'ObamaCare repeal'.
30 Luce, 'On life support'.
31 Lionel Barber, 'The year of the demagogue', *Financial Times*, 17–18 December 2016.
32 Denis MacShane, *Brexit: How Britain Will Leave Europe* (London: I.B. Tauris & Co Ltd, 2015).
33 Jonathan Eyal, 'Europe yet to realise how badly Brexit will hurt', *Straits Times*, 12 September 2016.
34 MacShane, *Brexit*.
35 Nick Clegg, *Politics: Between the Extremes* (London: The Bodley Head, 2016).
36 Barber, 'Year of the demagogue'.
37 Bagehot, 'Tony Blair is right on Brexit. Now he should get into the trenches or back off', *The Economist*, Bagehot's notebook, 17 February 2017.
38 Gideon Rachman, 'The crisis in Anglo-American democracy', *Financial Times*, reproduced in *Straits Times*, 24 August 2016.
39 J. O. Prochaska and C. C. DiClemente, *The Transtheoretical Approach: Crossing Traditional Boundaries of Therapy* (Homewood, IL: Dow Jones-Irwin), 1984.
40 Vinson, 'Congress and the media', p. 143.
41 Bagehot, 'Tony Blair', 2017.
42 Alex Barker, 'EU negotiators steeled for Brexit crisis after UK election', *Financial Times*, 8 June 2017, p. 4.
43 Walter Lippmann, *Public Opinion* (New York: Free Press, 1922), p. 11.
44 Hunt, 'Obama wins traction'.
45 Nick Timothy, 'Why I have resigned as the Prime Minister's adviser', available at: www.conservativehome, 6 June 2017.
46 'A healthy dose of reality enters the Brexit debate', *Financial Times*, Editorial, 22/23 July 2017.

3

INSTITUTIONS AND POLITICAL STRUCTURES

It's the source and channel of communication

The attraction of institutions, to policy-makers, the people and policy analysts, is that they give a structure to a world that is complex, and where there is a multitude of temporal processes underway at different levels. Institutions help provide a buffer against the uncertainty of interaction among policy actors and the perturbations external to the policy process. Institutions are enduring, regular and tend to be difficult to change.[1] Policy actors make use of institutions and are shaped by them. Political structures affect the behaviour of elected officials towards one another, towards the citizens and the respective groupings and associations. In reviewing Donald Trump's 100 days as president of the USA, we see a policy leader transforming the nation's highest office by pushing the traditional boundaries, ignoring long-standing protocol and discarding historical antecedents, but he has also adapted his approach to both the job and the momentous challenges it entails.[2]

At the macro level, the core institutions on governance in a country are generally related to the respective roles of the legislative (the power to enact laws), the judicial (the power to interpret laws), and the executive (the power to enforce laws). The three institutions are supported by a fourth less clearly defined institution called the Fourth Estate: the media are the fourth institution. Media, the information flow and the communication structure in a country are an important guide to the way the power of the public can make policy by having a voice via consultation, town hall or focus group meetings, various feedback mechanisms and legitimate avenues for grievances. Social media have accentuated the complexity quotient of social policies, policy actors, and the public. In this chapter, we will look broadly at the key aspects of institutions, such as the people who are governed, and also choose who should govern, the various institutions, including people power, the policy elites, the media, the marketplace and global institutions. The next two sections examine the role of these institutions in two vastly different forms of political structure: democracies with a focus on the USA, and a communist structure, namely, China, where institutions exist for the nation's and its public's good but without the democratic credentials. The final section is a further discussion on institutions and complexity.

Understanding institutions

In discussing institutions and complexity, this section looks at several structures:

- the *people* in the policy process and their empowerment in the governance process;
- the *policy elites and their networks*[3] are responsible for policy formulation till its execution and the evaluation of success or failure;
- *core institutions* in the country, such as parliaments, political parties, the courts, the bureaucracy and other entities involved in the governance of the nation;
- the *media* as an institution for information flow, access and communication to government;
- *markets* are an important institution for the nation's economy, income distribution and its links to the global entities;
- *global institutions* that create a rule-based international framework for nations to interact and seek mutual benefits;
- *other institutions*, such as religion, the military or an active sovereign wealth fund that may be uniquely dominant in some countries.

Each section, people power, elite networks, and so on, should not be taken to be in a silo, as they intersect and sometimes are indistinguishable as distinct processes. For example, the media are interlinked with people power and the elite network. Every political leader has cited a growing litany of interfering forces that limit their ability to govern: not just factions within their parties and the ruling coalition or uncooperative legislators and increasingly free-wheeling judges, but also aggressive bondholders and other agents of global capital markets, international regulators, multilateral institutions, investigative journalists and social media campaigners and an ever-widening circle of activists.[4] Additionally, different patterns of institutions in nations are deeply embedded in the past, usually based on the ideologies laid down by the founding fathers of the nation. These ideologies, social norms, traditions and historical antecedents, expressed as core values and the nation's exceptionalism, are relevant in shaping institutions. They are also relevant to how the country is organised to meet future challenges. Graham Room, in his (2011) book, *Complexity, Institutions and Public Policy*, maintains that no policy is made on a *tabula rasa*: any policy is an intervention in a tangled web of institutions that have developed incrementally over extended periods of time and that gives each policy its specificity. Thus, history shapes the constraints and the opportunities within which policy interventions can then unfold.[5]

People power

People are at the centre of political activities whether in controlled or democratic structures. In policy systems based on democratic norms, citizens remain the primary source of sovereignty. Citizens adopt different roles in each system, capable of influencing the policy development process, for example, individuals act as voters; as political party members; community activists; parents; community leaders; activists on social issues; campaign workers; workplace executives and opinion leaders; respondents to opinion surveys; union or association members; audience members for the mass media, and so on. People participating in the democratic political systems have specific institutional methods for deciding who will become the popular representatives, which leadership will obtain executive office, and what form of majority will hold power inside the legislature.

In non-democratic countries, people are still the centre and the beneficiaries of the policy process, except that as, in the case of China, the people are not expected to be at the centre of political activities and policy decision-making. At the core of the debate is the question whether countries with more pluralist and divided institutions have achieved better outcomes because of greater responsiveness and legitimacy or whether pluralism prevents political leaders from guiding those outcomes.[6] The political institutions of a society are key determinants through which a society chooses the rules that will govern it. People vote in democracies and leaders attract their votes not by addressing needs or presenting long-term visions, but rather by offering a sense of belonging, nostalgia for simpler times or a return to national roots.[7] Whatever the political structure, the complexity is in winning the hearts and minds of the public as the policy process is deeply intertwined with politics. Even in communist countries, when push comes to shove, people will stand up and express their needs, wants and sense of belonging.

Policy elites and networks

A significant part of policy-making is the elite structure within a nation that affects the institutions, people and the politics. There is close fit between professional elites and their policy discourses as knowledge and power (and wealth) are monopolised by interest groups or elites. Whether open and democratic or closed and communist, but not despotic, institutions help provide a buffer against the uncertainty of interaction among policy elites to ensure a high degree of consistency and coherence. Using policy institutions, policy elites oversee the budget rules, policy networks, standard operating procedures in government departments and agencies and also past and current policies that act as structures to shape current policy options. The elite's policy actors' network has four characteristics: (1) networks are based on actual ties; (2) networks extend across a range of actors; (3) networks are semiformal or informal; and (4) networks are not simply hierarchical. Working between established institutional processes and across rules and conventions of several different organisations, and given their networks, elites make things happen with their organising skills.[8] The complexity is that with pluralist's elite network there could be disputes and demarcations between groups and an absence of consensus of interests in particular with the policy-making organs of government.

Core institutions

The core institutions of the executive, the judiciary and the legislature with a fairly independent media form the core institutions for governance of the nation. Institutions have both a constraining role and a steering one. These core institutions – through parliaments, political parties, bureaucracies – lay down strict codes by which policy actors engage in decision-making. Well-recognised institutions are the constitutional rules in force in a nation state, such as the electoral system, or institutions charged with decision-making, such as a supreme court that adjudicates on fundamental political disputes or the central bank that decides interest rates.[9] Complexity or critical juncture is the presence of an array of potent interacting institutions, capable of checking each other. This elevates the need for compromise, and tests the political skills of their incumbents. Impasse and deadlock may overtake interactions; a sizeable policy change is costly, requiring large investments of time, effort and political talent.[10]

The media as an institution

In an open, democratic society, there are several forces that engender complexity, an active media structure is one of them. In western democracies, there is a wide range of views by independently run media networks (in contrast to official news and views only), robust rebuttal (in contrast to control of opinions and views), and people make up their own minds based on their partisanship and convictions. There are also impartial institutions tasked with producing the statistics for the facts to be checked. Against the backdrop of the different ways and means to connect with the public, western democracies have tended to describe and categorise their art of communication, winning hearts and minds, as persuasion. Politicians, however, do lie or spin the truth for their own benefit. In China, control and censorship of media are aimed at being absolute and for social media communication in the country, it has created the Great Firewall for the censorship of news.

Markets as an institution

After almost several decades, the complexity of market-oriented globalisation is seen as undermining national institutions, for example, the US multinational companies have been criticised for profiting at the expense of the American workforce. Thomas Friedman, in the *Lexus and the Olive Tree*,[11] used the term Golden Straitjacket as the golden rule on how the markets dictate policy formulation:

> Making the private sector the primary engine of its economic growth, maintaining low rate of inflation and price stability, shrinking the size of its

bureaucracy, maintaining as close to a balanced budget as possible, if not surplus, eliminating and lowering tariffs on imported goods, removing restrictions on foreign investment, getting rid of quotas and domestic monopolies, increasing exports, privatising state-owned industries and utilities, deregulating its economy capital markets, making its currency convertible, opening its industries, stocks and bonds markets to direct foreign ownership and investment, deregulating its economy to promote as much domestic competition as possible.

The complexity is the alarming growth of corporacy and the increasing gap between the haves and the have-nots in a society. The whole idea of welfare, the common good, happiness and satisfaction implicit in the market theory is often hijacked by vested interest elite groups and their networks. It is hard to occupy or drain the 'Wall Street' swamp.

Global institutions

The global institutions that govern today's global policy-making are generally recognised as being a creation of the USA. In his memoir, *Present at the Creation* (1969), Dean Acheson,[12] a former US Secretary of State, describes how he and his fellow 'Wise Men' helped President Harry Truman build a new liberal, rule-based order after the Second World War. Internationally, a new set of institutions was founded: the United Nations (UN), the International Monetary Fund (IMF), the World Bank, and the North Atlantic Treaty Organisation (NATO) alliance. The Organisation for European Economic Co-operation (OECD), the vehicle for the Marshall Plan, later renamed the Organisation for Economic Co-operation, oversaw the reconstruction of Europe and promoted global economic development. The formation of the European Common Market, signed in 1957, saw the progressive abandonment of controls by 27 nations in the EU on capital, goods, services and labour. It was a vision of a cooperative world, a market-oriented globalisation.

The challenge to global institutions in recent times is growing nationalism, as people in many countries have not benefited from globalisation. In the USA, Donald Trump as president issued a series of executive orders that are related to an 'America First' mantra, a focus on bilateral relations rather than multinational institutions and seemingly the abrogation of US global leadership. These deglobalisation moves are seen as undermining global norms, cultures and conventions. Ironically, Communist China's President Xi Jinping has promised to assume leadership from the western democracies, proclaiming that Communist China will lead in support of democratic international institutions related to free trade and globalisation.

The United States: institutions and ideologies

People power

As noted earlier, in all policy systems based on democratic norms, the citizens remain the primary source of sovereignty. People use specific institutional methods to decide, for example, who will become their popular representative, and what form of majority will hold power inside the legislature. In addition, there are profound values, standards and norms with regard to people power in the policy process, and many of these standards and norms have deep philosophical roots. German, French, British and American expectations of majority rule are all different. Those derived from the philosophies of Immanuel Kant will be concerned to prevent despotic acts by majorities; while those sympathetic to the 'general will' ideals of Jean-Jacques Rousseau will expect consensus rather than dissent and disobedience from the majoritarian rule. In the USA, the American founding fathers sought ways to create a check on majoritarian power while still allowing factionalism to play a role in decision-making. People in these democracies define their own interests, organise themselves, persuade others to support their cause, gain access to government officials, influence decision-making, and watch over the implementation of government policies and programmes.[13]

Generally, the uncertainty and polarisation would be contained by the fact that the western democracies have strong core institutions and the rule of law. In the USA, working on the basis that he has the popular mandate fresh from winning the 2016 elections, Trump was effectively trying to rewrite the pillars of American institutions. According to John Boehner, former Republican Speaker of the US Congress, the US presidents have limited powers. They do not get things done unless they have got a Congress which will work with them.[14] Unlike the unwritten rules of campaigning, the legal rules come with a full-blown ecosystem of institutions and actors.[15] Take, for example, President Trump's campaign promise and executive orders within his 100 days of taking over as president to ban Muslims travelling to America. It had a serious impact on various US institutions: the executive, the judiciary and the legislature. The executive order directs the Secretary of Homeland Security to conduct a 30-day review to determine which countries are to be issued visas to enter the USA. In addition, preference would go to refugees who are Christians, as he wanted to admit those who would not bear hostile attitudes towards the USA and its founding principles, resonating with his popular base. However, on the executive front, the administration failed to give the US Customs and Border Protection department guidance on what they were required to do; the order omitted, for example, to mention lawful permanent residents and affected as many as 500,000 lawful US residents from the countries on the list.

On the judiciary front, Trump and team did not run the executive order past lawyers at the Department of Justice, whose office of Legal Counsel reviews all presidential actions that are potentially unlawful. Trump sacked his acting Attorney General for refusing to enforce the ruling. One judge in Brooklyn New York blocked the federal government from deporting people detained at the airport; International Refugee Assistance had lawyers stationed at airports telling residents, refugees and visitors to file legal challenges. Regarding the legislative aspects, Chicago mayor, Rahm Emanuel denounced the executive order while Senate Minority Leader Chuck Schumer urged the Homeland Secretary to rescind the relevant executive measures. Anti-Trump policy people power manifested itself with activism – New York Taxi Workers Alliance stopped pick-up for one hour; and protestors blocked roads leading to international airports.

Policy elites and networks

A significant part of policy-making within western democracies is the elite structure that affects the institutions, policies and the politics. However, in the USA, the Trump presidency is like no other in the 230-year history of the nation. He hired the wealthiest cabinet in history, which includes Wall Street top executives despite a campaign promise to drain the swamp of Wall Street's network of elite influence peddling. His family members play key roles in his administration. His elite network base is non-traditional – knowledge and power are monopolised by alternative rights groups (a term for an informal and ill-defined collection of Internet-based radicals), comprising primarily white, rural, religious Americans. Consequently the discourses are no longer to stand up for pluralism, tolerance of dissent, equality, and the rule of law. His administration lacks the high degree of consistency and coherence expected of US elite networks. He sees no need to read briefing reports from his intelligence committee; he has a strong sense of self-capability to know situations, watching TV gives him enough insight into world affairs. Most important, his elite intellectual alter ego is Steve Bannon, Chief Strategist, who believes in the deconstruction of the administrative state. However, Bannon has now left the White House appointment. Trump's advisers are working on ways to bypass Congress mainly through a series of executive orders and other actions.[16]

Core institutions

The executive, the judiciary and the legislature with a fairly independent media form the core institutions for governance of the nation. Institutions have both a constraining role and a steering one. By the end of January 2017, Trump was already challenging both domestic and international institutions. His anti-trade tirade campaign message is a departure for a traditionally free-trade Republican Party but Trump's message resonated with voters in the industrial states. Domestically, even a sacred institution, the integrity of the US election voting system is being challenged by Trump. Worse still, Trump mockingly puts the 'intelligence' in quotes when referring to the US intelligence community to challenge the expertise of the FBI and CIA, highly respected institutions charged with safeguarding the nation's security and freedom. Questions arise whether the legislative arms of governance would weigh in to stop Trump's undermining of domestic and international institutions. By undermining core institutions, Mark Lilla, Professor of Humanities at Columbia University, said that President Trump was creating a kind of moral panic about racial, gender and sexual identity, and US interests in world affairs. This is in addition to other concepts in social movements like Black Lives Matter, which was a wake-up call to every American with a conscience, and the founding fathers' achievements in establishing a system of government based on the guarantee of rights.[17]

Media

In an open, democratic society, an active media system engenders complexity. The Fourth Estate in the USA is regarded as a check and balance institution in American politics and it is common in the USA for mainstream media to be on a collision course with the executive arm of government. Steve Bannon, President Trump's former Chief Strategist, told the mainstream media to shut up as the media had questioned the series of fake news emanating from the president's communication staff. His media institution is his own 101 million followers shared between Facebook, Twitter and Instagram; the Brietbart News and related sites; and FOX TV is his mainstream form of media. The 2016 presidential elections saw the growth of fake information as part of the social media communication strategy. As presidential hopeful, Donald Trump was always getting massive free mainstream coverage by making outrageous claims. This includes pithy and painful insulting descriptors about his opponents and their capabilities and competence. Even after winning the presidency, he continues to make unverifiable claims, for example, that he had the largest turnout for his swearing into office than any previous president. He has a good grasp and understanding of the power of communication. He surrounds himself with people who have the same drive and communication infrastructure (Brietbart News, owners of FOX TV) to make news and claims that resonate among his voting base. Political theorist at Harvard University, Danielle Allen wrote:

> Mr Donald Trump campaigned to an America largely dependent on televisual and social media-provisioned sources of information and misinformation. Institutions – such as newspapers, political parties and universities – that have traditionally helped test and vet evidence and arguments hit, and must face, the limits of their influence.[18]

Markets

There are different schools of thought within western democracies regarding an unfettered market, which is neutral and free, and the key driver for progressive and democratic nations. *Wall Street Journal* columnist Andy Kessler thinks so, seeing it as the greatest enforcer (implicitly on all entities involved in the market) since no person controls that market, investors separately make decisions every day to buy and sell. And that collectively enforces discipline on corporations as buy and sell orders have more sway over CEOs than corporate boards, Congress or the White House. The market as enforcer shakes politicians and ensures capital is allocated efficiently. When, for instance, federal deficits get too large, the bond market will squawk, driving interest rates up, forcing budget discipline on Washington.[19] On the other hand, leaving markets to self-organise may produce negative social consequences, in terms of social inequality and polarisation. William and Susan Roth, in their (2014) book, *The Assault on Social Policy*, maintain that an unfettered market-driven nation suffers from corporacy, which is market-linked institutions, abetted by the media, propaganda and lobbying activities. The organisational power of modern media outlets, social media and the online community negatively affect the way America thinks, particularly when their myths correspond to the bureaucratic corporate structures.[20] Graham Room, in his book, *Complexity, Institutions and Public Policy*, maintains that only the state can provide the stability within which capitalist entrepreneurs and their 'animal spirit' can flourish. Unfettered markets will undermine social consent and threaten a backlash against the market institutions on which prosperity is said to depend.[21]

Global institutions

As noted earlier, global institutions that govern today's global policy-making are generally recognised as being a creation of the USA as a superior military, economic, and cultural power. Roger Cohen, a *New York Times* columnist, noted that President Trump is not interested in the rules-based international order that the United States has spent seven decades building and defending. The president is also agnostic on human rights, freedom and democracy and he notes that America, by suspending moral judgement, will behave a lot more like China on the world stage.[22]

Under Donald Trump's presidency, international institutions are being undermined and this has had an impact on other democracies in Europe. Trump dismissed NATO as obsolete; building on white Americans' sense of insecurity, he pledged and signed an executive order to build a 'beautiful' wall on the Mexican border, while describing Mexicans as rapists and murderers. He vigorously has pursued border security measures by reducing the number of refugees accepted by the USA, deporting undocumented immigrants, and placed a temporary ban on people from Syria and some other Muslim-majority countries from entering America. Trump denounced the Trans-Pacific Partnership (TPP) pact between the USA and 11 Pacific countries and the North American Free Trade Agreement (NAFTA) with Canada and Mexico. The long-held institutions and ideologies of the USA and democratic nations are being revisited. Martin Wolf, *Financial Times* correspondent, notes that we are living once again in an era of strident nationalism and xenophobia and that the brave new world of progress, harmony and democracy, raised by the market opening of the 1980s and the collapse of Soviet Communism between 1989 and 1991, has turned to ashes. He adds that by succumbing to the lure of false solutions, born of disillusion and rage, the West might even destroy the intellectual and institutional pillars on which the post-war economic and political order has rested.[23]

China: institutions and ideologies

People power

In all policy systems based on democratic norms, the citizens remain the primary source of sovereignty. Not so in China. Under communist rule the core institutions of the legislature, the judiciary and the executive come under the control of the Communist Party, not the people. More so under President Xi Jinping's leadership; he himself has assumed the status of 'core leader', a status mantle accorded previously only to Chairman Mao Tse Tung and Deng Xiao Ping. His policy leadership is bent on tackling widespread corruption and the conspicuous wealth gap, strengthening state institutions before contempt for officialdom erupts into a class-based rioting, and he encourages the greatest participation in economic activities to advance the people's livelihood, that include secure private property, an unbiased system of law and the provision of public services. People are empowered in most matters affecting their lives and livelihood but never criticise the Communist Party is the bottom line.

President Xi's Party's policy aim is to create the China Dream; it has gone down well with the public, in part, there are profound traditional values, standards, and norms. One deep philosophical root that resonates with the people is to return China to its rightful, historical place as the greatest power in Asia. The Party slogan is 'never forget national humiliation' (*wuwang guochi*), a concept that is even taught in schools, and accepted by all Chinese. Tom Miller in his book, *China's Asian Dream*,[24] quotes Liu Mingfu, a retired People's Liberation Army (PLA) colonel who first postulated this concept in his book, *The China Dream: Great Power Thinking and Strategic Posture in the Post-America Era*,[25] which is to restore China as the superior state, with its neighbouring states as vassal states maintained through a relationship of tribute and rewards.

China's people power has been galvanised around this appeal of ancient China's political, economic and cultural advantages and the desire that neighbouring states would naturally fall into the Chinese orbit. Nonetheless, when corrupt officials deny the provision of goods and services, steal land and perpetrate other official abuses, especially in villages in such a large country, the people rebel. In addition, despite the control of all the levers of institutions, including civic societies, there still are anti-government people power expressions, such as the neo-Maoist movement. Maoists attract support from within the Party and at the grassroots level. There are several neo-Maoist websites and these sites have tens of millions of followers on Weibo, the Chinese equivalent of Twitter. The movement is estimated to enjoy the sympathy of hundreds of millions of China's 1.4 billion people.[26]

Policy elites and networks

In China, policy elites and networks do exist but not with the same kind of openness found in western countries. All elites and their networks should be in total congruence, from policy formulations to policy executions, with the Party-controlled state apparatus. The central institution is the Communist Party of China, and all elites and their networks, whether as individuals or interest groups and enterprises, must follow these three principles, namely: (1) the Party controls the armed forces; (2) the Party controls the cadres; and (3) the Party controls the news. President Xi's ongoing reform agenda since his inauguration, including 'deepening economic reforms' and a strong 'anti-corruption' campaign, touches upon many sensitive issues related to existing interest groups and leadership politics in China. Tom Mitchell, writing in his article, 'Smothering dissent',[27] notes that an internal document after Xi became president in March 2013 indicated that the very notion of civil society is an attempt to dismantle the Party's social foundation. China has ordered that all private think tanks must register with the Ministry of Civil Affairs and that a think tank's objective is to serve the Communist Party and aid government decision-making. Think tanks looking to publish statistical analyses of government data must consult China's Bureau of Statistics, and failure to do so means that the institution will be placed on a public list of 'abnormal' social enterprises.[28]

Core institutions

In China, politics is the process by which the Party chooses the rules that will govern the nation and ensure the nation's economic prosperity. China's institutions support economic growth and prosperity and are tasked to ensure China's international outreach. China's core institutions were initially agrarian in nature, focused on growing the rural economy. Institutional changes to market incentives for agriculture and industry dramatically increased agricultural productivity. In the 1980s, it grew with the help of foreign direct investments and technology. China made radical changes to its economic institutions but not so to its political institutions, after the Chinese leaders saw what happened to the Russian economy and its politics after *perestroika*. Institutions in Communist countries are weak or non-existent. As part of creating a strong market-driven economy with the Communist Party in full control, China increased its dependence on strong multilateral trading arrangement like the World Trade Organisation for its economic success.[29]

China has cultural institutional structures to project its soft power. One is the concept of the Han Chinese. In the eyes of its Party leadership, all Chinese who have migrated to other nations, and despite being citizens of other countries, are still Han Chinese and China's Foreign Minister was quoted as saying that Lee Bo, a British passport holder, was first and foremost a Chinese citizen. Even ethnic Han, whose families left for other countries generations ago, are often regarded as part of a coherent national group, both by China's government and its people. In a speech in 2014, quoted in *The Economist*, President Xi Jinping said: 'Generations of overseas Chinese never forget their home country, their origins or the blood of the Chinese flowing in their veins.' In 2015, in Malaysia, where the Han population is 25 per cent, the Malaysian government censured the Chinese Ambassador when he declared that China would not sit idly by if its national interests and the interests of Chinese citizens were violated.[30]

Media

In China, the media are totally controlled, they have to follow Party lines. The choice is to comply or quit, as did *Yanhuang Chunqiu*, a traditionally liberal political magazine, which stopped publication after the Chinese National Academy of Arts sacked the publisher and demoted the chief editor under the security law. Xu Zhiyong, a prominent civil society activist for causes related to China's migrant workers, was sentenced to four years jail for gathering a crowd to disrupt public order. China's human rights lawyers are also under similar pressure. In the past, the stars for activism were netizens on Weibo who drew attention to corruption and abuses of power, leading to a crackdown on the spreading of 'online rumours'.[31] China continually introduces new regulations to tighten both the mainstream media and social media. It also shuts down platforms that produce relatively independent reporting and opinion pieces. Cyberspace Administration of China has laid down strict rules for online news portals and network providers. President Xi has made China's 'cyber sovereignty' a top priority in his sweeping campaign to bolster security. He has reasserted the ruling party's role in limiting and guiding online discussion on all other platforms that select or edit news and information, including diplomatic reports, or opinion articles on blogs, websites, or instant messaging apps. Editorial staff must be approved by the national or local government Internet and information offices, while their workers must gain training and reporting credentials from the central government.[32]

Markets

Historically under the Ming and Qing dynasties, the domestic market was taxed lightly and the leaders exchanged the development of a mercantile or industrial prosperity for political stability. The consequence of the absolutist control of the economy was economic stagnancy throughout the nineteenth and twentieth centuries. By the time Mao had set up his Communist regime in 1949, China had become one of the poorest countries in the world. In 1961, Deng Xiaoping, as the Chairman of the Communist Party, famously argued that it does not matter whether the cat is black or white so long as it catches the mice. It did not matter whether policies appeared Communist or not as China needed policies that would encourage production so that it could feed its people. The combination of growth, stability and potential set off a tidal wave of foreign enthusiasm for China.

Markets as an institution thrive in China but as part of the state and Party apparatus. There is a bird cage analogy of Chinese entrepreneurs and their enterprises, namely, China's economy is the bird; the Party's control is the cage and it will enlarge the cage to make the bird healthier and more dynamic but the cage cannot be unlocked or removed lest the bird fly away. In addition, big state companies can get involved in huge projects but when private companies compete with the state's enterprise, there will be trouble.[33] China's leaders have expanded its markets and crystallised them under the development concept of the Belt and Road Initiative (BRI). This has effectively replicated the present global institutions, such as the Asian Development Bank (ADB), and China has managed its own global institutions with its own financial support and its own managerial skills. By accepting globalisation by joining the World Trade Organisation (WTO), China's 660 million people have escaped poverty and it has created 670 million middle-class citizens. China, which, in the past, exported Chinese communism to Asian states, is now exporting its 'capitalist' credentials, benefiting nations like Cambodia, Laos and the Philippines.

Global institutions

While it is possible that China lacks the full range of capabilities and competencies to take the place of US institutional, economic, political and military powers, nonetheless its intent is to be the global beacon upholding international institutions and initiating new ones. The Regional Comprehensive Economic Partnership (RCEP) replaces for the time being the previously US-led Trans Pacific Partnership (TPP), which was aborted by the Trump presidency; the China-led Asian International Infrastructure Bank (AIIB) is a close parallel to the Asian Development Bank (ADB), which is headed by the Japanese and strongly supported by the USA.

There are new China-led global initiatives, for example, its Belt and Road Initiative (BRI), which is a significant effort to rebuild a global institutional structure. And it has been effective. Take, for example, China's role in Cambodia (soon to be replicated in Malaysia and the Philippines) and compare this with western nations' model of development assistance. In Cambodia, since 1992, the western countries' model support has been linked to democratic institutions being in place first. Elections were held, and the donor nations delivered some US$12 billion in loans and grants, despite rigged elections. However, the bulk of the donation was never spent on actual development but went to pay the salaries of cronies and expensive consultants, according to journalist Sebastian Strangio, author of *Hun Sen's Cambodia*.[34] On the other hand, China has invested US$9.6 billion over the last decade and delivered crucial infrastructure projects in Cambodia, and without delay. This of course comes at the expense of the nation's institutions and normative values, such as human rights and democratic credentials. China's companies pumping in money into development work are awarded land that exceeds the legal size limits, putting aside the protests of dispossessed farmers. Cambodian government officials say that western investments come with attachments, related to democracy or human rights, when the country has been through a civil war ('if you have no food in your stomach, you cannot have human rights').[35] China's global financial firepower for these bilateral infrastructure projects comes from two lending institutions, the China Development Bank (CDB) and the Import-Export Bank of China (Ex-Im Bank), which have a combined loan pot of US$684 million in 2014, far more than that of all six western-backed multilateral lending organisations put together. Their help, however, comes with the condition that the projects they finance should be executed by Chinese contractors.

Other institutions

Another institutional structure is the military and foreign policy that is closely associated with Chinese domestic politics – President Xi needs a strong foreign policy posture in order to strengthen his domestic power base and defuse internal criticisms of his various domestic agendas. President Xi has transformed the People's Liberation Army (PLA) into a political power base. China's foreign policy has also its own characteristics with a strong China First focus. Its foreign policy institution is based on its understanding of history – it has drawn nine dotted lines in the map of the South China Sea (the 9-dash rule) from Japan to East Malaysia that represent its territorial rights, which, according to the UN Convention on Law of the Sea (UNCLOS) agreement, are regarded as illegal. Though a signatory to UNCLOS, it ignores an arbitration ruling, claiming these islands based on historical reckoning. Here it is China projecting its military might. .

Institutions and complexity

All these issues – people power, policy elites, core institutions, media, markets, global institutions – reflect what complexity theorist Jeff Conklin calls fragmentation. Moises Naim describes it as micropower. The concept of fragmentation notes that the fragmented character of policy-making, owing to its dispersal among and dependence on powerful interacting institutions, imparts incoherence to policy-making. This is because of the necessity to resort to compromise and ambiguity to achieve the consensus on which the policy is founded. Fragmentation suggests a condition in which the people involved see themselves as more separate than united, and in which information and knowledge are chaotic and scattered. Fragmentation is when the stakeholders in a project are all convinced that their version of the problem is correct.[36] Micropower is not that massive, overwhelming and often coercive power of large and expert organisations but the counter-power that comes from being able to oppose and constrain what those big players can do. A world where players have enough power to block everyone else's initiatives but no one has the power to impose their own preferred course of action is a world where decisions are not taken, or taken too late, or watered down to the point of ineffectiveness.[37]

In western democracies, we see the campaign and communication messages have created:

[a] belief in the corruptibility of all institutions [which] leads to a dead end of universal distrust ... all democracy will not survive a lack of belief in the possibility of impartial institutions; instead partisan political combat will come to pervade every aspect of life.[38]

Western ideologies and idealism have changed and the long-held institutions are being revisited. Martin Wolf, *Financial Times* columnist, notes that it is possible that by succumbing to the lure of false solutions, a product of disillusion and rage, the West might even bring down the intellectual and institutional pillars on which the post-war economic and political order has rested.[39] The USA has been downgraded to a flawed democracy, because of the continued erosion of trust in government and elected officials.[40] If institutions and interpersonal relationships fail to deliver well-being, they do not merit trust. Low-trust environments are ill-suited for boisterous democracy: it quickly descends into infighting and paralysis.[41]

In China, people are thinking of ways and means to move money out of the country, reflecting a lack of confidence in a Party-dominated state. Talent is also flowing out of the country. According to the Ministry of Education, of the four million Chinese who have left to study abroad since 1978, half have not returned home.[42] The Chinese society is divided into two, based on the Great Firewall, an Internet firewall created in 1998. One world stands for free information and the exchange of ideas, and the other for censoring and monitoring. The government fosters an Internet society that does not concern itself with politics and current affairs.[43] Acemoglu and Robinson discuss inclusive and extractive institutions in the context of politics and political structures surrounding institutions. In nations with extractive institutions, policy elites control all the institutions and there is no room for an unbiased system of law, no level playing field where people can exchange and enter contracts. On the other hand, countries with inclusive institutions pave the way for sustained economic growth accompanied by technological improvements that enable people (labour), land, and existing capital (buildings, existing machines, and so on) to become more productive. They maintain that 'our theory also suggests that growth under extractive political institutions, as in China, will not bring sustained growth, and is likely to run out of steam'.[44] Perhaps China may be unique in that a consumption-focused middle class may be prepared to accept restrictions on civil liberties to attain the China Dream.

Conclusion: complexity, hurts and minefields

The study of winning the 'hearts and the minds' of the people turning into 'hurts and minefields' is a study of politics, policy processes and political decision-making. Institutions play a significant part to ensure that people have the power to elect their leaders and have a say in the policy process. The media as an institution provide both a regular information flow for the people and a check and balance on governance, while core institutions relate to the functioning of the executive, the judiciary, and the legislature. Marketplace dynamics and global entities are other aspects of institutions subject to critical junctures (complexity, volatility, social mess). Based on the two contrasting political structures – the USA, representing western democracies, and China, representing government's control of institutions – we observed that the key institutions of people power, policy elites, core institutions, media, markets, and global institutions will still have a say in the policy process.

Understanding the functions of institutions in a country helps understand the gap between private interests and public interests. It is positive for hearts and minds when the public interest (common good for the masses) exceeds the private interests (elite groups, interest groups). Inclusive institutions provide broad-based social equality when people are well oxygenated with information, have control over the levers of governance, and the leaders enjoy loyalty and cooperation of the largest number of electorates. The study of institutions is also the study of information, ideas and alliances. Is information interpretative, incomplete and strategically controlled? How does the politics of the nation shape, build and maintain alliances? Are the institutions supportive of people expressing their ideas and enabling them to implement these ideas? Do the institutions support an environment for ideas to gather political support and maybe diminish the support of opponents? It is also about trust. Communism and the control of institutions destroy trust. However, in democracies, if institutions and interpersonal relationships fail to deliver well-being, they do not merit trust. Low-trust environments negatively affect democracy: it quickly descends into infighting and paralysis.[45]

Notes

1 Adrian Kay, *The Dynamics of Public Policy* (Cheltenham: Edward Elgar, 2006), pp. 13–14.
2 Peter Barber, 'In reshaping presidency, Trump has changed, too', *New York Times*, international edn, 2 May 2017, p. 1.
3 The terms 'policy planners', 'policy leadership', and 'policy elites' are also used interchangeably.
4 Moises Naim, *The End of Power* (New York: Basic Books, 2013), p. 78.
5 Graham Room, *Complexity, Institutions and Public Policy: Agile Decision-making in a Turbulent World* (Cheltenham: Edward Elgar, 2011), p. 63.
6 Peter John, *Making Public Policy* (London: Routledge, 2011), p. 92.
7 Daron Acemoglu and James A. Robinson, *Why Nations Fail: The Origins of Power, Prosperity and Poverty* (New York: Crown Business, 2012).
8 Mark Considine, *Making Public Policy: Institutions, Actors, Strategies* (Cambridge: Polity Press, 2005), p. 202.
9 John, *Making Public Policy*, p. 88.
10 Louis Koenig, *An Introduction to Public Policy* (Englewood Cliffs, NJ: Prentice Hall, 1986).
11 Thomas Friedman, *Lexus and the Olive Tree* (New York: Anchor Books, 2000), pp. 101–111.
12 Dean Acheson, *Present at the Creation: My Years in the State Department* (New York: W. W. Norton and Company, 1987).
13 Ulrich Beck, *The Reinvention of Politics: Rethinking Modernity in the Global Social Order* (Cambridge: Polity Press, 1997), p. 45.
14 Gillian Tett, 'Emerging markets offer clues for investors in 2017', *Financial Times*, Comment, 1 January 2017, p. 7.

15 Noah Feldman, 'Rule of Law: 1, president's immigration order: 0', *Bloomberg*, reproduced in *Straits Times*, Opinion, 31 January 2017, p. A22.
16 Lionel Barber, Demetri Sevastopulo and Gillian Gett, 'The imperious presidency', *Financial Times*, 3 April 2017, p. 9.
17 Mark Lilla, 'The end of identity liberalism', *New York Times*, international edn, 21 November 2016, p. 15.
18 Danielle Allen, 'Defend America the indivisible', *Washington Post*, reproduced in *Straits Times*, Opinion, 13 January 2017, p. A28.
19 Andy Kessler, 'The markets tough love delivers', *Wall Street Journal*, 23 May 2017, p, A11.
20 William Roth and Susan J. Roth, *The Assault on Social Policy*, 2nd edn (New York: Columbia University Press, 2014).
21 Room, *Complexity, Institutions and Public Policy*, p. 64.
22 Roger Cohen, 'Trump's Chinese foreign policy', *New York Times*, international edn, 17–18 December 2017, p. 13.
23 Martin Wolf, 'The march to world disorder', *Financial Times*, 6 January 2017.
24 Tom Miller, *China's Asian Dream: Empire Building Along the New Silk Road* (London: ZED Books, 2017), p. 18.
25 Liu Mingfu, *The China Dream: Great Power Thinking and Strategic Posture in the Post-American Era* (New York: CN Times Books, 2015), quoted in Tom Miller, *China's Asian Dream: Empire Building Along the New Silk Road*.
26 Jamil Anderlini, 'The return of Mao', *Financial Times*, Weekend, Arts and Society, 1–2 October 2016, p. 1.
27 Tom Mitchell, 'Smothering dissent', *Financial Times*, FT Series Xi's China, 28 July 2016.
28 Reuters, 'China toughens rules on private think-tanks in ongoing crackdown', quoted in *Straits Times*, 6 May 2017, p. A16.
29 Miller, *China's Asian Dream*, p. 211.
30 *The Economist*, 'The upper Han: who is Chinese?', 19 November 2016, pp. 20–22.
31 John Gapper, 'China's internet is flourishing inside the Wall', *Financial Times*, 24 November 2016, p. 9.
32 Reuters, 'China's grip on online news, network providers tightens', reported in *Straits Times*, 3 May 2017, p. A11.
33 Acemoglu and Robinson, *Why Nations Fail*, p. 438.
34 Sebastian Strangio, *Hun Sen's Cambodia* (New Haven, CT: Yale University Press, 2014).
35 James Kynge, Leila Haddou and Michael Peel, 'The pivot to Phnom Penh', *Financial Times*, 9 September 2016.
36 Jeff Conklin, 'Paper on wicked problems and social complexity', available at: www.cognexus.org.
37 Moises Naim, *The End of Power* (New York: Basic Books, 2013), pp. 17–18.
38 Francis Fukuyama, 'The emergence of a post-fact world', Project Syndicate, reproduced in *Straits Times*, Opinion, 28 December 2017, p. A22.
39 Wolf, 'The march to world disorder'.
40 *The Economist*, 'Declining trust in government is denting democracy', 25 January 2017.
41 Leonid Bershidsky, 'The West's biggest problem is dwindling trust', *Bloomberg View*, reproduced in *Straits Times*, Opinion, 13 January 2017, p. 28.
42 *The Economist*, 'The upper Han', pp. 20–22.
43 Murong Xuecan, 'Scaling China's firewall', *New York Times*, international edn, 18 August 2015, p. 7.
44 Acemoglu and Robinson, *Why Nations Fail*, p. 436.
45 Bershidsky, 'The West's biggest problem'.

PART II

Communication practice

4

AGENDA SETTING, FRAMING AND PRIMING

It's about managing your message

Public policy leaders, lobbyists and others engaged in the formulation and execution of policies consciously or unconsciously adopt the agenda setting, framing and priming of the communication strategy. All policies are messages to the public that the leadership thinks, claims to think, are in the public's interest. Public policy management is a continuum, with the policy first constructed as a *public agenda*, and then political actors and interest group elites deem it necessary to have a strong public support by *framing public issues* into communication 'sound bites' for easy public understanding and acceptance. *Priming* is to bring about behaviour and opinion change, the acceptance of the policy. In the public policy process, agenda setting and framing are policy message management, while priming is behaviour and change management. Agenda refers to the policy content, framing is to facilitate adoption of the policy, and priming is the implementation or execution of the policy content. In this book, social marketing, activism, lobbying, nudging, persuasion and other planned and sustained communication strategies are regarded and discussed as priming activities.

Policy actors when pursuing framing and priming strategies are looking at hearts and minds shifts in thoughts, emotions and action tendencies. It is a model of the rational decision-making process. The hurts and minefields of complexity problems, the reality of the policy-making process, appear in the implementation of public policies, which has two dimensions: technical and political. Technical complexity means the underlying causal processes are not fully understood or involves a number of interactions of individuals and social factors, while political complexity means there are multiple and conflicting interests involved in the policy domain.[1] This chapter examines the core concepts of agenda setting, framing and priming, followed by thumbnail sketches of framing and priming strategies in India, Indonesia and China.

Within the agenda setting-framing-priming continuum, there are additional communication strategies. For instance, the best way policy analysts can find out the real problems in a complicated issue of many unknowns is not by asking directly 'What's the problem?' but rather asking 'What's the story?' behind the issue.[2] Policy narratives are structured storytelling to explain the complex policy dynamics for better public consumption. Persuasion tactics are also treated as priming the change in behaviour and opinion as part of policy implementation and are planned around three elements: the media, the message and the source.[3] In recent years, social media have aggravated policy complexity; the final section discusses the role of social media, such as Facebook and Twitter, in the agenda setting, framing and priming context.

From agenda setting to framing

What is agenda setting?

Agenda setting was first articulated in the communication field by two young professors, Don Shaw and Maxwell McCombs, at the University of North Carolina's School of Journalism in their research investigation on the role of the media in the 1968 US presidential campaign. They concluded that the media set the agenda by influencing the salience of issues among the voters. 'Setting the agenda' is now a common phrase in discussions on politics and public opinion. This phrase summarises the continuing dialogue and debate in every community, from local neighbourhoods to the international arena, over what should be at the centre of public attention and action.[4] An agenda is dynamic, often changing based on the needs of the nation and its people. This is the Gallup Poll-type agenda setting based on the bottom-up priorities of the people. Since the 1930s, according to McCombs, the Gallup Poll question has been replicated by many nations, think tank institutions and academics, with polling based on the agenda-setting question: 'What do you think is the most important problem facing this country today?'

Louis Koenig[5] and Cobb and Elder[6] have noted that there are two agenda-setting functions: systemic and institutional. The *systemic agenda* is the agenda of society; in a sense, the Gallup Poll-type polling on policy agenda. It consists of all wants or issues commonly perceived by the general body of citizens as meriting public attention and possibly policy action by public officials. It is a bottom-up agenda-setting discussed in conceptual models such as claims making, interest group representations, and public choice. *The institutional agenda* comprises the more concrete orders of the business of the executive, the legislature and the courts. This is the top-down approach to setting the agenda discussed in conceptual models like incrementalism, polyarchy and elite models. In several countries, it is common for the leaders to articulate an annual review of the state of the nation; a top-down approach to convey policy intent on where the nation will be heading, and the national priorities, often with immediate, multi-year or long-term time frames. In Singapore's case, the agenda setting is during National Day rallies some time in the month of August. In China, it is after the leaders' Retreat to discuss Five Year Plans, usually in November. In the USA, it is during the State of the Union address, and there is similar institutional agenda setting by government leadership in many countries. Sometimes the proposed policies form the backdrop to budget sessions and before the budget is presented so that the national agenda coincides with the dispensation of the budget.

What is framing?

Framing is redefining information from the broad agenda to the specifics by calling attention to some matters while ignoring others; making some issues more salient than others and giving meaning and order to complex problems, actions, and events. Professional policy planners generally work closely with the media to convey dominant meanings, make sense of the facts, focus the headlines, and structure the story line. Diana Kandall in her (2005) book, *Framing Class: Media Representatives of Wealth and Poverty in America*, notes that framing is an important way in which the media emphasise some ideological perspectives over others and manipulate salience by directing people's attention to some ideas while ignoring others. As such, a frame constitutes a strong line or an unfolding narrative about an issue, what this means is that we are not receiving 'raw' information or 'just' entertainment that accurately reflects the realities of life in different classes.[7] Framing matters because individuals almost always focus only on a subset of possible ways to think about an issue, event, or campaign. Thus, the frame they have in mind determines their opinions and behaviours. Gatekeepers, the media, interest groups and policy elites (such as think tank organisations) are equally active in setting the public agenda; they too are engaged in framing the dominant themes which may contradict the policy leadership's objectives. Policy complexity is compounded by the target public's two separate behaviours: the first is selective exposure, that is, avoiding contradictory messages, and the second is selective approach, where people seek confirmatory messages.[8]

To answer the question of who frames the issues, policy analysts maintain that *citizens* typically receive multiple frames concerning an issue from different sides due either to media exposure or access to general political debate. Citizens are engaged in framing, by making demands for goods and services and that demand is considered by the politicians and policy leaders, with the media keeping the demand salient by news coverage and keeping a larger community interested in the public demand. Besides citizens, *policy elites* frame the issues. Klar, Robison and Druckman, in 'Political dynamics of framing', say policy elites in a nation are continuously framing the issues for the nation. They make people think about the issues with greater intensity. However, elite political actors actively formulate frames in competition with one another, before communicating to the media, and finally to the public.[9] However, most writers agree that it is the mainstream *media* that put together the separately occurring events and frame them as unity, as a movement of a particular kind. In the process of constructing the reality for the society, mass media do more than monitor: they dramatise. They create vivid images, impute leadership, and heighten the sense of conflict between movements and the institutions of society.[10] Bernard Cohen

(1963) adds that the media may not tell us *what to think*, but they are successful in telling the public *what to think about*.[11]

From framing to priming

What is priming?

Priming is moving the needle for public opinion or behaviour change after the agenda has been set and the messages framed. The professional makes priming an art form, for example, understanding the master frame of issues. In *New Social Movements: From Ideology to Identity*, Enrique Larana and others point out that the anti-war movement, the student movements, womens movements and the black movement drew heavily upon the civil rights social movement as a master frame, mapping their understanding of their situations on the general framework first, before putting forward the specifics of their civil rights activism.[12]

Priming is part of implementation and policy implementation suffers endless disparagement, not because of intrinsic shortcomings but because it is the victim of expectations, suffering from overload which stakeholders impose on it and trade-off accommodation and bargaining, with relentless give-and-take. A supportive political environment, which originally produced a favourably inclined policy by the public, may wither and vanish in the stages of implementation. Public opinion that once rallied behind public goals slackens when the costs and rough edges of implementation are exposed.[13] Herein is the 'hurts and minefields' issue in the policy process.

Case studies on agenda setting, framing and priming

In every nation, as mentioned earlier, there are larger universal agendas and those engaged in this agenda, framing and priming strategy draw heavily upon this master frame, mapping their understanding of their specific situations on the general framework first, before putting forward the specifics of their activism. We will look at several examples to better appreciate the importance of knowing the universal frames and the ability of policy leadership to manage specific policy frames within the agenda, framing and priming strategy in implementing complex public policies. Three cases are discussed: Prime Minister Narendra Modi's unique attempt to remove corruption in India, President Jokowi Widodo's management of ethnic and religious tensions in Indonesia, and President Xi strengthening the Communist Party's control over domestic matters in China. These present a rich tapestry of complexity, and the thumbnail narrative is along the lines of agenda framing and priming communication strategy and the management of policy complexity. Lippmann, in his book, *Public Opinion*, points out that the analysts of public opinion must begin by recognising the triangular relationship between the scene of action (the uniqueness of the nation's policy problems), the human picture of that scene (the policy leadership in each country implementing the policies), and the human response to that picture working itself out upon the scene (the conflict among stakeholders – from initiation to implementation). He adds that in each of these innumerable centres of authority (the elite and the interest groups), there are parties. These parties are themselves hierarchies with their roots in classes, sections, cliques; and within these are the individual politicians, each the personal centre of a web of connection and memories and fears and hopes.[14]

Case study 4.1: India

In India, Prime Minister Narendra Modi and his supporters (the policy elites) kept to their election campaign agenda messages, one of which was to transform the economy (a policy message). Modi came to power in 2014 in a landslide victory, promising bold steps to boost economic growth and employment and root out corruption. Within that broad-based, universal agenda he initiated several policies, and the most controversial one was the announcement and implementation of the demonetisation of the 500 rupee and 1,000 rupee banknotes. On 8 November 2016, the Prime Minister personally announced the demonetisation of the 500 rupee and 1,000 rupee banknotes, since he was confident of controlling the national agenda. In fact, he did control the agenda, informing his own Cabinet Ministers only a few hours before the public announcement; at that particular Cabinet meeting, the ministers were not allowed to bring in their mobile phones. Earlier in the year, he had received parliamentary approval for the Goods and Services Tax legislation, convincing a hostile opposition to support it. He was therefore confident that he could carry the groundswell of public opinion regarding the controversial demonetisation.

He framed the demonetisation as 'a long-term structural transformation' to clean up the economy. In media interviews and public declarations, he continuously conveyed the message that the black economy is estimated to be equal to, if not bigger than, the size of the formal economy, with unaccounted-for money used in property transactions and to buy gold. He spoke in religious terms of a great cleansing sacrifice that would transform India's behaviour and attitudes.[15] This was a narrative that resonated with the people who were sick and tired of the corrupt elites. Folksy speeches and story-telling from someone who used to be a tea boy and poor won the hearts and minds of those in the rural areas. Describing PM Modi as the Pied Piper of India's politics, *Straits Times'* Associate Editor Ravi Vellor wrote that painting the move as an attack on the privileged class and pronouncing that he was convinced that the toiling masses would accept temporary hardship for a greater cause, PM Modi spun his magic web over an India that has undeniably responded to his call.[16]

Priming in implementation was a tougher call, knowing that the Indian economy is heavily reliant on cash for most transactions and removing the high-value notes meant that 86 per cent of banknotes would be taken out of circulation. In terms of priming, he kept the narrative continuously in the public domain even if the outcome was something of a crisis management. The November demonetisation of the 500 rupee and 1,000 rupee banknotes caused deep frustration, with long queues outside banks. For millions of Indians, the measure was painful ('the human picture of the scene'). There was anger in rural areas where farmers were unable to sell crops while small traders reported a huge drop in earnings owing to a lack of paper currency in the system. It affected famers who needed to restock their seeds, and 36 million small and medium businesses that contribute 40 per cent of exports and employ more than 80 million workers.

His priming message was consistently that the implementation, while it has caused hardship, should be considered a temporary evil for a larger good. At a rally two months after implementation PM Modi asked for another 50 days, and stated that if after 30 December, there were shortcomings in his work or if there were mistakes or bad intentions found in his work, he would be prepared for any punishment at any crossroads of the country that the people decide for him. While demonetisation was politically popular, critics had warned the move could cut India's growth rate. The outcome is that he not only looked durable but, as surveys showed, in the midst of the implementation, 87 per cent of Indians still viewed him favourably. He was seen as the most promising of Indian leaders in terms of his ability to follow through on commitments. There was no serious challenge to either his government or his control over his Bharatiya Janata Party (BJP). In fact, after the whole exercise, 80 per cent of the black money found its way into the banking system. Despite this major economically painful policy initiative, his reputation was not dented. His BJP party won 312 out of 403 seats in India's biggest state assembly in March 2017. Commenting on the victory, the *Straits Times* editorial said:

> Putting his credibility on the line, he had campaigned vigorously, in the wake of his surprise decision last November to cancel high denomination notes in an effort to wipe out illicit stash. That move caused immense hardship to all. It bodes well for India that Mr Modi was not made to pay a price for this, as he has more work left to do.[17]

In short, as mentioned earlier, the universal value frame must first be understood and leveraged upon ('elite corruption is rampant and should be curtailed') and then comes the specific framing ('withdrawing 500 rupee and 1,000 rupee banknotes solves the problem'). This approach matters because individuals almost always focus only on a subset of possible ways to think about an issue, event, or campaign. The frame they have in mind – top-level corruption is endemic – determines their opinions and behaviour and in this case, PM Modi's painful policy action resonated with the masses. Generally, in democratic societies, like India, solutions cannot be commanded by a hierarchical control system, nor can they be reliably achieved by bargaining and persuasion that rest on a foundation of power. Rather, solutions are achieved by skilled assertion on the intrinsic merits of a given response to a policy problem. This demonstrates that in democratic societies, the solutions on which implementation depend can be found only through the exercise of imagination, analysis, experiment and criticism. Commands and orders and preoccupation with the power leverages of bargaining impede and distort the search for solutions.[18]

Case study 4.2: Indonesia

The universal frame set by Indonesia's founding father, President Sukarno, is that politics and religion should not be mixed. Indonesians, after attaining independence in 1945, firmly agreed that Indonesia did not represent one ethnic group or one faith. The founding father, Sukarno, as a 26-year-old revolutionary thinker, penned an article in 1925, 'Nationalism, Islam and Marxism', about synthesising these three ideologies, which he saw as the main political pillars for the independence struggle. The combination of these three competing ideologies, Sukarno wrote, could portend a force against the Dutch colonial rulers. While Marxism and Communism were effectively crushed post Sukarno, nationalism and religion-based political parties flourished, but the fact is that parties pushing forth purely Islamic credentials have consistently failed to win a majority of votes, despite the fact that more than 88 per cent of the people are Muslims. Sukarno also laid out the 'Five Principles' or Pancasila, namely, belief in God, nationalism, internationalism, democracy, and social justice.[19]

However, there are still deep divisions within the frames based on religion, race, ethnicity, centre-periphery provinces tension, economic well-being, social inequality, and business-media owners rivalry. This is despite the fact that, by 2004, at the time of the presidency of Susilo Bambang Yudoyono's government, destabilising identity politics had been successfully contained and the dominant political actors had been largely reconciled to the democratic rules of the game.[20] This universal frame and the specific frames on tension form the backdrop to the policy agendas pursued by the successive policy leadership, particularly when seeking high offices like parliamentary positions and the presidency.

When Jokowi Widodo was running for the presidential office, he was accused on social media of being a Chinese Christian and a communist – a severe criticism in the deeply Muslim country (a typical religious frame in Indonesia). He had to prove he was not a Christian and he made a pilgrimage to Mecca just before the voting started. Framing by fake news played a big part in the Indonesian 2014 presidential elections.[21] With regards to the military as a key political force in Indonesia, in 1998, after the fall of President Suharto, significant political changes took place in Jakarta. The military, though deeply embedded in the socio-political and economic aspects of Indonesian politics, decided to play a lesser role during the transition from a military-controlled political system to a civilian presidential leadership. Indonesia is a functioning democracy where the sovereignty of power has long passed from a single autocratic ruler to a multitude of political players vying legitimately for power. This change has helped the military to strengthen and not subvert the Indonesian presidency because of the credibility that only a free, popular mandate can bring a candidate to the highest political office of a country.[22] President Jokowi, with no political party as a power base, won the presidency; a remarkable continuation of the Indonesian democratic journey.

However, it takes little to spark the polarisation and the tension to bring out all the deep divisions into the open. In January 1999, following a quarrel between a Christian bus driver and a Muslim passenger in Ambon Town in the Moluccas, violence erupted, lasting for four years, from 1999 till 2003, with an estimated death toll of around 8,000–15,000 and over 700,000 people forced to flee from their homes, and hundreds of churches and mosques destroyed. The bloodiest theatre of the Maluku wars was centred in the north, on the large island of Halmahera.[23] During the 2017 Jakarta Governor elections to undermine the President, a proxy war broke out. Charlotte Setjadi, an Indonesian academic, said that like so many conflicts before, it was started with a seemingly innocuous comment on 26 September, by the incumbent Governor Basuki Tjahaja Purnama (better known as Ahok), who was Jokowi's deputy when he was the Governor of Jakarta. Ahok told a small crowd in Jakarta not to be fooled by those who say that it would be a sin for a Muslim to vote for a non-Muslim. Referring specifically to verse 51 Al-Madiah of the Koran, Ahok said that voters should follow their guts when voting and not be influenced by religious provocation. When footage of his comment went viral on social media, his opponent got the loaded gun they had been waiting for. More than 150,000 Muslims took to the streets of downtown Jakarta to demand Ahok's prosecution for blasphemy against Islam.[24]

Just as in the Moluccas violence, the age-old dissatisfaction among locals and between religious and ethnic groups came to the forefront. Another academic who writes extensively on Indonesia, Leo Suryadinata, saw the blasphemy accusation as Indonesia's 'ideological war'.[25] On one side are the entrenched interests and their supporters using Islam (the militant version of the religion) to counter the pluralists and the reformists group. Ordinary Indonesians may not understand the complicated power struggle but the simple slogan (message framing) pitched it as a struggle between Islam and non-Islam or anti-Islam supporters. Priming by the extremists group included weekly demonstrations, often violent, after Friday prayer to stop Ahok from contesting, and to keep repeating that he had insulted Islam. On the other hand, the agenda setting, framing and priming of the so-called pluralist group was to let the courts decide on Ahok's blasphemy case. And that Indonesians of all religions and ethnicity should keep national unity intact whatever the courts decided. This group's priming included a peaceful demonstration in a park; singing national songs; and a national prayer for the unity of the Archipelago.

While in the Moluccas case, the generals and their business cronies played an active part, complaining that Ambonese Christians were controlling civil service jobs, key positions and running the economy, in the 2017 Ahok blasphemy case, the military played a supportive role, keeping the nation free for democracy. During the Moluccas riots, the military distributed religiously provocative pamphlets. The police and military were even-handed in dealing with the volatile racial and ethnic issues. The police continued their investigations of Ahok and the religious leaders, who were deemed a public nuisance. The court were not constrained and based on their findings, the Indonesian court ruled that there was a blasphemy case to pursue against Ahok. However, it also ruled that he could continue to contest the elections while his court case was pending. President Jokowi met the top leaders of the military, to secure their support, telling them that he was fighting against the forces that are undermining the Unitary State of the Republic of Indonesia (NKRI), and ensured that the Special Forces quelled any threat to the state's pluralistic status. In contrast, during the Moluccas violence, the military openly supported the Muslim faction, and even allowed a fundamentalist group, Laskar Jihad paramilitaries, to board ships to Ambon, and Kopassus (the Special Forces) fought alongside Laskar Jihad troops on campus.[26] Laskar Jihad or Defenders of Islam is the same militant Islamic party that organised the 2017 mass rallies against Ahok, but with their wings clipped.

As President of Indonesia, Jokowi Widodo clearly laid out the leadership position that politics and religion should be separate so people can know what religion is and what politics is. All moderate leaders maintained that the majority Muslim population prefers the national agenda to be based on the theme of pluralism or Unity in Diversity (Bhineka Tunggal Ika or previously Pancasila). He met the two largest Islamic social organisations to make the leaders publicly denounce forces that threaten national unity. He affirmed that the judiciary's decision would be upheld; the judiciary eventually convicted Ahok and sent him to jail for blasphemy. Like the pluralist group, Jokowi focused on the institutions in Indonesia having the final say, and that the country should not be turned into a theocratic state.[27] Polarisation in framing and priming persist. The media in Indonesia, for example, are part of the powerful business and political interests. As in the past, the business owners of the media organisation use the legal system and defamation laws to defeat journalists and media outlets through high profile defamation suits, thus shaping the behaviour of both media organisations and individual journalists.[28] Ahok, a good friend of President Jokowi, was found guilty and jailed. Many read it as a proxy war to undermine Jokowi's presidency.

The whole episode was handled by President Jokowi to ensure that the social political spaces created by civil society were strengthened. People's representative capacities, post Suharto, had gradually widened their networks, and transformed sectarian-based conflicts into more strategic issues involving productive political collaboration. These are non-party, broad alliances and alternative channels of popular representation, which can be established from the village to the national level. Democratic political blocs have also functioned as alternatives to exercise popular control over the state's institutions, including parliament, as people can access wide-ranging public issues and mobilise extra-parliamentary alliances behind their crucial demands. Nonetheless, both dominant and alternative actors support the democratic institutions so long as those rules and regulations are relevant to their respective positions.[29] It will not be easy in an Internet age. Indonesia is one of the largest Muslim populations in the world, spread over 17,000 islands, has the world's fourth largest mobile phone market, and two-thirds of its 255 million people have smartphones.[30]

Case study 4.3: China

In China, the significant and substantive role of President Xi Jinping in guiding China's growth and development is a case example of effective agenda setting, framing and priming policy implementation. President Xi set the policy agendas, namely, an anti-graft drive, to curtail civil society which is attempting to dismantle the Chinese Communist Party's (CCP) social foundation, and to project power abroad. This policy agenda has to date been successfully framed and executed. This was framed against China's backdrop of unique universal values, namely, after centuries of humiliation by colonial powers, China must regain its natural, rightful and historical position as the greatest power in Asia, and domestically achieve a China Dream. The quest for wealth and power has been a common refrain among Chinese political leaders and intellectuals since the nineteenth century, a phrase that dates back 2,000 years to the Warring States period, which laid the way for a unified Chinese empire. In 1800, China regarded itself as blessed by heaven and China sat at the centre of the world; its very name, *Zhongguo*, means 'middle kingdom'. That position unravelled in a series of catastrophic events, primarily involving Britain and the European nations.[31]

What were the successful priming-in-implementation strategies of President Xi? Mid-term through his presidency, he strengthened his political position by pursuing and was accorded a 'core' leader status. This was an important development, as now he could stay longer in office as President and appoint more of his own political appointees to key positions in all the institutions controlled by the Party. He made the thoughts of Mao Zedong of fundamental importance (framing the policy position), incorporating Mao's quotes and ideas in his speeches. He made numerous televised pilgrimages to important revolutionary sites and commanded party officials to forever hold high the banner of Mao Zedong's thoughts. This was to counteract a strong grassroots movement of neo-Maoism that had a separate agenda – a return to a less capitalist and market-driven economy ('bourgeois fascist dictatorship led by bureaucrat monopolist capitalists'), and unlike other human rights civil movements was much deeper and stronger, with millions of peasants and workers as followers.[32]

China's Facebook and Twitter equivalents are controlled so that they do not negate his policy agenda and implementation of the policies. He ran a sustained publicity programme particularly on television, for example, a documentary series *Always on the Road* to emphasise that the president is serious about wiping out graft. Some of the most notorious fallen officials are shown on camera, repenting, warning of the misery that comes from dirty wealth and imprisonment. The sustained anti-graft move led to the fall of more than 150 senior officials of vice ministerial rank or higher, plus thousands of other lower-ranking figures. At the same time, the president portrays himself as Spartan, humble and happy with a simple diet. He intones in the documentary series that corruption must be punished and graft must be purged. His campaign included clearing the rot in the People's Liberation Army and transforming it into a lean military force capable of enforcing the country's territorial claims.

Domestic achievements are also intertwined with external relations. His inter-national agenda was to project China's power across the South China Sea and the East Asia Sea; and its soft power agenda extended through the Belt and Road Initi-ative (BRI) development strategy. His new foreign policy championed *fenfa youwei* (striving for achievement). BRI was now a way of spreading China's commercial tentacles and soft power, extending its global power to Pakistan, Tajikistan, and Uzbekistan, and other Silk Route countries, and ensuring that China's control of the South China Sea was not challenged by competing claimants like the Philip-pines and Malaysia. The unstated aim was to create a network of economic dependent nations to consolidate its international position (in Asia, Central Asia and the Middle East); help the state commodity producers, engineering firms and capital goods makers find a lucrative new source of growth; and use the renminbi for trade settlement and gradually let the renminbi (RMB) take its place alongside the dollar and the Euro. The priming of this foreign policy was wide and fairly suc-cessful. President Xi presented China's geostrategic ambitions at a series of regional meetings: The Silk Route project was first mentioned by President Xi in September 2013 in Kazakhstan, followed by similar speech to the Indonesian Parliament on a proposed twenty-first-century Maritime Silk Road through the South China Sea and the Indian Ocean, and then at the APEC (Asia-Pacific Economic Cooperation) meeting in 2014 in Beijing. Just before APEC, he announced the formation of the Asian Infrastructure Investment Fund (AIIB).[33] Domestically every province has to set its own BRI investment plan.

Financial Times correspondent, Tom Mitchell, said. ask any man or woman on the street in China what they think of their president and the most common reply is that he is a strong leader, who is *fan fubai* – opposed to corruption.[34] He has been able to successfully win the hearts and minds of his people. Louis Koenig notes:

> As the more discretion the leader has under statutes and higher administrative orders, the more consequential will be the sense of commitment and the exercise of managerial skills. The gifted political leader maintains a reasonable calm over the regulated groups, or at least convinces them and other critics that they are treated fairly.[35]

The narrative art in priming

In his (1994) book, *Narrative Policy Analysis*, Emery Roe writes that policy narrat-ives have an important role in public policy, and that narrative allows one to refor-mulate increasingly intractable policy problems in ways that make policies more amenable than the conventional policy analytical approaches. Stories commonly used in describing and analysing policy issues are themselves a force and must be considered explicitly in assessing policy options. The starting point of narrative policy analysis is the reality of uncertainty and complexity in the polarised issues and controversies.[36] India's Prime Minister Narendra Modi's agenda was to cancel the 500 rupee and 1,000 rupee denominations and his narrative was India must eradicate privileged class corruption that will free the economy to grow and increase employment. President Jokowi Widodo's narrative is that, as the largest Muslim nation, Indonesia can be pluralistic, democratic and progressive without being weighed down by Islamic extremism. President Xi Jinping's narrative is the China Dream, based on trusting the supremacy of the Communist Party, eradicating corruption, and regaining China's rightful historical place as *zhongguo*, the middle kingdom, through several policy initiatives, including the Belt and Road Initiative.

Adrian Kay, in *The Dynamic of Public Policy*, writes that a structured narrative helps to understand and explain policy dynamics. The basic material of a narrative is a chronicle: a list of things that happened in a chronological order. The list has some minimal organising principle, such as the facts that the events happened in a particular place or to a particular organisation or person. Crucially, chronicles do not attempt to make sense of what happened, whereas narratives, in contrast, are a single coherent story, sometimes with subplots. A narrative is a selection of elements such as events, steps and processes from a chronicle; the long sequence of things that happened, which can be organised by some interpretive frame to make sense as an overall story.[37] Emery Roe elaborates that many policy issues become so uncertain and complex that the only things left to examine are the different stories that policy-makers and their critics use to articulate and make sense of that uncertainty and complexity. First, the analysts start with the conventional definition of stories or narratives, which is to have beginnings, middles, and endings, and if they are stories in the form of arguments or persuasion, they have premises and conclusions. Next, the analysts could identify other stories regarding the policy issue that do not conform to the conventional definition (called the non-story) or run counter to the policy issue's dominant policy narratives (the counter-stories). Third, the analysts compare two sets of narratives (for example, the story with the counter-stories) in order to generate the meta-narrative. Next, the analysts determine if and how the meta-narrative once generated recasts the issue in such a way as to make it more amenable to decision-making and policy-making. Narratives or story telling are more important than numbers; colourful parables resonate better with the listeners than considered policy statements.[38]

President Donald Trump is a master of this art. Journalism lecturer in New York University, Sukutu Mehta compares Donald Trump's style of communication with Hillary Clinton's, when both were presidential hopefuls in the 2016 elections. Noting that most voters are bored and do not respond to policy statements, Mehta writes about the two candidates' reactions after a Bollywood show to woo Americans of Indian origin. Hillary Clinton's address to a Bollywood show in New Jersey read like an academic paper on multiculturalism, while Trump was succinct: 'It's a weakness. I love the beautiful Indian actresses. There's nothing like them.'[39]

Katy Waldman in a *Slate Magazine* article, 'Trump's Tower of Babble', writes of Trump's narrative as working for him as vast swaths of Americans find themselves in Trump's verbal thrall, nodding along as his mind empties its baleful, inchoate contents. For thoughtful readers and writers, Trump's language is incendiary garbage. It's not just that the ideas he wants to communicate are awful but that they come out as saturnine gibberish or lewd smearing or racist gobbledygook. What's the secret to Trump's accidental brilliance? A few theories: simple component parts, weaponised unintelligibility, dark innuendo, and power signifiers. Despite the often-complicated work they do, Trump's speeches are built from basic, readily understood elements: loosely woven sentences, simple sentences and cramped, simplistic vocabulary. His narratives talk just below a sixth-grade reading level, compared with the eighth- to tenth-grade reading levels at which his competitors speak. Trump tends to place the most viscerally resonant words at the end of his statements, allowing them to vibrate in our ears. The unplanned detours and intentional, nerve-fraying vagueness; the emotional chiaroscuro of ominous terms set afloat in nonsense, like a word salad where the lettuce leaves are nightshade – they *work*. Even the ornamental word stuff gives Trump an air of authority. Trump is unconventional, and he's unconventionally adept at the blunt force transmission of fear and rage. Consider his reliance on dog whistles and buzzwords. Trump returns again and again to 'radical Islamic terror', as if the incantatory phrase presented an argument in itself. Urging his supporters to monitor polling places in urban districts, he said: 'Go down to certain areas … Make sure other people don't come in and vote five times'– '*certain areas*', '*other people*'. Leaving things provocatively undefined is a powerful strategy, allowing people's fantasies to swirl into the gaps between his words. In a world where everyone shares your perspective, there's no need to belabour the racist claims behind your allusions.[40]

The art of persuasion in priming

Persuasion tactics are also priming change in behaviour and opinion and are planned around three elements: (1) the media; (2) the message; and (3) the source. In a society where the media are free and communication is open, the person being persuaded chooses, for example, which messages to attend to, which policy source to be trusted, and which media to turn to for information. Persuasion is to bridge the gap between personal interests and public interests and also conflicting interests. It is to win people over (winning hearts and minds). William McGuire, writing on motivational theories behind persuasion, notes that, to be persuasive, a message (a policy) has to be something of value to the target public. If the target public has to make adjustments to accept the complex policy, the policy leaders should provide a clear statement of that adjustment and the rationale for making it. The policy narrative style would resonate better in explaining complex policy issues. It must also be compatible with the public's motives. If the policy issue has been rejected before and is being represented to the same audience, then the policy planner must offer value that can be adopted to replace it or rationalise it.[41] Some of this can be explained by cognitive dissonance where something we are persuaded to accept collides with what we think we should do; we resolve the conflict by justifying our action, rationalising our behaviour and modifying our opinion. The cognitive strategy maintains that learning factual information can be persuasive if the information is retained. As it is cognitive, suitable alternatives have to be proposed, and the policy issue has to be presented as part of a bigger picture.[42]

Earl Newson, writing on persuasion and communication theories, suggests four principles of persuasion built on the concept of personal identification with an idea or policy position. First is *identification*, where people relate to a new idea, opinion or policy position only if they can see it as having some direct effect on their own hopes, fears, desires or aspirations. Second, *suggestions of action* when people will endorse ideas only if the ideas or policies are accompanied by a proposed action from the policy originator; the people would have asked for this policy change and then become more receptive to its adoption. Third, *familiarity and trust* mean people are willing to accept ideas, policies from sources they trust and unwilling if they do not trust the source. Trust and credibility of the source are a crucial factor in persuasion as priming strategy. Finally, *clarity* of the idea in the policy proposal, situation or message in order to be persuasive. In making persuasive appeals to various human motives, the policy planner must consider the possibilities of cognitive dissonance occurring and that the truth is personal to the receiver of the message.[43]

Conclusion: complexity, hurts and minefields

The agenda setting, framing and priming strategy is to move policy or political agenda from the margins to the mainstream. Framing is pursued on the basis that the more controversial the issue, the greater the need to inform the public and to gauge public reactions to the proposed changes. Priming is to ensure that perception is managed so that it is the reality, and that reality is primed to generate positive perception and reception. We examined the successful implementation of wicked problems: Prime Minister Narendra Modi, President Jokowi, and President Xi Jinping framed their specific domestic policy issues within a larger universal frame and these frames resonated with the groundswell. They managed influence, obtained cooperation with allies in order to compete with their opponents, and, above all, enjoyed trust and loyalty of the majority of the people. In part, they were seen as different leaders, above the political fray, selfless and not seeking popularity for personal aggrandisement, and, above all, to be trusted to look after the interests of the people. In such situations, the chances of winning the hearts and minds of the people and carrying the ground are good, despite polarisation, competition for power, complexity, and chaos in the course of the implementation.

The Achilles' heel, the hurts and minefields in policy process, is the continued priming-in-implementation. Wicked problems cannot be solved, only managed in constantly renewed steps in an endless process of adaptations and adjustments. India's Modi still has a long way to go to reduce corruption among the privileged, and to control the upper-caste Hindu nationals who rule the roost at the expense of the rural masses. Indonesia's Jokowi has still to deal with complex centre and provincial differences, racial and religious tensions, and an economy in the hands of the business-media-military-politician elites, whom he wanted to take on but has to accommodate. And there is no shortage of people wanting to take over institutions and impose *Shari'ah* law. Xi Jinping's China Dream is challenged when the top young talent and their capital find ways and means to leave China for greener pastures in the USA, Canada, the UK and other European countries, and when China's Great Firewall and other censorship mechanisms create self-centred, crass, consumerist citizens with a limited worldview. His Belt and Road Initiative operates in several unfamiliar unfriendly territories, and it has a very long gestation period.

Notes

1 Guy Peters, *Advanced Introduction to Public Policy* (Cheltenham: Edward Elgar Publishing, 2015), p. 23.
2 Richard Neustadt and Ernest May, *Thinking in Time: The Uses of History for Decision-Makers* (New York: Free Press, 1986), p. 106.
3 Doug Newsom, Judy VanSlyke Turk and Dean Kruckeberg, *This Is PR: The Realities of Public Relations*, 7th edn (Belmont, CA: Wadsworth/Thomson Learning, 2000), p. 188.
4 Maxwell McCombs, *Setting the Agenda: The Mass Media and Public Opinion* (Cambridge: Polity Press, 2004), Preface.
5 Louis W. Koenig, *An Introduction to Public Policy* (Englewood Cliffs, NJ: Prentice Hall, 1986), p. 149.
6 R. W. Cobb and C. D. Elder, *Participation in American Politics: The Dynamics of Agenda Setting* (Baltimore, MD: Johns Hopkins University Press, 1972).
7 Diana Kandall *Framing Class: Media Representatives of Wealth and Poverty in America* (Lanham, MD: Rowman & Littlefield Publishers, 2005), p. 5.
8 Natalie Jamini Stroud and Ashley Muddiman, 'The American media system today: is the public fragmenting?', in Travis N. Ridout (ed.), *New Directions in Media and Politics* (New York: Routledge, 2013), p. 16.
9 Samara Klar, Joshua Robison and James Druckman, 'Political dynamics of framing', in Travis N. Ridout (ed.), *New Directions in Media and Politics* (New York: Routledge, 2013), pp. 183–192.
10 Enrique Larana, Hank Johnston and Joseph Gusfield (eds), *New Social Movements: From Ideology to Identity* (Philadelphia, PA: Temple University Press, 1994).
11 Bernard Cohen, *The Press and Foreign Policy* (Princeton, NJ: Princeton University Press, 1963), p. 13.
12 Larana *et al.*, *New Social Movements*, p. 42.
13 Koenig, *Introduction to Public Policy*, p. 149.
14 Walter Lippmann, *Public Opinion* (New York: Free Press, 1922), p. 13.
15 Mihir Sharma, 'Indians need a nudge, not a shove, to go cashless', *Bloomberg View*, 18 February 2017.
16 Ravi Velloor, 'Pied Piper of India's politics', *Straits Times*, Opinion, 17 March 2017.
17 *Straits Times*, 'Worrying risk as Modi waves surges on', Editorial, 25 March 2017.
18 Koenig, *Introduction to Public Policy*, p. 170.
19 Audrey Kahin, 'Natsir and Sukarno: their clash over nationalism, religion and democracy, 1928–1958', in Hui Yew-Foong (ed.), *Encountering Islam: The Politics of Religious Identities in Southeast Asia* (Singapore: ISEAS Publishing, 2013), pp. 191–217.
20 Amalinda Savirani and Olle Tornquist (eds), *Reclaiming the State: Overcoming Problems of Democracy in Post-Soeharto Indonesia* (Yogyakarta: Penerbit PolGov, 2015), p. 5.
21 Paul Mozer and Mark Scott, 'Friction over fiction on Facebook', *New York Times*, quoted in *Straits Times*, 20 November 2016, p. B9.
22 Luhut B. Pandjaitan, 'Indonesia may have a Trump card in the new America', *Straits Times*, Opinion, 18 January 2017, p. A21.
23 Steve Sharp, *Journalism and Conflict in Indonesia: From Reporting Violence to Promoting Peace* (New York: Routledge, 2013), p. 134.

24 Charlotte Setjadi, 'Big party politics and discontent of urban poor behind Jakarta unrest', *Straits Times*, 8 November 2016, p. A24.
25 Leo Suryadinata, 'Indonesia's ideological war', *Straits Times*, 2 December 2016, p. A31.
26 Sharp, *Journalism and Conflict*, pp. 128–132.
27 Endy Bayuni, 'Jokowi turns to Islam-nationalism to preserve Indonesia's diversity', *The Jakarta Post*, reproduced in *Straits Times*, 15 April 2017, p. A37.
28 Krishna Sen and Donald T. Hill (eds), *Politics and the Media in Twenty-First Century Indonesia: Decades of Democracy* (London: Routledge, 2011), p. 7.
29 Savirani and Tornquist, *Reclaiming the State*, pp. 15–16.
30 Jon Fasman, 'Jokowi's moment', *The Economist*, Special Report on Indonesia, 27 February 2016.
31 Tom Miller, *China's Asian Dream: Empire Building Along the New Silk Road* (London: Zed Books, 2017).
32 Jamil Anderlini, 'The return of Mao', *Financial Times*, Weekend, Arts and Society, 1–2 October 2016, pp. 1, 2.
33 Miller, *China's Asian Dream*, p. 30.
34 Tom Mitchell, 'The rise of party politics', FT Series: Xi's China, *Financial Times*, 26 July 2016, p. 7.
35 Koenig, *Introduction to Public Policy*, p. 178.
36 Emery Roe, *Narrative Policy Analysis: Theory and Practice* (Durham, NC: Duke University Press, 1994), p. 10.
37 Adrian Kay, *The Dynamics of Public Policy* (Cheltenham: Edward Elgar, 2006).
38 Roe, *Narrative Policy Analysis*, pp. 3–4.
39 Suketu Mehta, 'A Bombay strongman's lessons', *New York Times*, international edn, 7–8 January 2017.
40 Katy Waldman, 'Trump's Tower of Babble: it may sound like gibberish, but there's an accidental brilliance to Trump's style of speech', *Slate Magazine*, 2 November 2016.
41 William J. McGuire, 'Persuasion, resistance, and attitude change', in Ithiel de Sola *et al.* (eds), *Handbook of Communications* (Chicago: Rand McNally, 1973).
42 Leon Festinger, 'The theory of cognitive dissonance', in Wilbur Schramm (ed.), *The Science of Human Communications* (New York: Basic Books, 1963).
43 Earl Newsom, 'Elements of a good public relations program', 3 December, 1994, speech, quoted in Doug Newsom, Judy VanSlyke Turk and Dean Kruckeberg, *This Is PR: The Realities of Public Relations*, 7th edn (Belmont, CA: Wadsworth/Thomson Learning, 2000), p. 198.

5

SOCIAL MARKETING

It's about managing your public's behaviour

In social marketing, the fundamental assumption is that complexity is built into the policy execution. Negative demand, highly sensitive, invisible benefits, intangible solutions that are difficult to portray, culture conflicts and public scrutiny, multiple publics are all examples of this complexity. In social marketing, there is high involvement of the target publics (the customers) in policy issues. The aim is to bring about behaviour and opinion change among the relevant publics affected by these complex public policies. The policy planners, having identified the national level social problems, address them systematically, often over a longer time horizon, and use the private sector strategies to market the policy. Campaigns are an essential part of civic culture of several countries, including the USA, addressing public issues, such as health, social issues, energy conservation and environmental protection, and these public service goals are widely supported by the public and the policy-makers.[1] It is also true of many Asian countries. For example, Singapore is sometimes called a campaign nation because of its numerous campaigns per year.

Social marketing differs from the agenda setting, framing and priming strategy where policy elites, interest groups and lobbyists influence stakeholders for commercial or political gains. In social marketing, the greater public good is the campaign objective. Social marketers, for example, will pursue anti-smoking campaigns with the general public health concerns, while interest group elites will apply agenda setting and framing strategies to ensure their tobacco company clients can influence the anti-smoking lawmakers. Social marketing is one of the priming-in-implementation strategies to bring about behaviour and opinion change for the betterment of society.

This chapter examines the use of social marketing to manage complex or wicked problems. The first section discusses social marketing and its development as a communication tool. Next is a detailed examination of barriers to action, based on a list of policy complexities faced by social marketers. One overriding question for social marketers is 'Why can't we sell human rights like we sell soap?'[2] The next section examines nudging principles based on the book, *Nudge: Improving Decisions about Health, Wealth and Happiness* by University of Chicago economist Richard Thaler and Harvard Law Professor Cass Sunstein (2009).[3] They describe how neuro-science, social psychology and behavioural economics can help policy-makers influence people's behaviour, make their lives longer, healthier and better, while remaining free to do what they like. Nudging incorporates many social marketing principles to bring about opinion and behaviour changes. Subsequent sections highlight two distinct social marketing approaches. First, that behaviour change takes time as citizens shift from ignorance or indifference to policy acceptance. Second is the appreciation of sense-making and segmentation to better influence behaviour and opinion change.

Understanding social marketing

Why is social marketing an appropriate communication approach to managing complex or wicked problems? Social marketing is the application of commercial marketing competencies to the analysis, planning, execution, and evaluation of programmes designed to influence the voluntary behaviour of target audiences, in order to improve their personal welfare and that of their society. Andreasen, in his (1995) book, *Marketing Social Change*, provides a comprehensive insight into social marketing and its developments. First, social marketing combines several past efforts to bring about behaviour and opinion changes to policies. Andreasen highlights four different approaches to solving social problems that are incorporated into social marketing. The *Education Approach* is based on the assumption that individuals will do the right thing if only they understand why they need to do what is being advo-cated, and know how to carry it out. The *Persuasion Approach* is based on arguments carefully thought out, cogently presented, and with motivational hot spots identi-fied. The *Behavioural Modification Approach* focuses on the individual's thoughts and feelings, often with emphasis on training and modelling of the desired behaviour, while the *Social Influence Approach* is usually effective where community ties are strong, as the campaign is directed at influencing community norms and collective behaviour. Social marketing combines these approaches with a marketing mindset in contrast to a product or policy-focused mindset. Organisations should not lead the target publics or customers. Target publics or customers must lead the organisation.[4]

Second, the public service delivery of goods and services has changed. The New Public Management (NPM) led to the introduction of new management concepts, with more widespread use of marketing tools (such as satisfaction analysis, fee systems, and promotional activities development of brands). NPM is discussed extensively in Pasquier and Villeneuve's (2012) book, *Marketing Management and Communications in the Public Sector*. Under NPM, solutions are focused on the growing autonomy of public organisations, putting them in competition with one another, and on the adoption of a 'consumer-driven' model for the provision of services. Public service quality is no longer measured by the authority but by the beneficiaries: the target public. Third, social marketers recognise that four different sets of factors must be in place before bottom-line behaviour can take place. These four elements are the 4Ps: Product (policy), Price (risk factor, degree of social mess), Place (the social policy context), and Promotion (communication initiatives). Market research is essential to designing, pre-testing and evaluating intervention programmes, and competition is always recognised. The Product is also products and services, such as the passport and identity documents; the Price is the cost for the service or, for example, the price of the passport; the Promotion is the communication activity for government services; and Place is where these public services are made available. To the 4Ps, the social marketer adds services or relationship marketing, as it involves people, personnel in charge of supplying the goods and services and the environment in which the service is delivered.[5]

In 1951, G. D. Weibe, writing on social advertising, asked the question whether we can sell brotherhood like we sell soap.[6] More than five decades later, Robert Hornik asked the question 'Why can't we sell human rights like we sell soap?'[7] His aim was to apply the field of communication for social and behavioural change to human rights issues, which is based on the 1948 Universal Declaration of Human Rights. Historically, the application of marketing principles to social or public policies dates back to the 1960s and early 1970s, when marketing scholars looked at the possible application of commercial sector marketing beyond its traditional confines. The early social marketers in this regard were Philip Kotler,[8] who noted that marketing could be applied to any social unit keen to exchange values with other units, and together with S. J. Levy, he broadened the concept of marketing to go beyond merely exchange of commercial goods and services to symbols, ideas and values, and made it possible to transpose these concepts to non-profit, social, political and public sectors.[9]

By the 1980s, these marketing concepts had caught the attention of non-profit organisations, universities, performing arts, hospital and healthcare administrations. In the 1980s and 1990s, communication scholars and practitioners shifted the emphasis from being merely informational to programmes that stressed behavioural changes. This was in line with commercial strategies which laid emphasis on purchase decisions; this 'purchase' application was to cause behavioural and attitude change. The lessons were drawn on why people buy a Big Mac or fly United Airlines, and social marketers tried to apply these commercial competencies to campaigns related to practising safe sex, or getting one's child immunised. The marketing lexicon included positioning statements, campaign missions, focus groups, and identifying the niche in the competitive marketplace.

Social marketers over time applied behavioural change strategies to public policy campaigns, anthropology, psychology, and economics. Innovation-Diffusion-Adoption theories, for example, advocated that those who tried something early in its product or policy lifecycle (innovators or early adopters) may be very different from those who consider adopting the product or policy later, called the Late Majority. Those who adopted reluctantly and much later are called Laggards, having personality attributes where they depended on external influencers for their decisions. The popular Health Belief Model and the social learning theory emphasised that the environment can influence behaviour, both by communicating norms and by making it possible and easy to act. Source role models explicitly demonstrated accepted behaviours, and depicted vicarious reinforcements to enhance the impact of the messages.[10] These communication strategies were deliberate attempts to inform or influence behaviour in large audiences within a specified time period using communication activities and featuring an array of messages through multiple channels to produce non-commercial benefits to individuals and society. This is a means of influencing public knowledge, attitudes and behaviour, and as an instrument of social change, according to public campaigners like William Paisley.[11]

Complexity, barriers to action

The complexity and barriers to action faced by social marketers and public communication campaigners are numerous, such as negative demand, highly sensitive, invisible benefits, intangibles solutions that are difficult to portray, culture conflicts and public scrutiny, and multiple publics.[12] Social marketer Alan Andreasen has studied marketing's application to several public issues, including health-related issues like anti-smoking, immunisation, disease prevention, environmental, healthy and gracious living, environmental matters, and productivity.

G. D. Weibe and Robert Hornik's earlier questions pose challenges to marketers: 'Why can't we sell brotherhood or human rights or migration issues like we sell soap?' Migrant issues, the rise of ethnic, religious and professional diasporas, are part of the mobility revolution taking place in this century. The United Nations estimates that there are 214 million migrants across the globe, an increase of 37 per cent in the last two decades, and the number of migrants grew by 41 per cent in Europe and by 80 per cent in North America. We are experiencing a mobility movement, more people moving than any time in world history.[13] Let us now apply these barriers to action to the migrant mobility problem:

- *Negative demand.* Unlike the marketing of commercial product, social problems attract adverse attitudes and consequently the rejection of the public policy. It is rare for a private sector marketer to be asked to market a product or service for which the target audience has distaste, such as persuading 'macho men' to wear seat belts, or taking medication, which is rumoured to have devastating effects on sexual potency.

    On migrant issues, the negativity towards foreigners is immense, in particular, due to overcrowded public transport systems, the depression of the wages of low-income earners, increased competition for jobs, and rising property prices. Yolanda Chin *et al.* (2012) have noted Singapore's attempt to encourage greater acceptance of the importance of having a migrant population. However, the challenges include transport overcrowding as a result of a large influx of foreign workers using the trains, rising prices of properties, and pressure and strains on the public infrastructure and social services.[14] In Europe, the far-right, anti-immigration parties depict themselves as the new defenders of the working class against the overwhelming influx of migrants. Europe faces the problem of an ageing population. It needs a younger workforce. Migrants are fleeing from countries facing long-drawn-out wars and poverty. However, the younger populations from Africa, the Middle East and South Asia are unskilled and poorly educated. This is a negative demand situation, given Europe's public anxiety about security and social problems that come with the influx of these migrants.

• *Highly sensitive topics.* When dealing with highly sensitive health issues like HIV infection and AIDS, it is difficult to speak frankly about sexual and drug habits, as these are surrounded by prior attitudes among the different stakeholders.

On migrant issues, pre-selection and old attitudes towards foreigners persist, making it tough to change the narrative to one where foreigners or new citizens are required to supplement both the nation's 'greying' population as well as improving the low birth fertility rate. One highly sensitive issue is the security and nuisance factors created by the large number of foreigners. In France, thousands of migrants and refugees from Afghanistan, Syria, Iraq and Africa have set up a sprawling camp, called the 'Jungle', in Calais, a French port near the Channel Tunnel. Their bad behaviour, becoming a nuisance to drivers and travellers, has reinforced old attitudes and deep suspicion towards these migrants.[15] In Europe, the nationalists maintain the conspiracy theory that the central government has abandoned them, wanting the middle class to be replaced by hard-working immigrants from North Africa and the Middle East.

• *Invisible benefits.* This means adopting a necessary but socially unobservable behaviour. However, people will not see the changes immediately or the benefits are not so transparent, for example, women in poor, developing countries taking a birth control pill. Moreover people may have difficulty knowing whether the behaviour action worked or if the same outcome would have occurred without the recommended course of action.

On migrant issues, given the bad behaviour and the seemingly overwhelming numbers of migrants, the locals cannot see the benefits of having refugees in their countries. For example, in the French town of Bezier, with a population of 9,000 migrants against the 75,000 total population, veiled women, unemployed Muslim youths roaming around, and male-only cafés with Moroccan customers seem visible signs that the town has been over-run by Mahgrebi migrants.[16] The central government should have addressed the issue by calibrating the inflow of foreigners, imposing more stringent caps, such as the number of foreigners companies can employ, and raising the eligibility criteria for higher-skilled foreigners. Policy leaders in most countries acknowledge the migrant issue should not be left unaddressed, otherwise it will have severe consequences on the nation's economy and quality of life in the not-too-distant future. This is a challenge faced by social marketers and the communication practice, namely, to sell policy changes where the benefits are not visible or where it seems that nothing happens immediately.

- *Benefits to third parties.* Generally people see other people benefiting while they are required to comply with a behavioural change. Productivity, energy conservation and long-term health campaigns suffer from this outcome, people affected feel that they only see other people, society or even the government benefit, not them.

  Migrant policies usually are seen by the larger citizen population as benefiting multinationals, big companies, and big cities but not the townsfolk living in smaller cities. It is difficult to motivate people to take action when they do not see the direct benefits, or worse, see direct downsides, like overcrowding. One reason for UK citizens opting to exit from the European Union was that their citizens in the smaller cities could not see the benefits to their communities, particularly overcrowding caused by migrants and the drop in wages for locals and severe pressure on property process. In contrast, for the cities like London, it was beneficial, almost essential, to have a migrant population.

- *Intangibles that are difficult to portray.* Symbols in communications, like family planning and use of condoms, to communicate intangibles often risk sending the wrong signals. Rural and traditionally-minded consumers are alienated by publicity and promotions that seem too Western. No amount of logical explanations from the authorities will be emotionally accepted if they fail to take into account personal situations and feelings. Well-intended efforts miss their mark because they do not deal with reality as the audience sees it or knows it.[17]

  On immigrants, for example, the German magazine *Der Spiegel* said even though Germany takes great pains to welcome hundreds of thousands of refugees, it is also accompanied by a wave of hatred that cannot be played down. It seems as though the time has come for a broad debate over Germany's future – and Chancellor Angela Merkel's mantra of 'We can do it' is no longer enough to suppress it.[18] Against the intangibles of compassion and competence to tackle the migration problem were social problems, such as sexual assaults. A major incident was the groping and robbing of young German women in Cologne, Germany, at New Year 2017, by predatory gangs of mostly foreign men, including refugees, which touched raw nerves and increased critical public scrutiny of government pro-migrant policies. The immediate negative tangibles were a more powerful image – the police's failure to stop the Cologne assaults as 'symbolic of the state's powerlessness in the face of chaos and crime'.[19]

- *Changes that take a long time.* As Andreasen has maintained, many behavioural changes involve or entail changing individuals from negative to positive and the process can take a very long time. Large amounts of information have to be communicated and on a sustained and planned basis in order to bring about basic values changes, often getting third parties or influencers to help.

  On migrant issues, in Germany, Chancellor Angela Merkel emphasised the moral imperative of accepting the migrants. Merkel, however, had failed to clearly articulate a plan for an integration process. A systemic, long-term approach to accommodate the refugees was not there. For example, early migrants who came 40 years in an orderly fashioned were trained and assigned jobs but after 40 years they still cannot speak German. Currently, many of the first Syrian refugees were doctors and engineers, but they were succeeded by many more who lack any skills. The question now how to absorb the 1.3 million migrants who have arrived is still one of the voters' key concerns.[20] The fact remains that the immediate downsides clearly continue to be palpable while the benefits remain obscure. The pro-immigration camp should sell, based on a multi-year campaign programme, the benefits of an open door, managed immigration policy and spell out the potential cost of a closed-door immigration policy. In the integration plan, the priority is not to provide employment as soon as possible but to ensure they learn German and acquire the skills needed for an advanced industrial economy.

- *Culture conflicts.* One complexity is the basic conflict between cultures, for example, the working style cultures between social service organisations and the social marketers. Andreasen advocates the six stages of implementation to manage such conflicts, which could have highly debilitating effects on social programmes. The communication steps include listen and learn cultural nuances, only then get into the planning mode, followed by structuring the processes, pre-testing to adjust and manage culture conflicts, and then implementing the marketing strategy but yet continuously monitoring the progress of the strategy; and repeating this strategic communication process for the duration of the campaign.[21]

On migrant issues, Europeans want to show compassion and are committed to decency, including a traditional welcome to accepting the migrants. However, there should be a shift in perception. There is a case that newcomers to the continent must learn to speak the language, be open to skills-based training, and accept 'European values', which include values training and acceptance of feminism, for example. This is important as many male immigrants from the Middle East and Africa bring much more conservative and sexist attitudes with them. It will be a challenge to integrate and acculturate the asylum seekers, most of them Muslims, and the majority of them single men.

- *Public scrutiny* (of government, funding agencies, the general public, and the media). The scrutiny makes it more difficult to take risks. Policy leaders have to be mindful of the stakeholders targeted and others, which means increasing the importance of public relations in the social marketing mix.

In migrant issues, there is public scrutiny by a wealthy but ageing Europe, public anxiety about security and social problems that come with the influx of migrants. For example, the locals are asking: are they genuine refugees?, are they able to be accommodated into society?, and can they contribute to European society? Or will they be a burden to the state welfare system? The public mood shifted from being accommodating to anti-migrant reactions, polarising at different levels – cities, communities and countries. Chancellor Angela

Merkel saw her poll ratings plummet in 2015 when she threw open Germany's borders. That also explains the popularity of the Alternative for Germany (Afd), an anti-immigrant party, which recorded electoral success in the 2017 German elections.

- *Limited budgets.* Social marketers, unlike private sector marketing, spend more time and effort leveraging their meagre budgets to engage service providers, like distributors, advertising agencies, to carry out their programmes. In fact, there are oversight committees or watchdog groups to scrutinise how the programme budget is spent, which is good for governance but may hamper creative marketing strategies.

  In social problems, like the migrant influx issue in Europe, limited government budgets constrain internal European arrangements; the burden of registering and feeding refugees was left to the front-line states of Hungary, Greece and Italy. Hungary, for example, was both unable and unwilling, the citizens turned hostile to the refugees. Instead of registering the hundreds of thousands who arrived, Hungary erected border fences. In Denmark, for example the government moved to confiscate valuables from arriving migrants to defray the cost of accommodating them.

- *Multiple publics.* In the typical social marketing programme, whether on health, environment, children and elder care, there are multiple publics and multiple opinions, which tend to weigh down on the implementation of the programme. Multiple stakeholders can be polarising and affect social marketing time to communicate with target customers.

  In the European migrant issue, in Germany, Chancellor Angela Merkel rallied ordinary Germans with her slogan, 'We can do it!' However, multiple publics opposed this policy position as the scale of refugee numbers became overwhelming. The resentment against the Muslims has already created multiple, polarised political groups within each European nation. *Financial Times* columnist Gideon Rachman noted that the big question in the coming decades is how Europe's faith in universal liberal values will withstand the impact of mass immigration. A battle between nativists and liberals is beginning to shape politics.[22]

- *Absence of a marketing mindset.* A major weakness in many organisations is the absence of a pervasive marketing mindset, the commitment to the bottom line of behavioural change. This is the crux of social marketers' strategy: organisations' policies should not lead customers (citizens): customers (citizens) must lead the organisations. It is not a populist approach but a pragmatic approach based on the Transtheoretical Model (TTM), an integrative model to conceptualise the process of intentional behavioural change, which is discussed in the section 'Behavioural change takes time'.

  On migrants, the marketing agenda is that a more seamless flow of goods and people across borders is good for the European host nations. It may be politically correct but ultimately irrelevant to compare the 200,000 Hungarian asylum seekers who fled their country when it was invaded by the Soviet

Union in 1956. Instead they should look at the economic and social target publics they need – professionals, professionals with families, young people who have skills and can be re-skilled, of the right temperament to fit culturally into the host countries and to be a labour supply for the European workforce, which is facing the problem of an ageing population. They should support refugee camps with training centres to skill them up for migration, make them learn the European language, and place a stronger focus on education and the correct social behaviour expected in western democracies. To further stem the refugee flow, they should invest in the home countries of the refugees, many former European colonies. The aim is to divert the millions of dollars and the resources of the European host countries spent in managing an intractable refugee problem to help individuals and build institutions in these home countries. These plans should find ways to bypass the corrupt governments of the refugees' home countries.

- *Few opportunities to modify.* Many products like social policies need long gestation periods to be successful or easily developed. Years of research are essential. Anti-smoking, drug abuse, vaccination, and other related, usually health, public campaigns are still ongoing after decades of implementation because of different circumstances, different target groups, and because these are social problems that will always be with us, no matter what the stage of economic progress.

   On migrant problems, it is generally difficult to modify the problem, especially in Europe. The EU's current asylum framework was put in place after the end of the Second World War, when most of the refugees were within Europe, and the solidarity and sympathy for those seeking asylum were very high. This time in the twenty-first century, the European publics were not ready for the millions from the Middle East and Africa, whose cultural and ethnic affinities were different. The German Chancellor displayed the same chutzpah as Tony Blair, the former UK Prime Minister, did when he openly welcomed migrants from Eastern Europe and found more than a million migrants without skills or with low skills flooding the various small towns in the UK. Germany is discovering that the present immigrants are not the labour migrants to fill the factories and companies that require foreign talent. Moreover, unless there is greater preparation for the integration of largely Muslim migrants, there will be severe unintended consequences for the western democracies.

Nudging: choice architects alter behaviour

Philip Kotler and Gerald Zaltman, in a (1971) article for the *Journal of Marketing*,[23] noted the availability of healthy snacks – fruit, vegetables, and the like – around the home or classroom will make it more likely that a child will learn healthy eating habits. Situational factors such as atmospherics play a role in consumer behaviour and provide behavioural change on public policies. Influencers play a role to alter people's behaviour in a predictable way, without forbidding any options or significantly changing economic incentives. Thaler and Sunstein, in their (2009) book, *Nudge*, define the role of influencers as choice architects, noting, for example, that if a bureaucrat defines the ballot that voters use to choose candidates, he is a choice architect; a doctor, who describes the alternative treatments available to a patient, is also a choice architect; or the person who designs the form that new employees must fill out to enrol in the company healthcare scheme. It is not possible to avoid choice architecture in the sense that it is not possible to avoid influencing people. The choice architect invests their time to know the citizens and their default bias, segment them as target publics, and understand their requirements in a detailed manner to be executed effectively and efficiently. They note that framing works because people tend to be mindless, passive decision-makers, and that message frames are powerful nudges.[24]

Peer pressure is a social influence to make people learn from others, and care about what other people think about their behaviour. People behave less than completely rationally: human fallibility, biases and preconceptions and their busyness when trying to cope in a complex world all make it difficult for them to think long and deeply on any topic. Instead, they are conditioned by environmental cues. To change behaviour, the environment may be structured to influence people subtly to make certain choices that experts know are better for the individual and society. The potential for beneficial nudging depends on the ability of the policy leaders (the nudgers) to make good estimates about what is best for the target audience (the nudgees). Massive social changes in markets and politics (for example, changes in attitudes towards migrants) start with small changes. Social influences involve information and peer pressure. Consistent and unwavering people (the influencers) can move groups and the groups' practices in the preferred direction.[25]

How should it be organised? Writing in the *Straits Times*, Nair writes that the nudging principle is premised on a solid 'whole of government' approach to policy planning and execution. The challenge is not just to have a centralised unit in charge of the behavioural change agenda. True, in France, the Centre d'Analyse Stratégique has established a neurological unit to explore the use of behaviour and cognitive sciences in the design of government policy. In the UK, a Behavioural Insights Team, parked within the Prime Minister's Strategy Unit, explores ways of mainstreaming the behaviour agenda in all public policy sectors. The more effective approach is to make the whole civil service understand that they are source architects: there is no ivory tower. As source architects, they are responsible for understanding the influencers and activists, who want a voice in the policy implementation. It requires reskilling, retraining the civil service for a hyper-connected citizenry. In the process, it lifts the quality and brand reputation of governments, in public policy planning and execution.[26]

Weibe and Hornik's challenge to the marketers is: 'Why can't we sell brotherhood or human rights or migration issues like we sell soap?' Nudge would look, for instance, at the social and choice architects in the refugee camps and create choice architecture there. In building the choice architecture like training schools, re-education, and re-skilling, Nudge would in the process find choice architects among the refugees, as well as choice architects from the European countries. In parallel, choice architects can be created in these home countries where the migrants are not refugees fleeing a war-torn area, but are economic migrants. The whole western programme should focus on job creation, entrepreneurship, and skills-based apprenticeship, founded on education. Choice architecture's pervasive and key question is: 'Who is responsible for starting and managing the programme?' Right now in the refugee movement, it is the mafias who are the source architects, planning the hazardous boat trips to Europe. Governments should take control of who is the choice architect for the refugee programmes. Choice architects chosen by the governments can nudge people in directions that will improve their lives.

Hornik has a five-fold perspective on communication difficulties related to human rights:

- Poor messages.
- Too little exposure.
- Over-focus on individual persuasion rather than social networks and institutional contexts.
- Communication perhaps is not the real problem.
- Confusing communication with action.

On *poor messages*, message producers need to choose messages that are persuasive to their target audience. More time should be spent on understanding how target audiences think about the behaviour of concern. On *too little exposure*, many serious communication efforts fail because their good messages are not seen or heard with sufficient frequency. On *persuasion and social networks*, some individual behavioural changes will happen quicker if they are influenced by shared norm change in their social network or the supporting institutions (such as changing the legal status of undocumented immigrants). On *not a communication problem*, this requires policy leaders to ask if the problem is one of lack of material resources to permit changes. Sometimes it is in the interest of policy actors, or the policy actor's constituents, not to change the policy. This is related to the fifth point that of *confusing communication with policy action*. Political decision-making actors turn to public communication with two possible outcomes. Ideally they are trying to make things better. The other outcome is to look like they are doing something, allowing the appearance of communication action to replace effective action.[27]

Behavioural change takes time

Social marketers are adamant that behavioural change takes time and must go through several stages. William McGuire proposed a six-staged concept to explain the challenges in trying to get someone to prefer a product or brand. He suggested that consumers go through six stages: (1) exposure to a message (policy); (2) attention; (3) understanding; (4) persuasion; (5) retention; and (6) behaviour.[28] To further understand the 'it takes time' process, one could look at the behavioural change advocated in the Transthereotical Model which discusses the process that citizens go through, from ignorance or indifference before policy acceptance.

The Transtheoretical Model (TTM) is an integrative model to conceptualise the process of intentional behaviour change. Whereas other models of behaviour change focus exclusively on certain dimensions of change (e.g. theories focusing mainly on social or biological influences), the TTM seeks to include and integrate key constructs from other theories into a comprehensive theory of change that can be applied to a variety of behaviours. Prochaska and DiClemente's behaviour modification model looks at five stages, namely, (1) pre-contemplation; (2) contemplation; (3) preparation; (4) action; and (5) maintenance/confirmation.[29]

- *Pre-contemplation*: At this stage, either the consumers are unaware of the new behavioural opportunity or they believe the policy is not appropriate for someone like them. The reason for the latter is often that the behaviour is perceived to contravene important values, including religious ones ('my people do not practise family planning'). Campaign initiatives at this stage will therefore be aimed at creating awareness and acceptance that the policy is relevant to them or to family or close friends. Individuals rely on past experiences and prior beliefs to determine whether the campaign messages are relevant. People are likely to ignore the message if it is perceived as irrelevant or insignificant, leaving no motivation to process the message.
- *Contemplation*: Consumers are actually thinking about and evaluating recommended behaviour options. At the contemplation stage, the challenge is to identify whether behavioural changes can be done directly by the affected target groups or if they will require additional support, such as third party involvement or engagement. If direct, the person only needs to have personal competence ('I will take responsibility' and 'attend the AA (Alcoholics Anonymous) session'. With indirect meaning (such as condom use), it requires help from the other person; success or self-efficacy involves a third party and also interpersonal competence. A campaign can induce talk with members from the social network about messages, message format and message topic, and these conversations can create awareness. People could process the information but with minimum cognitive effort. People process information that is congruent with their self-definitional beliefs.
- *Preparation*: Consumers have decided to act and are trying to put in place whatever is needed to carry out the behaviour. The decisions tend to be emotional decisions. The usual process is to emphasise benefits in the early stages and emphasise costs in the later stages. Consumers must 'feel' rewarded by their action, hence education, and constant repetition of the benefits, the cost of not doing so and positive social influences must be stressed. This results in deep, unbiased processing of the message and increases acceptance. Value researchers recommend that benefits should include the value benefits and linking the desired behavioural change to fundamental life-objectives. Values are mental

representations of the underlying needs and should take into account the realities of the world they live in.[30]

- *Action*: Consumers are doing the behaviour for the first time or several times. Education and persuasive strategies are applied to focus on the perceived benefits, the perceived costs, the perceived social influences, and the perceived behavioural control. They must also be subject to regular reminders until the new behaviours become an ingrained way of life and the old behaviour is no longer an option. Once an adoption process occurs, social marketers engage in redefining and structuring (adapting the innovation or changing support system to improve the innovation fit), clarifying (communicating changes to employees or customers), and making it a routine or part of the institutional behaviour.
- *Maintenance/confirmation*: Consumers are now committed to the behaviour and have no desire or intention to return to earlier behaviour. Having gone through the earlier series of steps, it is likely that the consumer/citizen has reached the social marketer's goal of permanent behavioural change. There is on-going two-way participation. Participatory discussion describes the information exchanges, the mutual understanding and the consensus building. Important components of participatory communication are capacity building, through personal responsibility, efficacy to deal with environmental threats, and the inclusion of groups who provide legitimacy to consumers' behavioural change efforts. Social marketers can create rewards for consumers as they undertake new behaviours. They also have to manage 'post-purchase' evaluation, meaning a comparison between the expectations during the contemplation stage and the reality as they perceive it during the action and maintenance stages.[31] This is why monitoring of customer satisfaction is so critical in social marketing programmes.

Sense-making and segmentation for change

Sense-making methodology (SMM) involves asking as many questions as possible to focus on gaps and ascertain the essence of the complexity. It is to understand the metaphor of a human (target public) moving through situations with history and past experiences, and finally moving towards an outcome. SMM assumes humans are constantly making and unmaking sense as they navigate the structural constraints of their situations. It assumes that the target audience control the interpretive gates – you listen to me, I will listen to you; you trust my narratives about my circumstances, I will trust your narratives based on your marketing expertise.[32]

Segmentation is sense-making the right audience to get the right message at the right time. Some fundamental questions are asked when navigating the structural constraints. Do people who do the work, control the workflow? Is management prepared to take the tensions when they find there are better measures for improving the systems? Is management prepared to be cheerleader for changes when their marketers find and present it? Segmentation assumes a high involvement of the target publics, which also implies competition. Marketers argue that one cannot develop a good policy without understanding the competitive demands faced by target publics. High involvement implies deep engagement with highly involved target publics for change. It means a fuller integration of citizens as stakeholders to be part of the decisional mechanisms.

The two types of segmentation are: (1) segmented markets (developing different strategies for different segments of the public); and (2) concentrated markets (or priority publics, selecting a few and targeting them with different strategies). Segmentation into priority markets, as practised effortlessly in the commercial sector, enables policy planners to first understand people on their own terms. Otherwise they see the consumers/citizens as nothing more than entities or statistics. In commercial marketing, segmentation looks at people in the context in which they live their lives and understands the circumstances in which the products are used. They help people to express their values, as well as meanings and motives for the purchase and use of the products. Understanding a person's lifestyle encompasses knowing how a product fits into that person's life and what is important about it for him or her. SRI International, a California research organisation, uses a system called Value-added Lifestyles (VALS) to profile consumers, in particular, discovering the motivation of people to choose what they buy, based on principles, status or action. These lifestyle decisions give insights into how a person evaluates and makes choices in a given situation. The conceptual framework is based on self-orientation and definition of resources. Self-orientation means people are motivated to choose what they buy based on principle, status and action. Resources refer not only to the material but also education, intelligence, energy, self-confidence and willingness to buy.[33]

Pasquier and Villeneuve, writing in *Marketing Management and Communications in the Public Sector*, note five criteria for segmentation. They are: (1) history; (2) heteronomy/autonomy; (3) uniformity/diversity; (4) participation; and (5) directionality/relationality. The first refers to the *historical relationship* that exists within the society (for example, a Confucian culture varies from the western Weberian culture; so the cultural ballast will influence the pre-contemplation stage). *Heteronomy and autonomy* represent the opposite ends of the continuum, from no or little influence (heteronomy) to higher degrees of influence by an autonomous citizen. The degree of pluralism and individualisation is reflected in the *uniformity and diversity* continuum. *Participation* follows as it defines the possibility of citizens taking part in the policy formulation and interaction. *Directionality and relationality* centre on the focus of power, namely, who effectively controls the relationship? The ability to control the relationship is the defining element that allows the activation or deactivation of the possibilities of the exchange.[34]

VALS could be based on astute observation by members of the public, which supports the need for a feedback mechanism in formulating public policies. *Participant observation* includes being perceptive and also listening to your consumers/citizens. It is sense-making methodology. How do we conceptualise audiences? How and to what end do we hear the voices of people? Participation observation typology is a quick and easy way to assess the target audience; this segmentation approach adds colour and clarity by making thumbnail sketches of the targeted publics. For instance, writing on the rise of China's new moneyed elite, a Singapore businessman, while criss-crossing China for two months to solicit investors for his China Hospitality Fund, segmented the Chinese nouveau riche he met into a nuanced collection of four archetypes: (1) Scholar-turned-Capitalist; (2) Farmer-turned-Industrialist; (3) Apparatchik-turned-Developer; and (4) Speculator-turned-Investor. With the help of such segmentation, the policy planner can build the theoretical descriptions to evoke powerful images of how the types are manifested within a particular culture. Based on the segmentation or archetype of China's elites, the Singapore businessman commented that the Chinese nouveau riche will play a profound role in shaping the new China, though he added that probably the Chinese elites do not see themselves in that light, preferring to keep a low profile. Most of the nouveau riche have a very limited sense of history, only of imperial China and post-Tiananmen China. They see themselves very much as supporting the status quo. But if they had studied history, they would have realised that a rising middle class with all its expectations is potentially the most destabilising force against the political status quo.[35]

The Economist magazine published a special report on Chinese society that affirmed the typology observation made by the Singapore businessman. Rosie Blau, the writer of the special report, said that political scientists have long argued that once individuals reach a certain level of affluence, they become interested in non-material values, including political choice. For the first time in China's history, a huge middle class (about 225 million households) sits between the ruling elites and the masses. While the population as a whole is ageing, the middle class is younger, with half of the people living in the cities. Many have an appetite for civic engagements, and arrays of groups are seeking to improve society in various ways.[36]

Conclusion: complexity, hurts and minefields

Social marketers approach complex policy issues or a social mess as being dynamically complex, ill-structured, extremely difficult to identify and model, but over time with the application of social marketing principles, a wicked problem should not be intractable and elusive. To appreciate social marketing is to appreciate its value in managing social complexity. The marketing mindset is that consumer behaviour is the bottom line; all public policy strategies begin and end with the customer, the public. Sense-making and segmentation are ways to know the customer. The marketing mindset is not just to manage the resources; it affirms that the market economy is the most successful mechanism for creating opportunities and progress for individuals and the communities. Policy leaders and planners cannot ignore this clear measurable guide: public satisfaction with policies designed to benefit them.

Social marketers expect the high involvement of the public in public policies. Humans behave less than completely rationally and to change behaviour, the environment may be structured to influence people subtly (Nudging) to make certain choices that experts know are better for the individual and society. Social marketers keep to the neat policy style of managing the public policy process but incorporate the hurts and minefield issues at the pre-contemplation and contemplation stages. And when it comes to the end, they maintain that there is no end, but instead it is an upward spiral of re-examining the hurts and minefields issues by listen-plan-pre-test-implement-monitor-plan-implement. It is a continuous policy-making cycle. It uses sense-making methodology and segmentation of the target audience to understand who has made the behavioural change, which group has not, why and what must be done for that group and how to do so. There is no ending or one size fits all public approach in social marketing. There is an opportunity to apply social marketing and nudge principles to difficult policy issues: 'Why can't we sell human rights like we sell soap?' or 'Why can't we sell migrant issues like we sell soap?'

Notes

1 William J Paisley, 'Public communications campaigns: the American experience', in Roland E. Rice and Charles K. Atkin (eds), *Public Communication Campaigns* (London: SAGE, 2013).
2 Robert C. Hornik, 'Why can't we sell human rights like we sell soap?', in Roland E. Rice and Charles K. Atkin (eds), *Public Communication Campaigns* (London: SAGE, 2013).
3 Richard H. Thaler and Cass R. Sunstein, *Nudge: Improving Decisions about Health, Wealth and Happiness* (London: Penguin Books, 2009).
4 Alan R. Andreasen, *Marketing Social Change: Changing Behavior to Promote Health, Social Development, and the Environment* (San Francisco: Jossey-Bass, 1995), pp. 7, 9–18.
5 Martial Pasquier and Jean-Patrick Villeneuve, *Marketing Management and Communications in the Public Sector* (New York: Routledge, 2012), pp. 70–72.
6 G. D. Wiebe, 'Merchandising commodities and citizenship on television', *Public Opinion Quarterly*, 15(4) (1951): 670–691.
7 Hornik, 'Why can't we sell?', pp. 35–52.
8 Philip Kotler, *Marketing Management: Analysis, Planning, and Control* (Englewood Cliffs, NJ: Prentice Hall, 1967).
9 Philip Kotler and S. J. Levy, 'Broadening the concept of marketing', *Journal of Marketing*, 33 (1969): 10–15.
10 Albert Bandura, *Social Foundation of Thought and Action* (Englewood Cliffs, NJ: Prentice Hall, 1986).
11 Paisley, 'Public communications campaigns', p. 10.
12 Andreasen, *Marketing Social Change*.
13 Moises Naim, *The End of Power* (New York: Basic Books, 2013).
14 Yolanda Chin, Nadica Pavlovska and Norman Vasu, 'An immigration bonus for Singaporeans? Making the foreigners more acceptable', Rajaratnam School of International Relations, No. 145/2012, 7 August 2012.
15 Noemie Bisserbe, 'Migrants return to France's "Jungle" in Calais', *Wall Street Journal*, 22 June 2016.
16 Anne-Sylvaine Chassany, 'Inside the French far-right's laboratory town', *Financial Times*, Big Read, 17 April 2017, p. 7.
17 Basskaran Nair, *Planning Successful PR Campaigns* (Singapore: Institute of Public Relations, 2001).
18 *Der Spiegel* staff, 'Germany's growing hate problem', Spiegel Online, 23 October 2015.
19 Steven Erlanger and James Kanter, 'Plan to distribute migrants strains limits of European unity', *New York Times*, international edn, 24 November 2015, p. 5.

20 Guy Chazan, 'Germany struggles to find employment for refugees', *Financial Times*, 23 June 2017, p. 6.
21 Andreasen, *Marketing Social Change*, p. 72.
22 Gideon Rachman, 'The unstoppable mass migration into Europe', *Financial Times*, 13 January 2016.
23 Philip Kotler and Gerald Zaltman, 'Social marketing: an approach to planned social change', *Journal of Marketing*, 35 (1971): 3–12.
24 Richard H. Thaler and Cass R. Sunstein, *Nudge: Improving Decisions about Health, Wealth and Happiness* (London: Penguin Books, 2009).
25 Ibid.
26 Basskaran Nair, 'Governance in wired world', *Business Times*, 12 July 2014, p. 26.
27 Hornik, 'Why can't we sell?', pp. 35–52.
28 W. J. McQuire, 'Some internal psychological factors influencing consumer choice', *Journal of Consumer Research*, 2 (1976): 302–319.
29 J. O. Prochaska and C. C. DiClemente, *The Transthereotical Approach: Crossing the Boundaries of Therapy* (Homewood, IL: Dow Jones-Irwin, 1984).
30 William L. Wilkie, *Consumer Research*, 2nd edn (New York: John Wiley & Sons, Inc., 1990).
31 Richard L. Oliver, 'A cognitive model of the antecedents and consequences of satisfaction decisions', *Journal of Marketing Research*, 17(4) (1980): 460–469.
32 Brenda Dervin and Lois Foreman-Wernet, 'Sense-making methodology as an approach to understanding and designing for campaign audiences', in Roland E. Rice and Charles K. Atkin (eds), *Public Communication Campaigns*, 4th edn (London: SAGE, 2013).
33 Doug Newsom, Judy VanSlyke Turk and Dean Kruckeburg, *This Is PR: The Realities of Public Relations* (Belmont, CA: Wadsworth/Thomson Learning, 2000), p. 96.
34 Pasquier and Villeneuve, *Marketing Management*, pp. 41–47.
35 Ho Kwon Ping, 'The rise of China's new money elite', *Straits Times*, 25 August 2010.
36 Rosie Blau, 'Chinese society: the new class war', *The Economist*, 9 July 2016, p. 4.

6

ACTIVISM, ADVOCACY AND PUBLIC OPINION

It's about managing social movements

The road is winding, full of bumps, and mostly uphill. These nuts and bolts are not events in themselves, but put together by the engine of a powerful people's machine fuelled by the energy of the collective action. And with a strong base in place, a community-driven process can begin organising the grassroots to power. This is activism. Activism is action that includes protests, political rhetoric, demonstrations, lobbying, debate, propaganda and the mobilisation of media resources.[1] Activism has its foundations in the everyday life of the people. In the midst of the mundane daily grind and the humdrum of policy execution, people are affected, reflecting perhaps deeper shifts in society. Activism covers the same complexity issues as social marketing but the approach is different. Policies from initiation to implementation involve politics, and in politics there are partisanships, enemies and friends (activism) while in the marketplace of exchange, there are products, buyers and sellers (social marketing).

Activism is helping those caught in the 'hurts and minefields', high emotion and passion, of social problems. Activism is driven by a social cause representing the interests of communities and individuals to make a positive impact on their behalf. These advocates and activists are better able to express the loss of rights, the social injustices and perhaps the irresponsible behaviour of public officials. Advocacy and activism are faster off the track in a volatile, uncertain, complex and ambiguous world, where agendas could represent 'the *known*, the *known unknown* and the *unknown*', following the terminology of former US Secretary of Defense, Donald Rumsfeld, to describe different levels of policy complexity.[2] For the purposes of this book, activism is a communication of activities and actions to bring about behaviour and opinion change. It is often the counter-power to domineering corporations and controlling institutions, where trust and credibility in the potential to look after minorities, the socially disadvantaged, and those affected by unbridled market forces have been eroded.

This chapter discusses concepts related to advocacy and activism, making a distinction between three types of activism, namely, single issue mobilisation (SIM), volcanic events, and social movements. This is followed by a discussion of activism in three countries where single issues and volcanic issues have become social movements. The three case studies covered are Egypt's Egyptian Movement for Change (popularly known by the slogan *Kifaya*), and the discussion includes harassment and violence against women protestors; France's Poujadists, related to industrialisation and loss of traditional ways of life, morphing into a nationalist social movement that has similarities to other European countries, such as the UK; and China, where despite total control by the communist regime, activism exists. Egypt represents the Middle East's so-called Arab Spring movements; France represents the western world's 'left behind' social movements; and China represents the human spirit seeking redress from social injustices, despite total government control. Finally, there is a discussion of how to approach the marketing of activism: (1) provoke a conversation in society; (2) build flexibility in problem solving; (3) oxygenate the public; (4) manage the media well; and (5) make the policy message simple and sticky.

Understanding advocacy and activism

What is the reason for activism?

Activists get involved in campaigning because they are concerned and they want to spread that concern to others. They want to motivate people to take action, and that requires a solution which looks feasible as well as a problem that is compelling. They then market these issues. Issue mapping is a complex beast. 'Its entrails will be a labyrinth with appendices that lead to nowhere, and branches that split into too many choices to handle. Debate explores mature issues and expands them to fill the available space.'[3] The activism issues are mobilised around specific issues, such as an incident with the police, unfair land acquisition, unfair suspension, toxic poisoning and related environmental problems.

In this book a distinction is made between advocates and activists and yet they are used interchangeably.[4] *Advocacy* is generally the reinforcement of present issues or policies, short-term with a heightened sense of immediacy. Advocacy employs non-confrontational campaign strategies. Advocates find a platform for the politicians or government senior officials to champion the public initiatives and strengthen the 'hero opportunity' for the policy planners. In addition, they develop and maintain trusting professional relationships with the leadership and the committee policy staff and engage them in mutual information-sharing about the issues. The advocacy coalition framework involves adjustments to existing policies rather than making policy entirely from scratch. Policy actors tend to bargain over changes in the status quo and most importantly they learn the ideas of the other actors and the potential for constructive change.[5]

Activism, on the other hand, is focused on social change based on the 'routes to power', revolution, revisionism, reinvention. Both advocacy and activism are based on making changes to existing social policies, public interests, social values, best practices, and right cultural norms.

Activism is gaining power for the less powerful. Social values, best practices and right cultural norms have been deeply violated and there is seething and simmering anger in the political landscape. The Occupy Movement is an example of an activism bent on bringing about a total change. The activists' leaders, in particular, an individual activist called David Graeber launched the Occupy revolution in 2011. His writings set the agenda for the Occupy Wall Street protestors, based on the influence of money politics and on debt; his (2011) book *Debt: The First 5,000 Years*,[6] provided the larger narrative for the social movement. It was aimed at corporacy and income distribution disparity. The Occupy Wall Street movement, which later became a popular worldwide movement, began with a small band of activists who quietly planned, then nosily executed the occupation of Lower Manhattan's Zuccotti Park. A mélange of freshly minted college graduates, older and laid-off blue-collar workers, young professionals and chronically homeless people called themselves the 99 per cent, proclaiming 'We are the 99 per cent that will no longer tolerate the greed and corruption of the 1 per cent.' The Occupy Movement soon spread to 1,400 cities across several continents. They changed the way politicians, the traditional media and much of the public perceived and conversed about social inequality in the United States. Over the years, the Occupy Movement has changed too. It now comprises multiple groups, each challenging social and political issues independently, for example, challenging home foreclosure, banking policies, Wall Street practices, and other issues affecting income inequality and economic fairness.[7]

What is the downside of activism?

It leads to micropower that undermines the proper running of institutions, nations, and companies. Moises Naim in his (2013) book, *The End of Power*, notes the corrosive effect of activism by micropower, which is the counter-power that comes from being able to oppose and constrain what the big entities can do. Activists in such instances have enough power to block everyone's initiatives but no one has enough power to impose their preferred course of action, leading to policy paralysis. Decisions are not taken, are taken too late, or are watered down to the point of ineffectiveness. Lives become governed by short-term incentives and fears, and less due to charted actions and plans for the future.[8] There are three approaches to activism: (1) single issue mobilisation (SIM); (2) volcanic events; and (3) social movements, with many variations or permutations in between. *Single issue mobilisation (SIM)* is an issue people care deeply enough about for them to grasp and which is winnable or realistic enough for them to get involved.[9] *Volcanic events* are events that erupt through the surface of the social life, and the focus is on the flow of human, organisational and resource-related magma. *Social movement* is a more protracted and complex response of aggrieved groups, such as the black civil rights movement, which began with single issues characterised by street demonstrations (often violently) in the 1960s.

Single issue mobilisation (SIM) is usually the initial building block for most activists groups. They tend to have a fluid and informal leadership structure, their membership tends to ebb and flow, and their relationship with the group is dependent on how 'hot' the issue is.[10] Turf guarding is one of the most common forms of single issue activism found in almost all cities and countries. An example of single issue and turf guarding activism is found in Nepal where a cartel of private bus owners regularly blocks the roads with their vehicles in protest against any government initiatives that does not suit their interest. The Nepalese government, on the other hand, is trying to tackle rising pollution levels in the smog-choked Kathmandu Valley. With the help of a US$30 million six-year programme funded by the Asian Development Bank, the government introduced newer buses into the transport system and larger ones in busy areas. They also planned to redraw over-lapping routes. Standing in the way is the activism by this powerful bus mafia, a web of transport syndicates made up of private bus owners. They own about 10,000 buses and minibuses. These buses cause congestion and pollution, and are responsible for the emission of microscopic particles harmful to human health, according to World Health Organization studies. The powerful bus mafia argues that the policy planners' modernisation plans amount to bullying small investors. They want competitive bids for the new bus and routing plans. They have refused to retire their buses older than 20 years, even after the introduction of policies that bans public vehicles older than 20 years from being on the road.[11]

Volcanic or flash points events (sometimes called passing events) are to reduce feelings of political isolation, and occur when people have little faith in the political process to achieve their goals. The purpose of such events is to demonstrate the activists' strength to the public, the constituencies and to the media. In Korea, a volcanic event occurred when hundreds of thousands of people took to the streets over several weekends starting in October 2016 to call for the resignation of President Park Guen-hye for allowing a close friend to influence government decision-making, meddling in state affairs, including budget proposals and policy drafts.[12] The deeper-seated narrative related to the complex business and political leaders' relationship and the attendant corruption. President Park had campaigned on the promise of curtailing the business–political leaders' relationship. She did not do so and added to this were the related issues of her reticent personality, relying on a small group of advisers, and students angry at lack of graduate jobs and unions angry at the loosening of labour laws to favour businesses. As a social movement, the outcome was the president was sentenced to jail and the chaebols, the large Korean business cartels, and their leaders were put under similar judicial scrutiny and were also jailed, and it led to a long-time activist being elected as the next president.

Case studies: activism and social movements

Social movements tend to become worlds unto themselves, characterised by distinctive ideologies, collective identities and actionable routines, and do not remain static over time. For policy leadership, the key thing is to manage single issues and stop volcanic events from becoming social movements. Once it morphs into a social movement, it can drastically change the complexion of the nation's future. Three case studies of social movement are explored, covering three different countries to appreciate the geo-strategic perspectives of activism.

Case study 6.1: Egypt

In Egypt, the activism movement is always seen by western democracies as the 'Arab Spring' – protestors taking to the streets at Egypt's Tahrir Square with a smartphone in their hand for Facebook, Twitter and YouTube postings. Egyptian activism is more than that. The 18 days of the 2011 Egyptian Tahrir Square protest, for example, were created by a confluence of events, including a deep political discourse and activism born in the culture, the renewal of an Emergency Law, which, among other things, prohibited street demonstrations, the availability of Al-Jazeera, a Qatari-based TV station that beamed regional events, in particular, Israeli oppression of the Palestinians, the increased activism of the Muslim Brotherhood, and the fear of President Hosni Mubarak passing the succession baton to his son, Gamal Mubarak. It led to *Kafiya* activism, the slogan for the Egyptian Movement for Change, and in parallel was the issue of harassment and violence against women, highlighted even more during street protests.

Egypt used to be progressive and an equal rights society with a relatively vocal feminism movement led by Egypt's National Council for Women (NCW). Unfortunately it has also one of the highest rates of reported cases of sexual harassment (Afghanistan is the highest), according to the United Nations Entity for Gender Equality and the Empowerment of Women. Activism operates within the constraints of military, legal and political suppression to prevent challenges to the leadership. By emasculating institutions, particularly political parties, trade unions, professional syndicates, independent media, non-government organisations or even popular personalities, it negates the proper functioning of the nation on behalf of the people.

The interconnectedness of the *Kafiya* activism and the sexual attacks against women are that hooligans and pro-government supporters target female protestors during demonstrations and protests. Public debate and the shame culture make it difficult for women to admit they were sexually harassed. Police discourage the girls from filing complaints, and their families also restrain them from complaining. Targeting women is also embedded in the security forces. In 1986, the security forces in their fight against Islamic forces, primarily the Muslim Brotherhood, rounded up the female members of the family, which the Islamists claim was degrading, as it was an attack on their honour. In the early days of the protests, for example, during the 2000 protests, in order to delegitimise the activists and vilify the protestors, the security forces hired thugs to mill among the crowd, wreaking havoc and shouting extremist slogans, to give the authorities an excuse to portray the protestors as terrorists, villains, or worse. However, when respectable middle-class women also took part, this portrayal was less convincing and the government changed its tactic to one aimed at harassing these women.[13] Women who joined the protest were tarnished by innuendos and accusations. They were recorded as prostitutes in court records and presented as sex criminals. Plain clothes police would pull women to the ground by their hair and hired thugs would attack women to abuse and rape them.[14]

Activist groups have now launched for the protection of women. In November 2012, groups such as OpAntiSH and Tahrir Bodyguard have launched online sites. They have well-connected and experienced activists in charge, and are able to garner official and international attention through online activism and can obtain Egyptian media coverage. Consequently there has been more vocal public outrage. During the June 2012 street demonstration at the election of President Abdel Fattah el Sisi, the protestors encountered sexual harassment, though to a lesser extent. Surprisingly, the President made a point of visiting one of the victims in hospital. New laws have been introduced to strengthen anti-sexual harassment although they are seen as inadequate by the activists. Neither protest activism nor sexual harassment will go away. On harassment, it is a culture where the Islamic politicians still maintain that the women are '100 per cent responsible' and that how can they be protected when they stand among men.[15]

Case study 6.2: France

In France, populist revolts have always been symptoms of deeper shifts in society. David Goodhart, in *The Road to Somewhere*, explores the rise of populism. One of his examples is the volcanic arrival of 'Poujadists', a revolt led by Pierre Poujade, triggered by the growing anxiety over industrialisation, economic modernisation and the loss of traditional ways of life. One of the early 'Poujadists' activists was Jean-Marie Le Pen, who decades later successfully pursued these nationalistic populist ideas in French politics. Continued by his daughter, Marine Le Pen, nationalistic populism became a social movement in France and even for the rest of Europe.[16]

Financial Times correspondent Anne-Sylvaine Chassany's article on Bezier, a French town of 75,000 people, captures the granular aspects of the nationalist movement. Historically it was a vibrant economic centre until its wine industry fell apart. Bezier is now 'peripheral France', a term used to describe struggling industrial bastions, the suburbs and the rural areas that feel abandoned by the central government. In these disillusioned territories, a right-wing counter-culture developed with the nostalgic desire for the vanishing French way of life and then also was translated into mounting anti-Islam sentiment. Like Bezier, crumbling French towns experienced an increase in the Muslim population and Muslim ways of life. For example, some cafés are male-only for Mahgrebi (a reference to North African Muslim nations) customers. Laundry is displayed in public view (a common habit of Mahgrebi residents). Bezier's mayor Robert Menard said: 'Minorities are never a problem as long as they stay minorities.' He claims that now the French middle class are being replaced by North African populations, although Muslims account for less than 10 per cent of the population. This local grievance was translated into the national arena; the mayor shifted his support to the far-right National Front, and for Marine Le Pen and her bid for the French presidential election in May 2017. Anti-migrant residents claimed that older French citizens have to live off a 1300 euro monthly pension while immigrants can access healthcare and other subsidies. Mayor Menard's local actions included mixing tough law-and-order measures, such as arming the local police and having posters to show police powers. He insisted that secular France should reaffirm its Christian roots. Understandably, Bezier's residents largely applaud Mr Menard and welcome the way he is shaking things up, strengthening security, restoring Catholicism and making the sleepy forgotten town of national consequence in light of the 2017 French presidential elections.[17]

In such a climate, France was all set to succumb to the same nationalist movement. The results of the first round of the presidential election saw Marine Le Pen's far-right National Front winning into the next round, while the incumbent centre-left Socialists and centre-right Republicans were resoundingly defeated. Finally, a centrist Europeanist candidate, Emmanuel Macron won the Presidency and his *République en Marche* won a convincing majority in Parliamentary seats. Nonetheless, western democracies are undergoing a social movement of ideas and identity shift. In France, the collapse of the traditional mainstream parties and the on-going realignment around a new axis of political competition pits advocates of openness to trade, immigration and liberal social values against advocates of 'closure' or 'protection'. This shift underpinned the Brexit vote in the UK, the very narrow victory of the left-wing candidate against the far-right candidate in the Austrian presidential elections and the gains made by Geert Wilder, leader of the Party for Freedom (PVV), in the recent parliamentary vote in the Netherlands.[18]

Activism that represents the deeper shifts in western democracies can be seen in both France and the USA with the elections of Emmanuel Macron and Donald Trump as presidents in their respective countries. President Emmanuel Macron's win is a case study of focusing on public-good policies in the midst of the cacophony of the web, the dilution of traditional political structures, and the rise of extremism politics. His 'marketing mindset approach' was to nurture a larger vision for France within Europe, which was going against the grain in a nationalistic-minded population unhappy with European liberalism, and for France to have a larger place in world politics. The vigour and vim in the messages helped him not only to win the presidency but also the majority of the parliamentary seats.

The contrasting study is the US President, Donald Trump. His 'marketing mindset approach' is to use the cacophony of the web effectively; he uses Twitter messages to communicate, often deflecting attention from the larger vision for the nation. He advocates polarisation when he rails against the Muslims, the Mexicans, and mainstream media, which resonated and coincided with activism by the alternative right. His activism mode was to keep nurturing the white, moral and religious Americans to make them think of themselves as a disadvantaged group and he is their saviour under the slogan, 'Make America Great Again'. It is the activism strength of the lone influential Twitter-blogger impacting upon the majority, including the global village.

Moreover, activism by elite networks, supported with cogent data, will be another key driver in the social movement issues. In his article on 'Citizens groups and the changing nature of interests groups politics in America', Jerry Berry takes the view that the rise of citizen groups and the rapid expansion of interest advocacy in general have had many important long-term consequences for the way policy is formulated by the government.[19] Policy-making is now best described as taking place within issue-focused activism networks rather than sub-governments. An issue network is a set of organisations that share expertise in a policy area and interact with each other over time as relevant issues are debated. Policy-making has become more open, and more broadly participatory. Unfortunately for the honest, people-centred, socially-conscious people, activism is in reality warped by money, particularly in the USA. It is now effectively controlled by the elite oligarchy, answerable primarily to ultra-rich donors. If these donors do not control branches of government, they are well positioned to block any agenda in order to maintain the status quo.[20]

Case study 6.3: China

In China, the second most powerful nation in the twenty-first century, there are 300–500 protests each day, with anywhere from ten to tens of thousands of participants, according to Human Right Watch's 2014 World Report. According to official police statistics, the number of annual protests rose to 87,000 in 2005 from approximately 8,700 in 1993, a ten-fold increase. The 2014 World Bank notes that the Chinese government places arbitrary curbs on expression, association, assembly and religion; prohibits independent labour unions and human rights organisations; and maintains Party control over all jurisdictions.[21]

Despite the massive communist control, China continues to experience the three facets of activism: single issue, volcanic and social movement. The typical single issues are demonstrators displaying banners against land grab or the location of environmentally dangerous toxic materials. For example, protests in Kunming, in South-West China's Yunnan Province, in May 2013 against plans for a factory which produces paraxylene (PX), a toxic petrochemical used to make fabrics.[22] Volcanic events are protests ranging from farmers contesting land grabs to environmental protests by the middle classes and to ethnic minority riots. Unlike in the USA and in Europe, these protests have involved the weakest, the poorest, the most marginalised sectors of Chinese society. They are poorly organised and their grievances are localised – so a protest might flare up in one particular location, but not spread like wildfire across the country.

Both single issues and volcanic issues are likely to become social movements. An example of the rise of a vocal political movement is the neo-Maoists militant leftists group. This underground social movement espouses the utopian egalitarian ideas that China's current leaders have abandoned. In the mid-1980s barely 60,000 people undertook the journey to pay homage to Mao in his Shaoshan hometown; in 2015, nearly 17 million people made pilgrimages to his hometown They see Mao as a symbol of a simpler, fairer society, and China's domestic politics currently faces an intense resentment towards the elites and the children of politicians who are described as 'princelings'.[23] Teng Biao, a law lecturer at China's University of Politics and Law, writes that large-scale environmental protests by the middle class, long viewed as a crucial government support, have caused alarm among the authorities. The way in which these demonstrations have rapidly formed using social media has clearly unnerved the authorities and made them wonder about how quickly middle-class unrest could spread. The problem for autocrats is that the censorship tools specifically designed for dissident use are politically easy for the state to shut down, whereas the tools in broad use become much harder to censor without risking politicising the larger group of otherwise apolitical actors.[24]

The protests by the minority group, the Uyghurs, are perpetually violent volcanic. In 2009, vicious Uyghur-led riots in Urumqi killed 197 people and injured nearly 2,000. In 2013, violence spread beyond Xinjiang when a jeep driven by a Uyghur protestor crashed through pedestrians on the edge of Beijing's Tiananmen Square and killed five people. In 2014, eight knife-wielding Uyghurs rampaged through a packed railway station in Kunming in South-West China, killing 29 people and wounding more than 140 others. It is a social movement since the Turkic-speaking Muslims, calling themselves the East Turkestan Islamic Movement, are protesting that Chinese of Han descent are occupying their land. Before 1949, the Muslim Uyghur comprised 90 per cent of Xinjiang's population but five decades later, they account for only 40 per cent of the population. Beijing has encouraged Han Chinese to migrate to Xinjiang. Most of the wealth flows into the pockets of Han immigrants, fuelling resentment among the Uyghurs. Beijing's fear of growing Islam militancy is justified. Leaks from the Islamic State (ISIS) reveal that of the 3,500 foreign fighters registered, a significant number are Uyghurs from Xinjiang, pursuing a global jihad, including against China.[25]

To compound China's social movement activism headache, Hong Kong and Taiwan, parts of Greater China, are prone to activism by student protestors. These anti-China protest movements are premised on the refusal to accept political and military control by China. Protestors in Taiwan and Hong Kong, mainly young people, want to enjoy the present democratic way of life and refuse to allow China to impose its Communist social values, political practices and cultural norms. Clement So and Joseph Man Chan, writing on social movements in Hong Kong, note that the demographic structure is influencing its democratic instincts. By the late 1990s, the locally born, educated and below 30 stratum comprised 60 per cent of the population. Although committed to the Chinese culture, they have accepted Hong Kong as their home and are much more concerned with local public affairs.[26]

Marketing of activism

Provoke a conversation in society

Start talking with society and it will end with the society talking to itself. Dialogue puts the activist in the driver's seat. When or if an activist builds strategically sound campaigns or movements for change, the elected officials will come.[27] Public dialogue provides powerful arguments for embracing talk as a form of communication activism. If participants are able to openly express and hear alternative points of view that would be a significant step forward, regardless of whether consensus was sought or achieved. In addition, the content of each dialogue should be documented and the reports of the entire process fed back to participants and distributed publicly. In cases where the activists or the interested groups or citizens have accepted the challenge of coming up with solutions; the organisation plays the role of facilitator or enabler. The consultation design calls for discussion among stakeholders.

Take, for example, Greensboro, USA. A group of spirited people organised the Greensboro Truth and Community Reconciliation Project (GTCRP). They felt strongly about repairing the damage to the fabric of the community caused by polemic dialogue among diverse groups, namely, the Communist Workers Party representing the textile workers, the Ku Klux Klan (KKK) and their affiliate, a neo-Nazi group, and the racially-minded black and white residents of Greensboro. The background is that on 3 November 1978, members of the Communist Workers gathered in Greensboro to organise the textile mill workers on work-related issues and to protest at the growing influence of the KKK in the neighbourhood. However, 35 members of the KKK in a nine-car caravan drove through the crowd of protestors, began shooting and killed five and wounded ten people. The community felt deeply the wounds of racial and ideological division. The GTCRP successfully pulled together a coalition of the different groups and facilitated a three-prong communication approach: first, educating, organising and questioning the various groups; second, maintaining dialogue that required each person to make a commitment to discover something new about the others (and, in the process, each person discovered many things about the community which never entered into official investigation, on public record, in public conversation or at a personal level); and third, opening the minds of the interested parties to the possibility of transformation. There were times when the groups lost interest but the GTCRP volunteers stayed the course, with focus directed at the root cause of the conflict, namely, no violation of the constitutional rights of any American citizen, whatever the creed, colour or conviction. They kept the discussion focused, ensuring people did not drift onto other issues of their own design or as a springboard to advance their own agendas. Another lesson from GTCRP is that top leaders, in this case, the mayor and the senior personnel, shared the vision and encouraged the activism vehicle. The mayor and his team supported and assisted in the process that promoted active dialogue.[28]

Build flexibility in problem solving

Helen Ingram and Dean Mann, in *Why Policies Succeed or Fail*, maintain that there is programmed implementation and adaptive implementation. Programmed implementation seeks to control the snares and problems in advance, that is by thorough examination of the programme before its implementation. Adaptive implementation adjusts the initial plans and procedures as the events and decisions unfold. Ideally, policies should be modified through public participation, with relevant actors giving feedback as it is implemented. This will enhance the policy process as more actors are drawn into the process, more information and input become available and pertinent points are incorporated into the problem-solving.[29]

Oxygenate the public

Supplying the public with a regular flow of information is particularly important. In managing the oxygen of publicity, the quantity and quality of information play a role in the public opinion dynamics. If the activism issue is ambiguous, the campaign messages may be interpreted in multiple ways; people read them in ways consistent with their own worldviews, goals, and needs. People with a special interest in an issue will seek more information, supporting arguments for and against the different options. They may hijack the agenda if the policy leadership is not alert. The strategy takes into consideration the time horizons, the nature of the population, and the desired policies when planning the activism message. There may be modifications to the policy concept because of practical difficulties of accurate or reliable measuring and the target groups affected by the policy. If the knowledge of or meaning of the policy is fuzzy, it is difficult to apply or interpret and it seldom leads to further understanding of problems.[30]

Manage the media well

Media management ensures that public expectations are constantly guided and the public opinion process is positively managed, both internally and externally. Internally, it includes the in-between levels of communication, such as larger community meetings, and the local media. The ability of a grassroots organising community (GOC) to get the message out entails internal communication, which includes word of mouth, networking, mailings, telephone calls, small community meetings and newsletters. And external communication is the larger public action and events, using major media outlets, video documentaries and books. External communications also will be essential for a GOC to get its opinions, positions and platforms to a wide assortment of audiences, including allies, opponents, third parties and the general public.

Framing

Selling the social movement's ideology is a function of framing: 'what must be done, who must do it and how it must be done', according to Hank Johnson in 'Social movements and old regional nationalists'. 'What must be done' – this is to present the demands and solutions, and to explain, defend or sell the programme or ideology. Each ideology is attached to some value, for example, equality, justice, liberty, progress, private property, free speech, right to privacy, right to life; it is crucial that these values are understood and defined by the ideology. 'Who must do it' – we are into leadership for the mobilisation. Activism elites capable of mobilisation guide the ordinary people and the grassroots movements for change or manage the resistance. 'How it must be done' – there must be a determination for adaptive strategies that are most appropriate and effective for the activism cause. Persuaders must convince large numbers of people to join the cause, to organise into effective groups, and to unify through coalitions. This requires orchestrating these conflicts among and within the interested parties. Equally important is to put the issue in a larger context. Nationalist movements share a strong affinity with the past values and norms that the subculture feels have been violated. The sense of injustice has its foundations in the everyday life. These identities are further elaborated within the dense networks of membership.[31]

Make it simple, make it sticky

Occupy Wall Street activism is a great case study of reframing a complex series of economic and social forces into a bumper sticker paradigm: *the 1 per cent versus the 99 per cent*. The make it simple, make it sticky principle. The organisers created an information flow environment for people to seek or sort information to better understand events and developments. Occupy activism also showed that grassroots energy can be tapped when activists aspire to transcend conventional wisdom about what is politically possible. Citizens cannot understand the intricate workings of issues, public policies and government. While the individual 'lives and works on a small part of the earth's surface' and sees 'at best only a phase and an aspect', it is still imperative that even the best-planned policies need to be marketed to the general public and the targeted public for effective and efficient implementation.[32]

It is the task of the leadership to be conscious of public policy execution – communicating to the public and getting their acceptance and support. A much-quoted author on activism strategy is Saul Alinsky. In his (1971) book, *Rules for Radicals*, he cites several action plans that have been used by Occupy movements or the Tea Party movements in the USA.[33] Here is a flavour of his direct action techniques:

- Power isn't what you have but what the enemy thinks you have.
- Never go outside the experience of your people.
- Wherever possible, go outside of the experience of the enemy.
- A good tactic is one that your people enjoy. Have fun!

- A tactic that drags on too long becomes a drag.
- Keep the pressure on with a variety of tactics and actions.
- The major premise for tactics is the development of operations that will maintain a constant on the opposition.
- If you push a negative hard and deep enough, it will break through ... the real action is in the enemy's reaction.
- Be prepared to offer an organisational solution to the issue if called upon.
- Tactics, like organisation and like life, require that you move with the action. Be flexible and imaginative.

Strong-arm tactics

There is the nasty side of activism, adversarial activism that aims to destroy institutions and support anarchism. In his (2004) book, *Roots to Power*, Les Staples advocates a strong offence to manage adversarial activism. He commends the use of the seven Ds of defence, namely:

- Deflecting (passing the buck, changing the subject, sending low-level staff to negotiate).
- Delaying (with a view to riding out the storm, buying time for a counter-strategy).
- Deceiving (using disingenuous tactics, from subterfuge to outright lies).
- Dividing (creating discord, dissension to diminish ability to wage the campaign).
- Denying (denying demands, and you need to escalate and put more pressure on when this happens).
- Discrediting.
- Destroying (in both discrediting and destroying, opponents attack either both the organisation or individuals or threaten its existence).

It is imperative, he maintains, that when dealing with the seven Ds, the policy official anticipates the hostility and prepares contingency plans, rehearsing the plans before rebutting, acting or implementing the strategies. It is also necessary to have action groups that can move quickly to preserve its action-reaction dynamics when encountering hostile and cantankerous activism. The coercive persuasive approach involves tactics ranging from threats to harassment which the persuaders are capable of and have the intent to use to the fullest to achieve legitimate and desirable ends. These strategies include: expulsion, restrictive legislation and policies, harassment, use of surrogates, infiltration and arrests and use of the courts.[34]

Conclusion: complexity, hurts and minefields

Fragmentation, micropowers, and powerful interest groups generate competitions, compromises, and ambiguities, sometimes incoherence, to upset well-meaning, public-good policies. They become wicked problems that cannot be solved but can only be managed in an endless cycle of adaption and adjustments. It is worsened as activists use the 24-hour media – online and offline – to sensationalise and amplify these dissensions which could be single issue mobilisations or volcanic events or both. They then lead to social movements. Egypt's Egyptian Movement for Change included activism to stop the harassment and violence against women protestors. Egypt's activism represents the activism in the Middle East, the so-called Arab Spring movements. France's Poujadists are related to industrialisation and loss of traditional ways of life, morphing into a nationalist social movement that has similarities to other European countries, such as the UK. France represents the western world's marginalised 'left behind' social activism. In China, despite total control by the communist regime, activism exists as the human spirit will find ways and means to seek redress from social injustices. Micropowers and powerful interest groups reside in all political structures, waiting to explode into activism.

In reviewing the communication strategies by activists, we see the need to have a marketing mindset, focusing on the public (citizens, customers), this is an essential attribute for policy leadership. Provoking a conversation with the widest possible target publics especially those 'left behind', oxygenating the public with a range of information, and framing issues as simple and sticky will help in the 'hearts and minds' battle in the policy process.

Notes

1 Les Staples, *Roots to Power: A Manual for Grassroots Organizing* (New York: Praeger Publishers, 2004), p. 101.
2 Errol Morris, 'The certainty of Donald Rumsfeld', available at: https://opinionator. blogs.nytimes.com/2014/03/25/the-certainty-of-donald-rumsfeld-part-1/?_r=0.
3 Chris Rose, *How to Win Campaigns: 100 Steps to Success* (London: Earthscan, 2008).
4 Advocacy is a specific issue addressed with a heightened sense of immediacy; activism is focused on social change based on the 'routes to power'.
5 Guy Peters, *Advanced Introduction to Public Policy* (Cheltenham: Edward Elgar Publishing, 2015), p. 58.
6 David Graeber, *Debt The First 5,000 Years* (New York: Melville House Publishing, 2011).
7 Randy Shaw, *The Activist's Handbook: Winning Social Change in the 21st Century*, 2nd edn (Berkeley, CA: University of California Press, 2013), p. 22.
8 Moises Naim, *The End of Power* (New York: Basic Books, 2013), pp. 17–18.
9 Saul D. Alinsky, *Rules for Radicals: A Pragmatic Primer for Realistic Radicals* (New York: Random House, 1971).
10 Gary Delgado, *Beyond the Politics of Place* (Oakland, CA: Applied Research Center, 1997), p. 31.
11 Agence News Presse/*The Kathmandu Post*, 'Bus mafia controlling Nepal's transport', 17 April 2017.
12 Song Jung-a, 'South Korean President Park Guen-hye offers to step down', *Financial Times*, 29 November 2016.
13 Maye Kaseem, *Egyptian Politics: The Dynamics of Authoritarian Rule* (Boulder, CO: Lynne Rienner Publishers, 2004).
14 Paul Amar, 'Turning the gendered politics of the security state inside out? Charging the police with sexual harassment in Egypt', *International Feminist Journal of Politics Issue*, 13(3) (2011): 299–328.

15 Jon Nordenson, *Online Activism in the Middle East: Political Power and Authoritarian Governments from Egypt to Kuwait* (London: I.B. Tauris, 2017), p. 92.
16 David Goodhart, *The Road to Somewhere: The Populist Revolts and the Future of Politics* (London: C. Hurst & Co, 2017).
17 Anne-Sylvaine Chassany, 'Inside the French far-right's laboratory town', *Financial Times*, Big Read, 17 April 2017, p. 7.
18 Carlo Invernizzi Accetti, 'The French elections and Europe's new normal: a choice between open and closed', *Foreign Affairs Today*, 25 April 2017.
19 Jerry Berry, 'Citizens groups and the changing nature of interests groups politics in America', *The Annals of the American Academy of Political and Social Sciences*, 528(1) (1993): 30–41.
20 Harold J. Smith, 'Warped US political system run by big money', *Financial Times*, 5 July 2017, p. 8.
21 World Bank Report 2016, 'China and Tibet', available at: www.hrww.org/world-report/2016/country-chapters/china-and-tibet.
22 Reuters, 'Hundreds protest at Chinese chemical factory', quoted in *Telegraph*, 4 April 2013.
23 Jamil Anderlini, 'The return of Mao', *Financial Times*, Weekend Arts and Society, 1 and 2 October 2016.
24 Teng Biao, ' "A hole to bury you": a first-hand account of how China's police treat the citizens it's supposed to serve and protect', *Wall Street Journal*, Opinion Asia, 28 December 2010.
25 Tom Miller, *China's Asian Dream: Empire Building Along the Silk Road* (London: ZED Books, 2017).
26 Clement Y. K. So and Joseph Man Chen, *Press and Politics in Hong Kong: Cases from 1967 to 1997* (Hong Kong: Hong Kong Institute of Asia-Pacific studies, The Chinese University of Hong Kong Press, 1999).
27 Rose, *How to Win Campaigns*.
28 Carey Adams, Charlene Berquist, Randy Dillion and Gloria Galanes, 'Public dialogue as communication activism', in Lawrence R. Frey and Kevin M. Carragee (eds), *Communication Activism: Communication for Social Change* (Cresskill, NJ: Hampton Press Inc., 2007).
29 Helen M. Ingram and Dean E. Mann (eds), *Why Policies Succeed or Fail* (Beverly Hills, CA: SAGE, 1980), pp. 205–240.
30 Judith Eleanor Innes, *Knowledge and Public Policy: The Search for Meaningful Indicators* (New Brunswick, NJ: Transaction Publishers, 1990).
31 Hank Johnson, 'Social movements and old regional nationalists', in Enrique Larana, Hank Johnston and Joseph R. Gusfield (eds), *New Social Movements: From Ideology to Identity* (Philadelphia, PA: Temple University Press, 1994). pp. 282–284.
32 Walter Lippmann, *Public Opinion* (New York: Free Press, 1922).
33 Alinsky, *Rules for Radicals*.
34 Staples, *Roots to Power*, pp. 333–337.

7

NEW MEDIA ARE MAINSTREAM

It's a new channel for communication

Welcome to the world of social media and its impact on public policy, political decision-making and politics. When David Cameron became Britain's PM, he wanted a few tips from someone who could tell him how it felt to be responsible for and accountable to many millions of people who expected things from him, even though in most cases he would never shake their hands. He turned not to a fellow head of government but to Mark Zuckerberg, the CEO of Facebook.[1] Assigned to be Barack Obama's campaign manager for the 2012 presidential elections, Jim Messina spoke to all the technology leaders for over six months, including Steve Jobs, who told him that mobile technology has to be central to the campaign's effort and that he has to programme content to a much wider variety of channels – Facebook, Tumblr, Twitter, YouTube, Google – because people are segmented in very different ways than they were four years ago.[2]

CNN Political Director Sam Fiest, writing a Foreword to a book, *The Big Book of Social Media: Case Studies, Stories, Perspectives*, said:

> In a remarkably short period of time, Twitter has helped journalism move from the '24-hour' news cycle to what I like to call the '1-minute' news cycle. The incredible shrinking news cycle has forced governments and politicians to be on alert every minute to respond to an opponent, respond to a news story, or simply respond to an errant tweet ... The '1-minute' news cycle is here to stay. This is one of the most important aspects of the social media confronting policy leadership.[3]

Moreover, the biggest change in the past two decades is the migration of news consumption to an online environment. More people seek out new online than read print newspaper or listen to the radio or watch television.

This chapter looks at complexity in the age of the Internet, exploring its impact and influence on policy formulation and execution. The Internet has created a global village where technology companies are almost nation states in their own rights. People are empowered by technology, and emboldened by living anonymously in a global village without leaving their nation states. The second section presents the application of cyber communication to social marketing, social activism, and the agenda setting, framing and priming strategy. The third section examines a unique phenomenon in western democracies, namely, alternative or fake news adopting strategies similar to rumour-mongering and propaganda. The final section examines challenges as governments grapple with their citizens as netizens in a post-fact global village. The policy politics issue is governance in a new media age.

Understanding social media

The World Wide Web, the foundation for social media, was first conceived in December 1990 by Tim Berners-Lee, a British computer scientist who sent the first successful communication between a Hypertext Transfer Protocol and a server via the Internet, thereby creating the Web. The founding members ensured that the management, technological acumen and administrative effectiveness of the Internet resided primarily with various international bodies, like the Internet Architect Board (IAB), the Internet Engineering Task Force (IETF), the International Corporation for Assigned Names and Numbers (ICANN), or the Internet Society (ISOC). It was independent of nations, even of superpowers. It has since sparked a global communications revolution, and become an agent for the new technologies and new global industries and markets. It has a history of developing deconstruction, disintermediation and disruption technologies. In deconstructing for example, it has disrupted fixed built environments and face-to-face human engagement. Physical collocation and geographic contiguity have been changed by online electronic proximity.

The World Wide Web has created a global village. The concept of a global village enabled by technology was first predicted in the 1960s by Marshall McLuhan, a media theorist and a futurist. He is famous for the phrase 'the medium is the message'. He had predicted a future that would integrate television, computer and database and said that instantaneous electronic communication would connect people across the world, blending together space and time to make possible a 'global village'.[4] We now have a global village, where information, knowledge and all the technological systems that accompany the information explosion have quantitatively exploded; and we live in a world in which online information and informational activities form an essential part in our daily organisation.[5] In this global village, netizens tell their friends what they do online, using social media websites like YouTube, Facebook, Instagram, and Twitter. Everything personal when conversed or shared in the Internet age is also public information. Privacy is almost a thing of the past; citizens live in a narcissistic social media world. Google knows, for example, what we searched for and when, knows more minute details about us than we do, details we have forgotten, discarded from our minds as irrelevant. Perhaps society should seek to establish expiration dates in the quest to forgetting and help humanise our digital world.[6]

Technology companies are almost nation states in their own right. Facebook has two billion people regularly using its flagship service. The user base is bigger than the population of any single country and of six of the seven continents. It represents more than a quarter of the world's 7.5 billion people. Twitter has 328 million users, while Snapchat has 166 million users. WeChat in China had 938 million users in the first quarter of 2017. These people, citizens of a nation state, are also part of cyber communities, united under the banner of connectivity and interactivity. It is due to social media because people of different race, gender, class, nationality or locality interact with their identities as a string of chat-text, synthesised speech or stylised graphics. Cyber culture is information, communication and technology (ICT) convergence; the PC, the telephone, the Internet and multimedia provide an integrated form of communication, where entertainment and information have become 'infotainment' and education and entertainment is 'edutainment'.[7]

People are empowered by technology, and emboldened by the anonymity of a global village without leaving the security of their nation states. People seek solutions to their problems online. A Canadian folk singer, Dave Carroll, after nine months of complaining about how United Airlines baggage handlers had damaged his $3,500 guitar, and when the airline refused to pay compensation, made a video and posted it on YouTube. Within three days it had been watched half a million times; within a month it reached five million. United Airlines had a massive public relations crisis on its hands, not least as thousands of other unhappy customers now came forward to vent their frustration. Similarly, in 2017, as seen on video, United Airlines violently threw off a paying passenger for its own crew members, and faced a barrage of online and mainstream media backlash. The CEO had to retract his earlier confident support for his company's policy.

Politicians now take advantage of these communication trends by creating personal online profiles on major social networking sites, uploading campaign advertisements and other multimedia materials. They are ready to embrace social media more than bureaucratic policy planners. Politicians treat social media and the chatter as a gigantic polling apparatus. The consequence is that these new forms of communication have changed the relationship between the governing and the governed. President Donald Trump is a classic example of a political leader making 'tweeting' his mode of communication for national policies, overriding the traditional structures, for example, intelligence reports and papers. Twitter communication overrides his respect for the legislature, the judiciary, the executive and the mainstream media. Similarly, in western democracies in Europe, politicians are making promises often online and catching the traditional institutional structures off-guard. The decision-making machinery is breaking down.

Bureaucratic policy-makers find the social media can be 'super-scary'; it is not advisable to enter social media before their departments, institution or organisations are ready. There is a lot that needs to be understood when they communicate public policies in the new media environment. There is the accelerant effect, where the process of policy-making is speeded up in response to the '24–7' news environment with the policy-makers having to act quicker.[8] Citizens' behaviour in the online media environment is similar to their viewership and readership pattern for mainstream media. There is the familiar selective exposure to pro-attitudinal messages and avoidance of counter-attitudinal messages. Even though social media permit ample opportunities to explore diverse views, citizens continue to gravitate towards like-minded political information. New media technologies have not completely absolved people from preferring views echoing their own and avoiding issues they find less compelling. Partisan exposure to both online and mainstream media strengthens partisan identities, partisan views towards political figures, and skews the issues that the nation should address.[9]

Trust and credibility, so critical in governance, have been eroded. There is a continued distrust of the media. Craig Crawford, in his (2006) book, *Attack the Messenger: How Politicians Turn You against the Media*, noted that the public distrust of the news media is one of the most hazardous political challenges now facing Americans.[10] According to the Pew Center for the People and the Press, Americans think their news organisations do not 'get their facts straight' and that mainstream media 'stories and reports are often inaccurate'. People are less trusting that the news media will provide accurate information. Media distrust contributes to the growing partisan polarisation of the American political system and this is an important determinant of the extent to which the Americans' partisan divide will grow wider in the years ahead.[11] This worrying trend is seen, though to a lesser extent, also in Europe and the UK, where the media are partisan but not overtly polarising compared to the toxic media environment in the USA.

New media and social marketing

What is social marketing in an Internet age?

Social marketing is the application of commercial marketing competencies to influence the voluntary behaviour of target audiences in order to improve their personal welfare and that of their society. For social marketers, history is filled with examples of technology changing how governments conduct campaigns. Public communication and campaigns will always find ways to take advantage of the newest communication technology. What is different now?

There are unique communication possibilities in this Internet age. Information Communication Technology (ICT) dramatically increases the amount of government information that is accessible to citizens and the ability of citizens to receive information, mobilise and interact with government.[12] Government agencies are leveraging on social media as a tool for constituent interactions, and enhancing service efficiencies. Public education now incorporates Internet tools as part of integrated marketing. The Web itself has multi-media channels and as part of the marketing mix, the Web has a greater capacity to create alternatives that by-passes traditional gatekeepers. Well-designed games use multi-media channels, creating powerful environments for learning and behavioural change. This involves mobile apps, websites, interpersonal interaction, such as home-to-clinic telehealth systems, and mainstream media coverage to complement social media and mobile technologies.

Well-designed games are particularly applicable, and extensively used, for health-care campaigns. Debra Lieberman writes extensively on the several applications of Internet-based commercial practices for public health campaigns. Digital games are interactive media that motivate and engage players by challenging them to reach goals. They are immersive, social, 'cool' and fun. There are thousands of digital games designed to motivate and support health behaviour change. Health games appear in social media, virtual worlds, on mobile apps, on health insurers' websites, in museum exhibits, in medical devices, and in robots, in addition to computers and video game consoles. She adds that the decision to develop a game for health campaigns and which style to develop depend to a great extent on the desired outcome. A game intended to change behaviour would be more expensive and time-consuming to produce. It would require a team of experts in game design, interactive and media-based processes. But if that game leads to players' improved health behaviours, especially aligned with the campaign's overall goals, it is worth the investment.[13] Singapore, a public campaign nation, actively promotes social marketing campaigns using social media channels extensively while still maintaining its traditional forms of communication. A YouTube video, for example, urges people to embrace the diversity in Singapore's society, keep an open mind, and get to know people for who they are. In this clip, a boy rushes to take an empty bus seat next to an 'auntie', a respectful term for older folks. She stops him and the two appear to struggle. The video's theme is 'Sometimes, things aren't what they seem'. It turns out the seat is wet. It enjoyed hits of over 2.8 million.[14]

Social marketers have taken note that young audiences are migrating from television to digital media and the advertising dollar follows them. The old-school entertainment giants are in for a slow and sad decline. Media companies need to re-imagine themselves as factories of video content. The new lucrative platforms include YouTube, Facebook Live and Snapchat. The new targeting capabilities combined with marketers' discomfort with the underbelly of online marketing – fake traffic and fraud – have slowed the shift of dollars from TV to digital.[15]

New media and activism

What is social activism in an Internet age?

There are do-it-yourself social networks. Activists with limited finances can use these tools to forge a 'netroots' base. This empowers individuals, especially in countries where the mainstream media is government controlled. These activists leap-frog with the help of social media, challenging establishments that control the mainstream media. Given its global nature, the Internet also doubles up as the international mass media. A YouTube video that goes viral generates more bangs for the buck and is more likely to be seen by the Millennials in most countries. For example, the Tunisian activists and their allies organised a 'digital sit-in', linking dozens of videos about civil liberties to the image of the presidential palace. That turned a low-key human rights story into a fashionable global campaign. The bottom line is that new media has a stickiness value, a hip factor or the X-factor attraction that few television, radio or print media can replicate.

Similar online activism has been successfully implemented in other countries in the Middle East. Jon Nordenson in his (2017) book, *Online Activism in the Middle East*, traces the online activism in Egypt. *Kafiya*, the pro-democracy movement, started in the late 1990s and was supported by online activists. When there was another protest movement in 2000, the online activists were on the scene, documenting offline events, and providing uncensored news and information to counter the state-controlled media. For example, one online story led to police officers being convicted for brutality. Online activism wrote stories and circulated a mobile video of police 'raping' a microbus driver with a stick (it was caught on a mobile by the police to humiliate him). The postings and the video were covered by a mainstream media. Another incident of successful online activism was when a gang of young men, in their hundreds, failing to get tickets to a cinema, went on the rampage. The hooligans besides the rampage also started to sexually harass women they accosted in the streets. Police who arrived to disperse the youth did nothing to help the women and ignored any attempts to investigate the incident further. The mainstream media too ignored the horrific event. However, online activism pursued the matter. Finally, they found their voice of protests on TV – their video postings were carried by television stations. Moreover, the newspapers started using the activists' blogs as a news source.

Soon these volcanic events, covered by online activists, widened into a social movement. The activists group lined up with labour movements, protesting against unemployment, labour and economic conditions. The Muslim Brotherhood, a religious organisation outlawed by the government for a long time, wanting to have a wider appeal, joined the online activists, to strengthen the offline protest. The authorities did shut down the Internet in Egypt but by this time, the offline protests were already successfully representing various interests, including groups representing 'anti-sexual harassment of women'. The Muslim Brotherhood did gain traction and even formed the next government. However, after winning the elections and forming the next government, the Muslim Brotherhood became just as repressive as President Mubarak's military regime. Following massive demonstrations and military intervention, President Muhammad Mursi, the Muslim Brotherhood leader, was soon ousted by the military.[16]

In Africa, there was deep concern for the plight of young boys abducted into the army in different parts of the African continent. Joseph Kony, leader of Northern Uganda's Lord's Resistance Army, was particularly notorious for kidnapping children to serve as sex slaves. A concerned individual made a 28-minute YouTube video describing the long-running military conflict in Northern Uganda and focused on Joseph Kony's atrocities. The YouTube video went viral. The video itself was viewed by over 100 million viewers. It graphically portrayed the violence and havoc caused by Joseph Kony. It described Kony's kidnapping of children to serve as sex slaves and forced soldiers. In terms of priming, the video made the *New York Times* front page and forced the White House and the Pentagon to respond. It ended with the arrest of Kony. However, without a sustained communication campaign on behalf of the children, it did not build a broader base, a social movement concerning the plight of young boys abducted into the army in other parts of the African continent.[17]

On the one hand, sustained one-off activism like the 'Color for Change' campaign in the USA has morphed into the Black Lives Matter movement. The 'Color for Change' campaign in 2007 highlighted the status of five African-American students charged with attempted murder after a school playground fight with a white student. Activists saw a racial bias in the decision to charge the African-American students. While the local media covered the incident, it did not get national coverage until Color for Change activists launched an online campaign. Similar examples include the Trayon Martin case, an unarmed African-American shot and killed on 26 February 2012 in a gated community, and the white alleged killer was questioned but released. After a sustained online petition, galvanising 2.3 million signatures across the country, the killer was re-arrested, found guilty and sentenced.[18] These series of single issues pursued as a sustained campaign maintain that the police are against Blacks. On the other hand, there are the alternative voices that are critical of the Black movement. Tomi Lahren, a conservative commentator, with more than 4.3 million followers on social media, maintains that the Black Lives Matter movement is aimed at murdering police officers.[19]

New media and agenda setting, framing and priming

What is the agenda setting, framing and priming strategy in the age of the new media?

Historically, election campaigns have used the media for agenda setting, framing and priming. This was first articulated by Maxwell McCombs in his (2004) book, *Setting the Agenda: The Mass Media and Public Opinion.*[20] Now new media are being harnessed for the same purpose by political campaigners and activists. In India, the BJP, the main Indian political party, uses social media to mobilise public opinion. The leader of the party, Narendra Modi favours tweets to get his message across to his voters and mainstream media. After his election, the Indian Prime Minister did not hold a single press conference; he tweets regularly on public issues and they are watched closely by the media for coverage and by others as policy guidance. He follows a clutch of Twitter accounts, mostly that of his BJP supporters, who are religious fanatics and often abusive in their tweets. Some of his Cabinet members openly endorse Twitter trolls. When asked in Parliament why he follows cyber-bullies, the Prime Minister replied that 'we are mainstream hating'.[21]

The priming is in the narratives

Since many public policy issues have become so uncertain, complex and polarised, it is left to storytelling or narratives, according to Emery Roe, in his (1994) book *Narrative and Policy Analysis*, to articulate and make sense of that uncertainty and complexity. Narratives are framing agendas, created and circulated to an online community. However, people lean towards social media narratives that fit or conform to their political, religious and personal preferences and bias. As a result, such narratives create an online echo chamber. Politicians exploit this channel of communication to avoid the gatekeeping functions of the mainstream media. Their narratives, often through Facebook and tweets, are aimed at making sense to their followers of the highly uncertain policy issues that dominate political life. Such an approach of using social media for agenda setting, framing and priming public issues is a meta-narrative that jump-starts decision-making, at least at that time when the meta-narrative itself comes under attack by polarising and complexifying positions.[22]

President Trump understands instinctively the concept of agenda setting, framing and priming, in particular, the value of online narratives, through Twitter-post, as priming. For example, he names and shames US manufacturing firms that relocate their production lines overseas. NBC TV news coverage on air-conditioning manufacturing firm Carrier, showed an interview clip of a Carrier worker challenging President Trump to keep his campaign promise and to stop the manufacturer from leaving the state. Trump watched the news and the film footage of him making that promise. Immediately, he tweeted his policy position and made arrangements to appear at the Carrier factory in Indiana. On TV, he explained why he was there: to ensure some of the company's operations did not move to Mexico in keeping with his campaign promise. Similarly, he told the NBC interviewer that he got his military advice by watching NBC's political show and then he tweets his views to reach out to his electorate base:

> He is in a strange meta way, a spectator of his own performance; we are living in a TV show that Mr. Trump is simultaneously starring in, consuming and live-tweeting; Mr. Trump pushes the news cycle, he seems to be pulled by it. Look at how many of his Twitter outbursts … have been about something on TV that made him mad.[23]

In priming his policy narratives, President Trump is amply supported by a strong following of an online community of his tweets which are retweeted and covered extensively by the media. He is also helped by the conservative Fox Television and Brietbart News, an online publication that played a pivotal role in the 2016 presidential elections. Southern Poverty Law Center, a non-profit organisation that tracks hate groups, says that Brietbart News is the media arm of the Alternative Right movement, publishing articles that promote popular white nationalist tropes. Using social media, Twitter in particular, President Trump sets the agenda, frames the messages and primes the messages, bypassing mainstream print and television media which he and his former Chief Strategist, Steve Bannon, call the manufacturers of fake news.

Fake news: influencing public opinion

What is fake news?

Fake news or alternative news using social media is false news framed as truth or near truth. Fake news is post-truth politics, turbocharged by technology, such as the smartphone. A single device allows individuals to project in real time an unfiltered version of the news and (often highly partisan) views across Facebook, Google and Twitter. Fake news has a purpose: Deliberately constructed lies, in the form of news articles, meant to mislead the public.[24] The disinformation, misinformation and hate speech goes to the crux of undermining the proper functioning of democratic institutions. It is easy to transmit information online to a wide audience, even if it is not true or accurate. Given that it is widely circulated on social media does not mean it is true. Often people in an online community, bombarded with a constant flow of news and views, fail to ask critical questions or to challenge their belief with careful reflection.

Fake news strategies are similar to rumour-mongering. In rumour-mongering, there are three broad categories: (1) divisive or wedge-drive; (2) wishful or pipe dream; and (3) bogies or anxiety rumours. *Wedge drive* divides groups; *wishful* express hopes; *bogie* mirrors fear and anxiety. In rumours, information is distorted in three ways, namely, (1) levelling; (2) sharpening; and (3) assimilation. In *levelling*, few words are circulated and the few details essential to understand the true situation are levelled down or deleted. In *sharpening*, the emphasis is on limited but dramatic details from a larger context. In *assimilation*, people receiving the rumour with its limited dramatic detail will add on others based on their own prior knowledge and biases. The add-on comments are assimilated into successive accounts. The rumour, like some shrinking missile, keeps getting shorter and sharper in its flight. How strong rumours are depends on the degree of control and the credibility of the formal news sources. Generally rumours are born within a certain emotional climate.[25]

Fake news employs strategies similar to propaganda. Propaganda devices include:

- *name calling*: 'Lying Ted', 'Crooked Hillary', or 'he's a character' which is open to negative interpretation;
- *glittering generalities*: nebulous words like 'largest crowds in any presidential inauguration', 'many people say';

- *transfer*: using movie stars' celebrity status to campaign and transfer their public aura to the lesser person or lower reputation politician;
- *testimonial or third party endorsement*: like transfer, using others with reputation to endorse;
- *plain folks*: using 'one of us' phrases, homey, addressing down-to-earth concerns to convince the public;
- *bandwagon*: a device to sway undecided people to go with the majority, 'we have the largest turnout you have ever seen';
- *card stacking*: telling one side of the story, obscuring facts, resulting in distortions and misrepresentations;
- *emotional stereotypes*: 'they are taking our jobs', 'Mexicans are rapists', 'drain the swamp';
- *illicit silence*: like innuendoes, insinuations, withholding information that would correct a false impression;
- *subversive rhetoric*: an offshoot of card stacking to discredit a person's motivation or an idea, or make nasty calls like 'lock her up'.

History offers numerous examples of skilful users wielding these tricks with great subtlety and effectiveness. Reared on television and other media (now social media), they know how to use propaganda devices and media effectively.[26]

Fake news has led to the rise of trolls, social media bullies threatening people surreptitiously. The rapid formation of cause-driven communities, engaged and enraged citizens, vocal in tone and thrust to the point of harassment and bullying will significantly impact the policy process. *Time* columnist Joe Stein notes that the Internet was once a geek with lofty ideals with a free flow of information. Now the Web is a sociopath with Asperger's.[27] In her book on trolling in India, broadcast journalist Swati Chaturvedi writes that she was a BJP cyber-volunteer (BJP is the ruling party in India) for two years until 2015, and during that time she and others posted a barrage of misogyny and Islamophobia. BJP has a network of volunteers who take instructions from the social media cell and BJP's social media cells principally target critical voices.[28] Studies have shown that online communities of like-minded people engaged in discussion among them are likely to adopt the more extreme than the more moderate variants of the group's shared beliefs. There are higher levels of polarisation when members meet anonymously. Trolling is a common problem on platforms such as Twitter, where one can openly purchase fake accounts, fake followers and marketing content, as well as misinformation and hate. Fake news and trolling are possible because disintermediation technologies like Twitter communication cut out mainstream media as the middlemen between the politicians and the public.

Fake news is a global phenomenon. Bogus news reports strategies are now being imported from the USA to Europe, abetted by the Russians to influence the election results in France, Germany and Italy. Brietbart News is bringing its brand of news formation – often regarded as racist, white supremacy advocacy – onto the international market with a focus on Europe. It has an office in London, headed by a

UK Independence Party (UKIP) member. It is anti-immigrant, white conservatism and anti-EU. It hopes to help far-right parties like the National Front in France and the Alternative for Germany party (Afd) in Germany in the 2017 elections in these countries. Russia and its various propaganda organs are experts in faking and framing lies as true news and radicalising politics. In the USA, Russian influence in the US 2016 elections and attempts to undermine American democratic values are under intensive security and legislative scrutiny. In Europe, the then Italian Prime Minster Matteo Renzi complained privately to his European counterparts about Russia's meddling in his country's politics by supporting anti-establishment parties. Russia has been helping the anti-establishment Five Star Movement. Buzzfeed, an online watchdog, and the Italian newspaper *La Stampa* have reported that blogs and web-sites in Russia connected to the Five Star Movement were spreading false news. The Five Star Movement started as an online movement, co-founded by Beppe Grillo and an entrepreneur, Gianroberto Casaleggio, now deceased; Casaleggio's Internet and publishing company Casaleggio controls several widely followed web-sites that often pick up sensational reports found on Sputnik Italia, an Italian version of the Kremlin website that projects President Vladimir Putin's worldview. Russia Today, a Russian TV station, for example, carried a video showing thousands of people protesting against a November Referendum when in fact the people were gathering to support PM Renzi and his reforms. It was widely reposted and retweeted in all the Five Star Movement online outlets. Another fake news item is a picture of a large gathering to hear Pope Francis speak but Beppe Grillo used it to caption: 'A sea of humanity in the square, the people can't take it any more.'[29]

Governance in the new media era

Reviewing his experiences in the First World War, General Smedley Butler of the US Marines claimed with some hyperbole that 'I'd rather fight an entire army than battle an idle rumour. At least in fighting an enemy, one knows where one stands.'[30] Fake news, like rumour-mongering and propaganda, has raised concerns among governments the world over. It has been contributing to a more volatile security environment, and more complex, uncertain and ambiguous public information flow. The UK, France and Germany have raised concerns, accusing the social media companies – Facebook, Google and Twitter – for failing to tackle terrorism and regulating hate content. In 2014, the British intelligence and security com-mittee of Members of Parliament criticised Facebook for failing to pass information that could have prevented the murder of a British soldier by Islamist terrorists. These are challenges posed, as nations and governments grapple with netizens, and a post-fact global village. Who governs?

The preference is for common, universally agreed standards of a legal and regu-latory framework to be agreed upon by the technology companies. In this position the technology companies are responsible. In his (2017) book, *Whose Global Village?*, Ramesh Srinivasan explains that digital technology companies are becoming the face of journalism and public information, they must be held accountable. These companies are treated as though they are public spaces and systems, or public utilities for the common good. Google, Facebook and Twitter are for-profit companies, not democratic institutions. Commercial priorities, rather than publics and cultures, shape how these tools are developed and the agendas they serve.[31] Facebook is a media company with more power and influence than the *Washington Post* and the *New York Times*, and yet it claims not to be a publisher and not to have responsibilities for what appears on its platform.

Technology companies maintain that a common standard for the whole Internet is not possible. They face policing millions of accounts and posts. YouTube, for example, has 400 hours of video uploaded every minute. Twitter says between July and December 2016 more than 376,000 accounts were suspended for violations related to the promotion of terrorism, while YouTube terminates any account that it reasonably believes is an agent of a foreign terrorist group. Facebook insists it uses a combination of technology and human review to thwart terrorists.[32] In the light of the backlash, Facebook and Google have pledged to do something about it. Facebook plans to build a safe, informed, civically engaged and inclusive community that fulfils the benevolent promise of social media, which is to spread democracy, community and freedom.

Italy's anti-trust chief, Giovanni Pitruzzella, has called for EU members to set up a network of public agencies to combat fake news. It should be done by the state and not by the social media organisations like Facebook and Twitter. He said that it is not the job of a private entity to control information. This is historically the job of the public sector. There should be a public third party, independent of the government, to intervene quickly if public interests are harmed. Germany and the UK are among the nations looking at legal measures to tackle the problem. Singapore too is preparing to introduce laws to rein in the disinformation, misinformation and the hate content. In Germany, the government is planning a law that would impose fines up to 500,000 euro on Facebook for distribution of fake news. Uzbekistan changed its media law to count all websites as 'mass media' – a category subject to draconian restriction. Belarus requires owners of Internet cafés to keep a log of all websites that their customers visit.

Governance is not easy. The diversity in social media technologies enables netizens to move to other online platforms. Faced with tighter restrictions, trolls and terrorists are changing their approach. Most jihadists are now using end-to-end encrypted messenger platforms such as Telegram. Trolls like Richard Spencer, a right-wing troll, when suspended from Twitter, hopped over to join Gab, the latest social network built like a hybrid Twitter and Reddit. Twitter cracks down on harassment trolls from the conversation but Gab does not. Gab has attracted Milo Yiannopoulos, the former Brietbart editor, and conservative commentators like Ann Coulter and Alex Jones, founders of Inforwars. While Twitter bans anti-Semitic slurs, Gab tolerates anti-Semitism. While mainstream social networks are promising to crack down on 'fake news', Gab clears the way for fake stories like the Pizzagate story, a conspiracy theory spinning lies about Democratic paedophiles operating out of a Washington, DC pizzeria.

Social media are not beyond legal scrutiny, not very different from mainstream media. In the UK, most Commonwealth countries and most of Europe, but less so in the USA, there is congruence in the application of the law for social media as it is for mainstream media. Luke Scanlon, writing in the *Guardian* newspaper, listed ten points on the legal ramifications of Twitter, which is generally applicable to other social media communication. The law of libel, applicable in England and in most Commonwealth countries, for example makes it an offence to communicate defamatory remarks where that communication takes some form of permanence. On social media, if a tweet lowers a person's standing 'in the estimation of right-thinking members of society', it will breach the law of libel. In addition, the UK law protects against harassment. Two or more tweets would be necessary for a claim of harassment to be made. If a reasonable person in possession of the same information thinks the course of conduct amounted to or involved harassment, it is harassment. Most countries have implemented data protection laws to protect against processing of personal information without consent.[33]

But how do you deal with a tweet that obviously looks dangerous from a security perspective but is deemed acceptable by the judiciary? The UK High Court overturned the conviction of a man, Paul Chambers, who sent a tweet threatening to blow up an airport. The Lord Chief Justice wrote:

> 'Tweets' include expressions of opinion, assertions of fact, gossip, jokes (bad ones as well as good ones), and descriptions of what the user is or has been doing or where he has been, or intends to go. Effectively it may communicate any information that the user wishes to send, and for some users, at any rate, it represents no more and no less than conversation without speech.

'Treat Tweets as nothing more than pub talk rather than publication', writes John Kampfner of the *Guardian* newspaper.[34]

The above governance issues refer to functioning democracies, which countries like China are not. China continues to control its social media, and independent media, including popular celebrity gossip accounts. Cyberspace Administration of China requires all online news portals, network providers and related content providers to ensure that all content are managed by party-sanctioned editorial staff. Communist China control's mechanism is called the Great Firewall. Nonetheless no nation state will be spared the impact of social media. Guo Long, a researcher at the Chinese Academy of Social Services, said: 'The Internet will affect China more deeply than other societies because China is a closed society and the Internet is an open technology.'[35] Talking in the context of country censorship of social media, Ethan Zuckerman, an Associate Professor at MIT, discusses the cute cat theory of Internet activism (*cute cat* is a term for any low value but popular online activity). Specific tools to counter censorship can be shut down but 'broader tools that the larger population uses to share pictures of cute cats are harder to shut down':

Cute cats are collateral damage when governments block sites. And even those who couldn't care less about presidential shenanigans are made aware that their government fears online speech so much that they're willing to censor the millions of banal videos … to block a few political ones.[36]

Conclusion: complexity, hurts and minefields

The Internet has created a huge global village, where commercial technology companies are almost nation states in their own right. People in the global village are empowered by the technology, and its promise of anonymity emboldens them to live in the global village without leaving their nation states. In the meantime, new media and the technology companies are now mainstream media and more. While policy leaders govern and plan the policy process for nation states with borders, there exists a parallel global village, communities without borders that live in the world of Facebook, Google, Twitter and related social technologies. Policy leaders will be hard put to win the hearts and minds of its people, if the communities on the Net think otherwise, influenced by ideas and identities that are different from the nation state. All the biases and prior selections normal in human behaviour and opinion formation will continue. Who governs is one of the challenges facing nations and governments, particularly in a VUCA (volatile, uncertain, complex ambiguous) world, with their citizens living in a post-fact global village.

Moreover, the Internet and social media have aggravated the already VUCA world with fake news as part of the information (misinformation) flow. Fake news adopts strategies similar to rumour-mongering and propaganda. It is complicated by the fact that in America fake news is practised with impunity, even by high-ranking politicians. Fake news has made it 'normal' that truth is what you get away with and makes people immune to facts by constant repetition of alternative news. This weakens and worsens the difficulties in the policy process as fake news is a global phenomenon. Bogus news reports, strategies and the rise of trolls, social media bullies, are now being imported from the USA to Europe, seemingly abetted by the Russians and their agents to influence, for example, the national elections results in European countries. Unchecked, social media will make 'hurts and minefields' the default outcome in policy implementation.

Notes

1 *The Economist*, 'The Future is another country', 24 July 2010, p. 49.
2 Joshua Green, 'Jim Messina has a president to sell', *Bloomberg BusinessWeek*, 18–24 June 2012, pp. 48–53.
3 Sam Fiest, 'Foreword', in Robert Fine, *The Big Book of Social Media: Case Studies, Stories, Perspectives* (Goole: Yorkshire Publishing, 2010).
4 Marshall McLuhan, *Understanding Media: The Extension of Man*, 1964, available at: web. mit.edu/allanmc/www/mcluhan.mediummessage.pdf.
5 Frank Webster *Theories of the Information Society* (London: Routledge, 2002), p. 58.
6 Viktor Mayer-Schonberger, *Delete: The Virtue of Forgetting in the Digital Age* (Princeton, NJ: Princeton University Press, 2009), pp. 7, 195.

7 Pramod K. Nayar (ed.), *The New Media and Cybercultures Anthology* (Oxford: Wiley-Blackwell, 2010).

8 Piers Robinson, *The CNN Effect: The Myth, Foreign Policy and Intervention* (London: Routledge, 2002).

9 Natalie Jomini Stroud and Ashley Muddiman, 'The system today: is the public fragmenting?', in Travis N. Ridout (ed.), *New Directions in Media and Politics* (New York: Routledge, 2013), pp. 6–23.

10 Craig Crawford, *Attack the Messenger: How Politicians Turn You Against the Media* (Lanham, MD: Rowman & Littlefield, 2006).

11 Jonathan Ladd, 'The era of media distrust and its consequences for perceptions of political reality', in Travis N. Ridout (ed.), *New Directions in Media and Politics* (New York: Routledge, 2013), pp. 24–44.

12 Robert J. Klotz, *The Politics of Internet Communication* (Lanham, MD: Rowman & Littlefield, 2004).

13 Debra A. Lieberman, 'Designing digital games, social media, and mobile technologies to motivate and support health behavior change', in Ronald E. Rice and Charles K. Atkin (eds), *Public Communication Campaigns*, 4th edn, (Los Angeles: SAGE, 2013), pp. 273–287.

14 Pearl Lee and Charissa Yong, 'New ways of reaching out: dialect for seniors and Facebook for young people', *Straits Times*, 27 November 2016.

15 Amol Sharma, 'Big media needs to embrace digital shift – not fight it', *Wall Street Journal*, 22 June 2016.

16 Jon Nordenson, *Online Activism in the Middle East: Political Power and Authoritarian Governments from Egypt to Kuwait* (London: I.B. Tauris, 2017).

17 Randy Shaw, *The Activist's Handbook: Winning Social Change in the 21st Century*, 2nd edn (Berkeley, CA: University of California Press, 2013).

18 Ibid.

19 Jonah Engel Bromwich, 'The America right's new, young and vocal media star', *New York Times*, international edn, 6 December 2016, p. 8.

20 Maxwell McCombs, *Setting the Agenda: The Mass Media and Public Opinion* (Cambridge: Polity Press, 2004).

21 Amy Kazmin, 'Cyberbullies shake Indian politics', *Financial Times*, 20 February 2017, p. 8.

22 Emery Roe, *Narrative and Policy Analysis: Theory and Practice* (Durham, NC: Duke University Press, 1994).

23 James Poniewozik, 'The new TV reality: all Trump, all the time', *New York Times*, international edn, 15 December 2016, p. 8.

24 Margaret Sullivan, 'It's time to retire the tainted term "fake news"', *Washington Post*, quoted in *Straits Times*, Opinion, 10 January 2017, p. A22.

25 Basskaran Nair, *A Primer on Public Relations Practice in Singapore* (Singapore: Institute of Public Relations of Singapore/Print and Publish Pte Ltd, 1986).

26 Doug Newsom, Judy VanSlyke Turk and Dean Kruckeburg, *This Is PR: The Realities of Public Relations*, 7th edn (Belmont, CA: Wadsworth/Thomson Learning, 2000), pp. 194–195.

27 Joe Stein, 'Tyranny of the mob', *Time*, 29 August 2016, pp. 25–30.

28 Swati Chaturvedi, *I Am a Troll: Inside the Secret World of the BJP's Digital Army* (New Delhi: Juggernaut Publications, 2017).

29 James Politi, 'Italy antitrust chief urges EU to help beat fake news', *Financial Times*, 30 December 2016, p. 3.

30 Quoted in Gary Alan Fine and Patricia A. Turner, *Whispers on the Color Line: Rumors and Race in America* (Berkeley, CA: University of California Press, 2001).

31 Ramesh Srinivasan, *Whose Global Village? Rethinking How Technology Shapes Our World* (New York: New York University Press, 2017).

32 David Bond, 'Social media groups defend record on hate content', *Financial Times*, 5 June 2017, p. 3.

33 Luke Scanlon, 'Twitter and the law; 10 legal risks, out-law.com', *Guardian*, Network, 10 August 2012.

34 John Kampfner, 'Twitter joke trial: for Paul Chambers common sense has finally prevailed', *Guardian*, Opinion, 27 July 2012.

35 Robert J. Klotz, *The Politics of Internet Communication* (Lanham, MD: Rowman & Littlefield, 2004).

36 Ethan Zuckerman, 'Cute cats to the rescue? Participatory media and political expression', 2013, available at: ethanzuckerman.com/papers/cutecats2013.pdf.

PART III

Issues management

8

NATIONAL INTERESTS AND TRADE-OFFS

It's communicating what is the best option

Trade-off is an integral part of the policy-making process. Policy issues are in essence a struggle of ideas, the constant struggle in trade-offs on the definition and execution on what is best for the people. Each issue-idea is an argument or a collection of arguments in favour of different ways of seeing the world. Trade-offs are not necessarily an exercise in rational problem-solving. They are deeply emotional and often characterised by high levels of anxiety, dissatisfaction and anger. Responsible leaders must recognise people's fears and anger as legitimate. Leaders need to develop a mindset of knowing their publics in order to address the pervasive issues. Take, for example, the political trade-off debate on globalisation in the USA and Europe. Anti-globalisation groups argue that globalisation has resulted in painful collateral damage, particularly for manufacturing-dependent communities in the USA and Europe. The low-skilled workers in these countries have been left behind as a result of low-cost competition from countries such as China. On the other hand, the pro-globalisation groups argue that many of the manufacturing and agricultural-related businesses are trade-dependent and the more this trade expands, the more people are going to be employed and wages will go up. In the political trade-off debate, this model of globalisation that governed the global economy is unravelling.[1]

In this chapter, complexity in trade-offs is examined in several contexts. Trade-offs, for example, take place in the policy-making environment where most policy-makers do not know what their people want. Multiple changes and severe disruptions create trade-offs, and policy-makers cannot attend to each piece of the policy in isolation. Trade-off is linked closely to the marketplace, global trade and geopolitics. The next two sections are case studies of trade-offs. One is on migration, identity and assimilation with an overarching question 'Why can't we sell human rights (migration) the way we sell soap?' Migration is an important global issue. The other case study is on the South and East China Seas and the various claimants' trade-off positions and postures, with China as the chief protagonist in the trade-off discussion. The final section looks at communication practices applicable in trade-offs. Policy leaders are required to rally the stakeholders, and persuade them to appreciate the policy vision and the policy challenges.

Complexity in trade-offs

In trade-offs, the complexity is embedded in the definition. For instance, it is assumed that citizens and communities and elite groups have two sides: a private, self-interest side and a more public-spirited side. Personal problems such as not having enough money to pay the monthly bills could also reflect a public issue – the result of a social problem that courses through society and affects many people, reflecting a systemic economic inequality. This can translate personal problems into policy issues.[2] People care about fairness at a personal and even at a community level. However, once in the marketplace, that idea becomes relative. People care much less about fairness as they seek maximum profit or benefits for themselves through legal, sometimes illegal, means, and this undermines society's moral sentiment. Discharging industrial waste into a lake is a cheap method of disposal for a factory owner (private interests) but ruins the water for everyone else. Clean lakes are a social benefit entailing the private costs of non-polluting waste disposal.[3]

Trade-offs take place in an environment where policy goals are usually multiple, conflicting and vague. Often policy-makers do not know what their people want. And they would not know how to attain the particular policy goals even if they did know what goals they were after. Many problems defy immediate solutions. There is no systematic connection between problem and solution as solutions are often the results of political choices and trade-offs. For instance, the Affordable Healthcare Act (ObamaCare) will be repealed and replaced by the American Health Care Act (TrumpCare). However, the non-partisan Congressional Budget Office (CBO) analysis is that the number of uninsured may increase by 23 million by 2026, and many more will experience a sharp reduction in healthcare support if TrumpCare replaces ObamaCare. Under the Trump presidency, many of the public policies are still impossible to predict. 'We live in a world the US made. Now it is unmaking it. We cannot ignore the grim reality.'[4]

In a trade-off, bureaucratic policy-makers cannot attend to each piece of the policy in isolation. It must be addressed with a whole of government approach, able to present skilfully how the dots of the policies connect to the people's benefit, at times with temporary dislocations and difficulties. Reimut Zohlnhofer and Friedbert W. Rub, in their (2016) book, *Decision-Making under Ambiguity and Time-Constraints*, maintain that often the policy-makers have little time to think through their decisions as the proposed solutions are challenged by alternative views, and subject to the pace of economic and social change. It becomes harder in an accelerated technology-laden environment, and continuous and intrusive media reporting. In the course of trade-off, policy leaders are under severe time constraints, which limit the number of issues a political system can deal with at any one time. This means that there are many more problems than the political system can attend to.[5] Policies are meant for the public good but the public seems divorced from the policy process, and negatively impacted by the policy execution.

Trade-offs are inevitable in open pluralistic societies which contain so many different groups with differing ideas and values. The functioning of modern, complex urban societies often depends on the tolerance of cultural differences, and equal rights and protection for all cultural groups. At some point, the cultural differences result in the pulling apart that exceeds the pulling together. Trade-off issues could be related to the gender roles and the family, the conflict between career and child-bearing, how to help successfully integrate family and career. It could be controversies regarding inequalities due to education premium, and policies are built with the view to encourage people to get more education and better themselves. It could be trade-off discussion on the kind of political economy and institutions relevant or necessary for a country.[6]

Trade-off is linked closely to the marketplace and global trade. The marketplace has produced powerful multinationals with concentrated powers, described as a corporacy. These powers have created their lobbying groups, supported by entities with deep pockets. Corporacy has a stronger say than government policy leaders, think tank institutions and the professional class. Consequently, they distort the trade-off environment between voters and officials elected to represent the public interests. Modern capitalism has also aggravated social and income inequality. Trade-off in such an environment is not perfectly self-correcting. There is a need to check the excesses of corporacy through extra-market institutions that transcend mere hedonism and profit maximisation. To temper corporacy, one must reclaim and strengthen civil society, and make clear government and civic vitality are allies not adversaries.[7]

Changes and disruptions create trade-offs. Changes in technology, organisations, the character of cities and industries, and domestic and foreign affairs affect everyday lives. What are the overall best interests for the people? What is the nation's limiting factors? Is it a large population, with a large rural poor who have been left behind by technological changes? Or, as in some countries, the problem is scarce land and scarce labour? Is the challenge economic policy, generating enough work for all who need work for income, purchasing power and dignity? What will this require? Lack of attention to find the right policy strategy, for example on employment means dissatisfaction mounts, conflicts swell, and social movements spring up to reform or defend the endangered order. Often established public policy lags behind new needs. Technology is allowing the production of far more output with far fewer people. Amazon Retail made its foray into Singapore with its two-hour delivery service. A Singapore media columnist downloaded Amazon Prime Now app and within minutes she had purchased a cart full of items. Then the questions and guilt set in: 'What have I done? Was I aiding a foreign e-commerce company to kill off local retailers?'[8]

Case study 8.1: trade-off on migration and assimilation

Migration is a significant global issue. It is also one of the most emotional public policy issues that has led to the rise of nationalism and voter revolt. It has led to European nativism, white-worker backlash at liberalism, and the rise of alternative right movements in the USA and Europe. The world is in the middle of the largest wave of human displacement since the Second World War. More people are entering countries as new citizens, or staying as economic immigrants. Around the world, 65 million – including 21 million refugees – are on the move, forced from home by war, violence, economic deprivation and climate change. If they all came together, the group would be the size of the UK. Instead they are spread across the planet – putting pressure on national borders; straining budgets, infrastructure and social services; reshaping economies and communities; and affecting nations' sense of their own security. It is a global problem and demands a global response. The United States has said no. Italy emphasised the obligation of developed nations to resettle more migrants and refugees. Most European countries are rallying behind Italy.[9]

In Italy, and the rest of Europe, there are at least two schools of thought. One, it is a humanitarian duty to care for the new arrivals and they offer an economic opportunity, given the country's demographic decline. Another is that it leads to 'ethnic substitution', 'attempted Islamisation' and the likelihood of social clashes between poor Italians and immigrants.[10] One of the complexities is how immigrants are categorised. That categorisation affects the public attitude and sentiments towards them. Are they to be regarded as intellectual capital? Will indigenous people with nativism instincts accept them as citizens or talents if they have shared identity? Compare the trade-off policies of Canada and the USA. Canada has a successful immigrant population policy. In 2016, Canada admitted 320,000 newcomers, one of the highest per-capita immigration rates in the world, about three times higher than the United States. However, it is based on hard-headed policy. They are admitted purely on economic grounds based on a nine-point rubric that ignores race, religion, and ethnicity and instead looks at their age, job skills, language ability and other attributes that define their potential contribution to the national workforce. Consequently, the foreign-born immigrants are more educated, work harder, and create more business opportunities. In contrast, in the USA, about two-thirds of the immigrants are admitted under family reunification; 27 per cent have college degrees (in Canada, 50 per cent of new immigrants have college degrees); and immigrant children do not read at the same level in America as native-born children, whereas in Canada almost all the children do.[11]

Public discourse on migrants shapes public attitudes, opinions and behaviour. In the USA, the terms used for foreigners portray the politics of the country: 'illegal alien', 'undocumented worker', 'guest worker', or 'first generation émigré' all convey different status. American public discourses are partisan and polarising, and the tension between the liberals and conservatives is extremely toxic. Political and social discourses speak of waves of immigrants in terms of competition, particularly with the lower class and have-nots for jobs and resources. Transnational corporations, automation, globalisation, hard and soft technologies and corporacy controlled by conservative interest groups determine the immigrant issues in the USA.[12] In Eastern European countries, the national public discourse was against endemic corruption and the fecklessness of their traditional political parties. However, in the course of the refugee crisis, the national public discourse changed dramatically and included issues related to anti-migrants and anti-Muslims. Right-wing parties' discourses have introduced vicious divisiveness, and animated an angry voter base.

There are endless trade-off decisions to be made. Should they be given citizenship or be treated as economic entities? In the USA, only 54 per cent of the recent immigrants are naturalised citizens, with Latin American migrants at the lowest rate at 32 per cent. In the Gulf countries, there is a clean-cut policy – only Arabs are granted citizenship. All other ethnic groups are regarded on entry as economic digits, even if these workers have lived and worked there for three generations. The Gulf policy option is not to assimilate them as citizens. In all other ways there are opportunities for these foreigners to be entrepreneurs and economically well off. In the USA and Europe, immigrants work hard and are provided with ample economic opportunities. However, they are often seen as a threat to the non-white local-poor citizens who embrace the culture of poverty. In the USA, for example, the children are born out of wedlock, and suffer teenage pregnancy, absent fathers, crime, and welfare dependency. The white local-poor too have an identity crisis and consequently, the Open Society Foundation, a think tank, studied white working classes, the mostly poor whites, who suffered discrimination for the way they looked and dressed, not just in the USA but also in Europe. They studied how and why locals, in the USA and in Europe, are treated poorly in comparison to migrants and skilled foreigners. For example, many poor whites complain that the 'elite' care about ethnic minorities and gay people, but not about them.[13]

'Why can't we sell human rights (migration) the way we sell soap?' carries the trade-off debate between two views, as expressed by Mark Krikorian (migrants are threat to American way of life)[14] and Jason Riley (there is a case for an open border).[15] The 1965 Amendments to the US Immigration Act put the entire world's people on an equal footing in terms of immigration. The new law gave preference to those with a family member already living in the United States. Decades earlier, in the 1920s, America narrowed its gates to people from certain regions of the world by imposing quotas designed to preserve the balance of races in America. The trade-offs debate includes, will the immigrants take jobs away from American workers? Or will they fill jobs that American workers do not want anyway and that will stimulate the economy? Behind these economic issues is a more profound cultural question: Will these immigrants add healthy new strains to America's cultural inheritance, broadening and revitalising it? Or will they cause the country to break up into separate units, destroying unity? The hearts and minds issue is the tension between unity and diversity.[16]

Krikorian maintains that the most important long-term measure of success in immigration is assimilation. It should be patriotic assimilation – the identification with Americans as the immigrants' new country, converting membership from one's national community to membership to another. The problem posed presently is a practical one. Technology enables newcomers to retain ties to their homelands, even to the extent of living in both countries simultaneously. It is transnationalism, living in a way as not rooted in one nation but living across two or more nations. The second problem is a political one. Political elites in modern societies, particularly in western democracies, have come to devalue their own nation and culture, supporting an ideology of multiculturalism which rejects the idea of bonds (patriotic bonds), tying together all members of a society. The economic problem is a porous immigration policy for low-skilled workers. A loose labour market reduces the bargaining powers of the native-born whites, blacks (badly hit by low-skilled immigrants), and Hispanic Americans (largest number affected). In short, migrants are a threat to the American way of life and this has greatest adverse impact on the most disadvantaged native-born minorities.

On the other hand, Jason Riley argues that immigrants keep the workforce young and strong. They also generate economic activities and entrepreneurship, fill in the niches in the workforce, making the economy efficient, and allow upward mobility for the native population. In other words, immigrants tend to expand the economic pie, not displace native workers. Studies between 1991 and 2006 show that immigrants started 25 per cent of the US public companies. These companies employed some 220,000 people in the United States and boasted a market capitalisation of $500 billion. On the touchy subject of assimilation, Peter D. Salinas, author of *Assimilation: American Style*, states that the USA should pursue assimilation and not acculturation of migrants to the country. Acculturation is the adoption of a common culture. On the other hand, *Assimilation, American Style* sets out three simple precepts: (1) accept the English language as the national language; (2) expect to take pride in the American identity and its liberal democratic and egalitarian principles; and (3) live by Protestant ethics (self-reliant, hard-working and morally upright).[17]

Case study 8.2: trade-offs with China

What is the trade-off issue?

China asserts that the East and South China Seas belong to China, based on historical records, not international law, namely, the United Nation Convention on Law of the Sea (UNCLOS). China is pushing forth its great power identity, its China Dream to its people, and challenging the post-war US-led unipolar structure of global politics. Historically, since the 1970s, China has accepted US strategic leadership in Asia. China maintained this position as its trade-off for domestic development and growth for almost 40 years. It is now one of the largest, if not the largest, economy in the world. It has built up during those decades one of the largest military capabilities to be a dominant power. It now challenges the Asian regional order based on US primacy. Similarly, Russia, China, Iran, cannot contest the

United States globally but they can challenge it diplomatically and militarily as a regional power: Russia in Eastern Europe, China in East Asia and eventually perhaps Iran in the Middle East.[18] China's basic reflex is to remake the world according to its image, just as the USA did in past decades. Previously, the colonial powers foisted their brand of dominant political structures onto the rest of the world.

For the rest of the East Asian and South-East Asian nations, China's regional power projection is best seen in their respective responses and trade-offs to China's claims. The Asian nations' positions and policies are based on whether they are claimants or not, their domestic imperatives, their security and geopolitical interests, and their relationship with both China (the rising regional power) and the USA (the slow-fading unipolar power). The trade-off positions of the Asian nations can be grouped as follows: Vietnam and the Philippines' security and geopolitics are directly affected by China's 9-dash line ruling on the South China Sea limits, indicating the maritime waters and islands that China claims as its own; Malaysia and Brunei are also affected by the 9-dash line ruling but decided to maintain a low-key approach; Indonesia and Singapore are not claimants but are interested in upholding international law and freedom of navigation; and Laos, Myanmar, and Cambodia as peninsular nations are not directly affected by the 9-dash line ruling but share a common land border with China. In North-East Asia, it is South Korea, Japan and Taiwan; Japan and the Taiwan islands are within the 9-dash line and therefore claimed by China.

What is China's position in these trade-offs?

Historically, a China Dream is embedded in the Qin Empire (221 BC–206 BC) and continued under the Han Empire (206 BC–AD 220). During these dynastic empires, China made great cultural advances and expanded into several 'barbarian' peripheral nations. For a short period, China also expanded into the maritime peripheries, under Admiral Zheng He during the Ming Dynasty. The land-based 'barbarian' peripheries were Vietnam, Burma (Myanmar), Thailand, and Korea. The maritime disputes in the East China and South China Seas grow out of these historical narratives. China unilaterally drew 9-dash lines on the maritime maps to claim these seas coercively. There is a kind of law in the 'sea-jungle' that once an area is occupied by a claimant territory, the other nation has to fight to get back the territories. Thomas Mahnken maintains that China's strategic culture has three tenets: (1) China is culturally superior; (2) China's natural posture is that of the Middle Kingdom; and (3) China must be unified internally and be free from external meddling.[19]

The China Dream narrative is nationalism linked to its historical ambition and its people's economic and social expectations. China's nationalism lenses see these nations failing to respect China's core interests, and their collusion with external powers to undermine its core interests. At the turn of the twenty-first century, China faced a host of domestic issues, including the need to adjust its economic model (for example, from being export-oriented to being a consumption-led economy), serious environmental degradation, food-related scandals, and economic resource misallocation due to pervasive and widespread corruption. In per capita terms, China is not a rich country, ranking around 80th in the world, depending on the method of calculations. However, it is world's largest economy with an impressively expanding military and naval power. China has politically elevated the 9-dash line and the disputes in the East and South China Seas as 'core' territorial interests.

In its trade-off, ambition and nationalism shape the negotiation. China prefers bilateral discussions. China does not want the Association of Southeast Asian Nations (ASEAN) to stand united against it. Its trade-off strategy is to offer economic inducements to win the ASEAN countries over, while still unilaterally and coercively advancing its 9-dash line territorial claims. China uses two divide-and-rule tactics. First is to shift the South China Sea Code of Conduct (COC) into a low-level dialogue unconnected with the high-level strategic and economic discussions. Second is to find at least one pliant ASEAN member, usually Cambodia, to block any ASEAN initiative that China dislikes.[20] Nationalism seems to narrow its policy options but China has brilliantly widened that option by offering largesse to the cooperating nations and engaging domestic issues by tying all 'goodies' to its domestic interests – use Chinese capital, material and labour when building the railways and roads in these countries.

China is exceptionally generous to nations that support its hegemonic aspirations in East Asia. When Cambodia was ASEAN Chair in 2012, for the first time in ASEAN history, no final communiqué was produced as there was a dispute over how China should be represented in the joint statement. President Duterte put aside the Arbitration ruling that China had violated international law. The Philippines will be enjoying China's largesse of roads, railways and other investments that Cambodia and Laos are currently enjoying. Malaysia, a claimant country, for not pushing sovereignty issues in the South China Sea, received a similar infrastructural boost – China agreed to build a new deepwater port in Malacca, and a new railway line between Malacca and Kelantan, while its private sector have increased their investments, especially in Kuala Lumpur and Johor. China's Belt and Road Initiative (BRI) is an umbrella trade-off counterbalance, providing an avenue for the claimants to accept China's infrastructural and economic development while giving China predominance in the South China Sea. The BRI is also a grand geopolitical and geo-economics strategy to expand China's influence further afield, into Central Asia, the Middle East and Europe.

What is China's trade-off with the USA?

In East Asia, China's framing of its negotiating/trade-off posture is that the USA is required to recognise China as a great power in East Asia with equal rights, prerogatives and recognition of the paramount nature of China's interest. In return, China will offer peaceful cooperative relations, and avoid the 'Thucydides Trap' that awaits a weakening predominant power (USA) and a rising challenger (China). An up-and-coming rising power causes an established power to be afraid and this can escalate into war, as happened with Athens and Sparta. China maintains that any conflict that arises on maritime issues should be resolved only by the Asian parties directly involved and that non-state, non-Asian countries and international law have no role in bilateral relationships. The USA should also give up its alliances and bases in Asia and yield it strategic dominance to China.[21] Peter Dean and Greg Raymond, writing on strategic culture, see a similarity in Sun Tzu's art of war strategy and Thucydides Trap narrative. They quote Sun Tzu's, 'If you know the enemy and you know yourself, you need not fear the result of a hundred battles. If you know yourself but not the enemy, for every victory gained you will suffer a defeat.' Thucydides argued in not too dissimilar a vein that scrutinising the political and cultural differences of the ancient Greek city states was critical in understanding their motivations and behaviour during the Peloponnesian War.[22]

What is the US trade-off position?

The USA is not a claimant in the East or South China Seas. The USA has treated China as an equal partner and established strategic and economic dialogue with China. Although accused of partiality and hypocrisy, the USA stands out as a champion of the international law, UNCLOS. It is not a signatory (hence the hypocrisy). The USA has characterised China's policy and action as a threat to the freedom of navigation in international waters. The USA has reasserted its right to sail and fly in these international waters, and insisted on freedom of navigation and rule of law based on UNCLOS. It has developed a closer relationship with the ASEAN countries, even with Vietnam, where there is still deep resentment against the USA for the Vietnam War. In addition, it has strengthened relationships with Japan, South Korea, Australia, and India besides the ASEAN countries; it beefed up US forces in Guam and Hawaii; appointed a permanent US Ambassador to the ASEAN Secretariat in Jakarta, and increased US military strength in Asia despite budgetary pressures. The Chinese, on the other hand, maintain that a country that has no sea coast in the region, like the USA, does not have the freedom of navigation or flight in the South China Sea; there is no international water in the South China Sea, according to the Chinese scholar, Pan Guoping.[23]

China's trade-off with the Philippines

The Philippines' negotiating priorities are generally domestic. The strategic culture, according to Renato Cruz De Castro, is an emphasis on internal security, which is a reflection of the preference of the elites who have dominated Philippine local culture since independence in 1946. Despite the tensions with China over territories in the South China Sea, their preference is not to adopt a more outward-looking defence posture.[24] The Filipinos generally are admirers of the USA and dislike China. During President Gloria Macapagal Arroyo's leadership, the phrase 'what is ours is ours' position against China's encroachment on its territories struck a chord among ordinary Filipinos who are increasingly aware of Chinese assertiveness. President Benigno Aquino, who became president in 2010, took note of China's warnings and hostile activities since 2007 towards the other East Asian nations, for example, warning the oil companies BP and Exxon from working with Vietnam in offshore areas; creating a special province to administer maritime territorial claims; and tensions with the Indonesian Navy over the Natuna Islands. President Aquino decided to challenge China's 9-dash line territorial claims and facility building, taking it before the International Tribunal on the Law of the Sea (ITLS) in January 2013. The Arbitration ruled in favour of the Philippines and among the ruling it stated that China has no rights to construct artificial islands or reefs or shoals in the Exclusive Economic Zone (EEZ) of another country. The court found that Chinese actions violated the Philippines' sovereign rights under UNCLOS and by implication those of other states in analogous positions.[25]

President Rodrigo Duterte, elected in May 2016, made a radical change to the nation's foreign policy priorities, based on his domestic agenda. He wanted to end the scourge of drugs-related social ills and build the nation's inadequate infrastructure. He wanted other countries to support him in his domestic drive on drugs-related social issues. He did not want to be criticised for extrajudicial killings of drug dealers and criminals. Western countries, particularly the USA, did not support President Duterte's extrajudicial killings. Duterte decided to be pragmatic and acceded to China's request for bilateral negotiations and willingly abandoned former President Aquino's demand that China should abide strictly by the arbitration ruling. He wanted China's assistance to build a railway in Mindanao, to issue work permits for Filipinos currently working illegally in China, the cessation of Chinese citizens' involvement in the shipment and sale of narcotics, and non-interference with fishermen's activities in the South China Sea. All this made Duterte popular among his people and the people were prepared to forgo their pro-US sentiments to embrace China-led growth. In October 2016, President Duterte visited China with a delegation that included 400 businessmen, had US$24 billion of trade deal contracts signed, and Filipino fishermen are permitted to fish in Scarborough Shoal.

China's trade-off with Vietnam

The ultimate political challenge for Vietnam's leadership is how to take geopolitical advantage of a rising economic power without alienating and antagonising China, a challenge that it has been dealing with over 2,000 years.[26] Vietnam rejects China's trade-off position that the disputes are exclusively bilateral in nature. Vietnam's position is that it is simultaneously bilateral, multilateral and international. The Parcels Islands are the source of a bilateral dispute between China and Vietnam. The Spratly Islands is the source of a multilateral dispute involving Taiwan, Malaysia, the Philippines and Brunei, besides China and Vietnam. Issues such as maritime security, safety of navigation and freedom of navigation are international. As for

China's 9-dash line historical claims, newly available sources suggest that until 1914, the Qing Dynasty (1644–1912) maps did not even show the Parcels or the Spratlys. They only showed Hainan Island as China's southernmost island. In contrast, maps in Vietnam's possession indicate as early as the seventeenth century that the Nguyen Dynasty of Vietnam administered both the Parcels and the Spratly Islands and exploited their resources.[27]

Vietnam passed a marine law in 2012 to reiterate its territorial claims in the Parcels and Spratly Islands which China naturally said was illegal and invalid. China in response raised the administrative status of Sansha – a body to govern territorial claims in the South China Sea – from country to prefectural level. While China assured its peaceful intentions, Vietnam sees assertiveness in its actual actions. China's state-run media, for example, have warned Vietnam not to play tricks and urged it to recognise China's claims in the South China Sea. In Vietnam there is deep resentment against China and it takes little to generate widespread anti-China sentiments. In May 2014, when China sent an oil rig to explore for oil in the disputed areas, violent demonstrations erupted in Vietnam against China. The May 2014 incident also exposed the fissures within the Communist Party of Vietnam on the best way to deal with China. On one side were leaders who advocated a harder line against China and a closer relationship with the USA (despite deep 'scars' within the Communist Party over America's Vietnam atrocities), while another group favoured a closer relationship with China, given the geopolitical realities and the historical and ideological ties. Vietnam has embarked on five strategies: (1) hold regular talks with China at government, party and military levels; (2) push to implement the Code of Conduct; (3) 'internationalise' the problem through regional and international forums; (4) accelerate defence modernisation; and (5) sign strategic and comprehensive partnerships with a broad range of countries such as the USA, Japan, India and Russia.[28]

China's trade-off with Thailand, Laos, Myanmar and Cambodia

China has focused on economic inducements to bring these countries into a dependence relationship, and displaced or reduced US strategic influence. In Thailand after US laws forbade the sale of weapons and required sanctions in the wake of the military coups in 2006 and 2014, China stepped in with increased economic and military assistance and more recently, the building of rail and road infrastructure. Thailand is still wary of overdependence on China. Laos, north of Thailand, shares its northern borders with China, Burma and Vietnam; it is a landlocked country. Vietnam dominated Laos from 1975 to 1990. Laos is now influenced by China as China is its largest foreign aid donor. However, it has planned its trade-offs well: When Laos assumed in 2016 the Chair of ASEAN, it did not block reference to the South China Sea in the final communiqué. At the ASEAN summit, President Obama visited Laos, giving it international coverage and at the same summit, China's Premier cut the cake to mark the 25th anniversary of ASEAN-China dialogue. For a small and relatively poor country, Laos showed its fellow ASEAN neighbours what deft diplomacy could accomplish.[29]

Myanmar is similarly cautious with China's economic generosity. China covets Myanmar's energy, natural resources and location on the Bay of Bengal. China has built a gas pipeline project, Myitsone hydropower, from the Bay of Bengal to Kunming. There is also a strong ethnic nationalism that is not pro-China. Myanmar has a complex, unpredictable decision-making process. For a period, Myanmar suspended its Myitsone hydropower project that will supply 90 per cent of its electricity back to China; and it repaired its relationship with western powers, in particular, the USA. In 2013, President Thein Sein was hosted at the White House, and western nation sanctions against the country were lifted. While still heavily dependent on China, it has made counterbalance trade-off efforts such as Japanese investments to build dams, logistical and industrial complexes, and a partnership with Thailand and India. India is building the Kaladan Multi-modal Transit Transport Project that links the North-East Indian state of Mizoram with Sittwe deepwater port in Myanmar. Japan and Thailand are building the Dawei port project.

Cambodia's present successes are due to the shrewd leadership of Prime Minister Hun Sen, who started off as a Khmer Rouge cadre, defected to become a quisling ruler under the Vietnamese occupation of Cambodia, and when Vietnam was forced to leave, he fought and won the Cambodian elections. Hun Sen switched his allegiance to China after the Vietnamese forces left, to increase Cambodia's geopolitical space vis-à-vis its traditional rivals of Thailand and Vietnam. Because it single-handedly blocked the ASEAN joint communiqué reference to China and the South China Sea arbitral ruling in 2012, Cambodia has received generous assistance from China. China has invested in its agriculture, mining, infrastructure projects, hydro-power dams and garment production.[30]

China's trade-off with Malaysia and Brunei

Malaysia and Brunei, as direct claimants, have taken different approaches to the dispute, compared to Vietnam or the Philippines. Malaysia claims 12 atolls and occupies five in the South China Sea. Both countries have downplayed tensions with China, in contrast to Vietnam and the Philippines. They are strong proponents of ASEAN's approach to the Code of Conduct on the South China Sea. Malaysia prefers to seek trade and investments and infrastructural support from China. China has agreed to build a deepwater port in the state of Malacca, which meets China's vested interest in the busy Malacca Straits. It is building a railway link between the states of Malacca and Kelantan, where it is building another port facing the South China Sea. Brunei has agreed to strengthen cooperation between their state-owned energy companies and explore joint explorations of oil and gas resources.

China's trade-off position with Indonesia

Neatly framing the issue, Indonesia states that it is not a claimant to the territorial disputes even though some of the islands are within China's 9-dash line territorial ambition. Indonesia's Natuna Islands contain significant reserves of natural gas. Nonetheless, it took action to assert that the 9-dashed line was incompatible with UNCLOS, increased its military presence on the Natuna Islands and has redrawn the map on the Natunas, a signal to China that it will uphold Indonesian sovereignty rights. It detained Chinese fishermen who operated illegally in the Natuna Exclusive Economic Zone (EEZ). China has not taken its claims off the table but has focused on economic inducements such as building rail infrastructure between key Indonesian cities. As in the other ASEAN countries, China's actions have led to an increase in Indonesian military spending, especially in strengthening air and maritime patrols, and naval capabilities (including submarines) with the help of the USA, Japan, Russia, India and other countries.

China's trade-off position with Singapore

While not a claimant, Singapore shares Indonesia's concerns over the legal status of the 9-dash line. It challenges the validity of the 9-dash line and is a strong advocate for the Code of Conduct. Singapore has actively facilitated the US military presence in Asia by regularly hosting visits by US ships and aircraft. In its trade-off position with China, Singapore as a small nation punches above its weight by cultivating soft power such as the respect for good governance, economic development, efficient stability of its institutions and skilful diplomacy.[31] Singapore has trained well over 200,000 Chinese mid-career civil servants, is one of the largest foreign investors, and plays a contributory role in China's development, a contrast to other countries that are dependent on China's largesse.

China's trade-off position with South Korea, Japan and Taiwan

China has no outstanding territorial disputes with South Korea but is keen to wean it from the USA and to displace the US presence in North Asia. It has focused on economic inducements. China has strengthened relations with South Korea, offered a bilateral free trade agreement, increased cross-border tourism and economic benefits, and pledged to push North Korean denuclearisation. However, when it became obvious that China was paying lip service to North Korea's denuclearisation, and continued to permit sufficient trade and investments to sustain North Korea, the South Korean government questioned China's role as an honest broker and effective manager of regional safety. South Korea allowed the USA to station THAAD missiles and began to rebuild security cooperation with Japan.

Japan and China are claimants to the disputed Senkaku/Diaoyu Islands. China cites the 1943 Cairo and the 1945 Potsdam declarations which revoked the Imperial Japanese government's sovereignty over territory it seized. Japan, on the other hand, quotes the 1952 San Francisco Peace Treaty under which the USA gained administrative control over the Senkaku/Diaoyu Islands which it then transferred to Japan under the 1972 US-Japan Reversion Agreement. In their trade-off postures, both countries are constrained by domestic lobbying groups. While placating international critics, the governments are also mindful of the nationalist backlash back home.[32] In their trade-off positions, China pursues its relationship with these countries within its ambitious China Dream and its BRI building infrastructure. Japan's desire is to counterbalance with almost similar support for infrastructure needs for these countries. It enhances Japan's economic and geopolitical interests, ensures US-Japan security cooperation, and keeps the USA firmly engaged in the region. In the minds of the Japanese policy-makers, the disputes in the South China Sea and the East China Sea are inextricably linked.[33]

Taiwan was the first country to claim sovereignty over several islands in the South China Sea soon after Japan's withdrawal from the islands at the end of the Second World War. Taiwan's position in the trade-off was undermined when the other South-East Asian countries adhered to the 'One China' policy. It has also to consider its domestic politics, as the cross-straits bilateral relationship with China is sensitive and divisive in Taiwanese politics. Taiwan has continued to maintain a cautious approach to cooperating with the PRC in terms of maritime boundary defence and joint development. Its policy-makers face a complicated dual challenge of protecting its interests without undermining thee cross-straits relationship with China or hampering its relations with the other claimants and the USA.[34]

Communication practices in trade-offs

Political scientist Harold Lasswell is often quoted on understanding complexities and controversies. In trade-off or negotiations involving changing attitudes, one must change the other party's opinion and that attempt requires communication. His famous line on knowing the other parties' opinion and attitude is: 'Who said what, to whom, and with what effect?'[35] In the 9-dash line issue, we have China's preference on 'Who said what, to whom, and with what effect?' in its bilateral negotiation with the respective Asian nation states. Other nation states prefer multilateral discussion, for example, within an ASEAN forum. The source, 'who', is the policy leader or nation initiating and making the policy overture. It is a complex situation as in the case of the Philippines. There were different policy leaders' responses – from Presidents Arroyo to Aquino and finally to Duterte who decided that domestic needs are better served by accepting the positive infrastructural support from China, despite deep negative public sentiments towards China among his people. To his credit, President Duterte was supported by the majority of his people as they accepted his trustworthiness, goodwill and dynamism as a leader. That helps as a factor in influencing the negotiation and trade-offs. In this political dictum, 'Who said what, to whom, and with what effect?', we see the final outcome which is 'with what effect' to the Philippines and to China. Policy leadership in this trade-off found the 'sweet spot' of winning the hearts and minds of its people.

Communication is trying to change attitudes. It involves convincing a person to relinquish one way of looking at the world (or part of the world) in exchange for another. What publics do with a message defines its effects. The effectiveness and effect of the policy message should be measurable at every step of the communication. There must be focus on the language of communication; one chooses words the receivers will feel jell with their needs and wants, fits with their frames of reference and images of national good (Walter Lippmann calls it the 'pseudo-environment'). In addition, there is the significance in repetition and consistency of the policy messages, making sure that it gets through, and stays to change opinion. Repetition increases the chances of accomplishing this goal. Chinese President Xi Jinping repeated his message on the Belt and Road Initiative at several international platforms on the infrastructure support China could provide nations under this policy politics. That resonated well with several of the South China Sea claimants. In this dictum, the source ('who', the policy leader) has to demonstrate power, competence, trustworthiness and idealism. 'Who' speaks on behalf of the entity is important, with the avoidance of jargon and obfuscation. It is for the leader to reduce discrepancies that exist within their own cognitive system.[36]

What about communication and the complex issue of migrant issues? One communication discussion is to focus on assimilation and integration. A picture of communication success is neatly captured in an Ireland case study. Irish voters chose Leo Varajhar as its new prime minister, who at 38 is not only unusually young, but also of immigrant stock (Indian ethnicity) and openly gay. Ireland used to be a homogeneous country where the Catholic Church was powerful and religiously conservative especially on the issue of sexuality. Ireland's success in assimilation is the communication strategy adopted to change public attitudes towards undesirable (immigrants) and conservative Christians' attitude towards lesbian, bisexual, gay and transsexual groups. Ireland's campaign was all about the person, not policy. The campaign consultants decided that everyone knows someone who is gay, and everyone recognises the importance of love. The campaigners started with the personal and then moved to the bigger picture of Ireland's desire to be a modern, pluralistic European country. People vote for the personal not the global; that was the lesson.[37] This focus on the person is supported in health campaigns of opinion and behavioural change. Finding the right message is central to the campaign and extremely important. The message, however, is almost always about personal change rather than social change, institutional accountability, or collective action.[38]

In the communication process, agenda setting encourages the media to focus and shape the debate on policy issues. Priming is the community organising, the activism, and the social marketing activities. Media advocacy understands and responds to problems as social issues rather than as personal problems. It is finding the source, the person, the group that have the power to articulate the message for the media. Policy battles are long and contentious and it is important to make use of the media to keep the issue on the media agenda. News media generally focus on the plight of the individual whereas policy advocates emphasise social conditions that create victims. The challenge is to present the story to journalists, and bloggers, with varied story elements that make it easier for them to tell the story from the people and policy perspective. The communication challenge is to frame and reframe from episodic to thematic frames, to position individuals or events in broader contexts that matter to readers and viewers.

Conclusion: complexity, hurts and minefields

In the twenty-first century, public policies operate in a capitalist market system which is good at creating wealth and innovations but not good at assigning non-economic values and distributing social or economic justice. That is where governments fill the gap. They play a role in problem definition, equity and trade-off issues. Migration, for example, is still a complex, emotional public policy that has led to the rise of nationalism and voter revolt, leading to Brexit, European nativism, white-worker backlash at liberalism and the rise of alternative right movements in the USA and Europe. In each country, each regional dialogue and international discussion, the trade-off is taking place; trying to change attitudes of citizens left behind by forces such as technological changes. It involves fair distribution of wealth (the left leaning, socialist policy) but faces resistance from strong lobbying of the marketplace dynamics. It is convincing citizens to relinquish one way of looking at the world (or part of the world) in exchange for another.

Another case study of trade-off is China's growth as a regional power and stamping its presence in the East China and South China Seas based on its 9-dash lines, which represent its historical rights. Present international laws do not count. It is the unilateral historical claims of global reach and the exercise of soft power that have their own unique characteristics. Take, for example, Hong Kong. Pundits said Hong Kong's return to China in 20 years' time would revolutionise China. Instead 20 years later, China is remaking Hong Kong in its own image: bullying the local press, silencing dissent, dousing hopes for real elections, teaching patriotic values, and buying subservience with pledges of swelling bank accounts to justify this 'Chinafication'.[39]

The trade-off in territorial disputes in the East China and South China Seas can be seen from the perspective of Hedley Bull's *The Anarchical Society*.[40] In an anarchical system, a mediating power could negotiate with another power to establish sustainable order, providing a way to manage their relationship peacefully. Bull maintains that every international system can be analysed in the context of cooperation and regulated intercourse among nation states. Each nation state seeks the sweet spot of common grounds with a dominating power (China), finding common grounds among themselves (ASEAN), and accommodating an existing global power in the region (the USA) that seems more benign than the up-and-coming regional dominant power. One advantage for the parties concerned is that China as a trade-off for its assertiveness is also providing a badly needed economic, financial and infrastructural boost to many of these South-East Asian nations.

Notes

1 Shawn Donnan, 'A political trade-off', *Financial Times*, 23 September 2016, p. 9.
2 C. Wright Mills, *The Sociological Imagination*, 40th anniversary edn (Oxford: Oxford University Press, 2000).

3 Deborah Stone, *Policy Paradox: The Art of Political Decision Making* (New York: W. W. Norton & Company, 2002).

4 Martin Wolf, 'Donald Trump and the surrendering of US leadership', *Financial Times*, reproduced in *Straits Times*, 1 June 2017.

5 Reimut Zohlnhofer and Friedbert W. Rub (eds), *Decision-Making under Ambiguity and Time-Constraints: Assessing the Multiple Streams Framework* (Colchester: ECPR Press, 2016).

6 Kurt Finsterbusch, *Taking Sides: Clashing Views on Social Issues*, 16th edn (New York: McGraw-Hill, 2011).

7 Christopher Jencks, 'Does inequality matter?' *Daedalus*, special issue on equality, 131(1) (2002): 49–65.

8 Chu Mui Hoong, 'The guilt of shopping at Amazon', *Straits Times*, 29 July, 2017.

9 Anthony J. Blinken, 'A ban is our loss', *New York Times*, international edn, 7 June 2017, p. 11.

10 James Politi, 'Migration opens door to Italy's populists', *Financial Times*, 7 August 2017, p. 7.

11 Jonathan Tepperman, 'Canada's ruthlessly smart immigration policy', *New York Times*, international edn, 29 June 2017, p. 11.

12 William Roth and Susan J. Peters, *The Assault on Public Policy* (New York: Columbia University Press, 2014).

13 Simon Kuper, 'Poor, white and no longer forgotten', *Financial Times*, Life and Arts, 17–18 December 2016, p. 2.

14 Mark Krikorian, *The New Case Against Immigration: Both Legal and Illegal* (New York: Sentinel, 2008).

15 Jason L. Riley, *Let Them In: The Case for Open Borders* (New York: Gotham Books, 2008).

16 Finsterbusch, *Taking Sides*.

17 Peter D. Salinas, *Assimilation, American Style* (New York: Basic Books, 1997).

18 Hugh White, 'War and order: thinking about military force in international affairs', in Nicolas Farrelly, Amy King and Michael Wesley (eds), *Muddy Boots and Smart Suits: Researching Asia Pacific Affairs* (Singapore: ISEAS Publishing, 2017).

19 Thomas Mahnken, *Secrecy and Stratagem: Understanding Chinese Strategic Culture* (Double Bay, Sydney: Lowy Institute for International Policy, 2011).

20 David Arase, *The Geopolitics of Xi Jinping's Chinese Dream: Problems and Prospects* (Singapore: ISEAS/Yusof Ishak Institute, 2016).

21 Ibid.

22 Peter J. Dean and Greg Raymond, 'Strategic culture in the Asia Pacific: putting policy in context', in Nicolas Farrelly, Amy King and Michael Wesley (eds), *Muddy Boots and Smart Suits: Researching Asia Pacific Affairs* (Singapore: ISEAS Publishing, 2017).

23 Denny Roy, 'The United States and the South China Sea', in Ian Storey and Lin Cheng-yi (eds), *The South China Sea Dispute: Navigating Diplomatic and Strategic Tensions* (Singapore: ISEAS Publishing, 2014), pp. 228–246.

24 Renato Cruz De Castro, 'Philippines' strategic culture: continuity in the face of changing regional dynamics', *Contemporary Security Policy*, 35(2) (2014): 246–249.

25 Arase, *Geopolitics of Xi Jinping's Chinese Dream*.

26 Kishore Mahbubani and Jeffery Sng, *The ASEAN Miracle: A Catalyst for Peace* (Singapore: Ridge Books, 2017).

27 Hoang Anh Tuan, 'A Vietnamese perspective on the South China Sea dispute', in Ian Storey and Lin Cheng-yi (eds), *The South China Sea Dispute: Navigating Diplomatic and Strategic Tensions* (Singapore: ISEAS Publishing, 2014), pp. 186–204.

28 Ian Storey, 'Rising tensions in the South China Sea: Southeast Asian responses', in Ian Storey and Lin Cheng-yi (eds), *The South China Sea Dispute: Navigating Diplomatic and Strategic Tensions* (Singapore: ISEAS Publishing, 2014), pp. 134–160.

29 Mahbubani and Sng, *ASEAN Miracle*.

30 Ibid.

31 *Straits Times*, 'Balancing pragmatism and principle', Editorial, 7 July 2017, p. A23.

32 Joan Beaumont, 'History, conflict and contexts: remembering World War II in Asia', in Nicolas Farrelly, Amy King and Michael Wesley (eds), *Muddy Boots and Smart Suits: Researching Asia Pacific Affairs* (Singapore: ISEAS Publishing, 2017), pp. 95–109.

33 Yoichiro Sato, 'Japan and the South China Sea dispute: a stakeholder's perspective', in Ian Storey and Lin Cheng-yi (eds), *The South China Sea Dispute: Navigating Diplomatic and Strategic Tensions* (Singapore: ISEAS Publishing, 2014), pp. 74–103.

34 Anne Hsiu-an and Cheng-yi Lin, 'Taiwan's evolving policy toward the South China Sea dispute, 1992–2016', in Ian Storey and Lin Cheng-yi (eds), *The South China Sea Dispute: Navigating Diplomatic and Strategic Tensions* (Singapore: ISEAS Publishing, 2014), pp. 272–290.

35 Harold Lasswell, 'The structure and function of communication in society', in Lyman Bryson (ed.), *The Communication of Ideas* (New York: Harper & Row, 1948), pp. 37–51.

36 Doug Newsom, Judy VanSlyke Turk and Dean Kruckeburg, *This Is PR: The Realities of Public Relations*, 7th edn (Belmont, CA: Wadsworth/Thomson Learning, 2000).

37 Gillian Tett, 'Politics and the power of the personal', *Financial Times*, 1–2 July 2017, p. 8.

38 Lory Dorman and Lawrence Wallack, 'Putting policy into health communication: the role of media advocacy', in Ronald E. Rice and Charles K. Atkin (eds), *Public Communication Campaigns*, 4th edn, (London: SAGE, 2013), pp. 335–348.

39 William Pesek, 'Beijing remaking Hong Kong in its image', *Straits Times*, Opinion, 4 July 2017, p. A25.

40 Hedley Bull, *The Anarchical Society: A Study of Order in World Politics* (London: Macmillan Publishers Limited, 1977).

REFERENCES

Accetti, Carlo Invernizzi, 'The French elections and Europe's new normal: a choice between open and closed', *Foreign Affairs Today*, 25 April 2017.

Acemoglu, Daron and Robinson, James A., *Why Nations Fail: The Origins of Power, Prosperity and Poverty*, Crown Business, New York, 2012.

Acheson, Dean, *Present at the Creation: My Years in the State Department*, W. W. Norton and Company, New York, 1987.

Adams, Carey, Berquist, Charlene, Dillion, Randy and Galanes, Gloria, 'Public dialogue as communication activism', in Lawrence R. Frey and Kevin M. Carragee (eds), *Communication Activism: Communication for Social Change*, Hampton Press Inc., Cresskill, NJ, 2007.

Agence News Presse/*The Kathmandu Post*, 'Bus mafia controlling Nepal's transport', 17 April 2017.

Alinsky, Saul D., *Rules for Radicals: A Pragmatic Primer for Realistic Radicals*. Random House, New York, 1971.

Allen, Danielle, 'Defend America the indivisible', *Washington Post*, reproduced in *Straits Times*, 13 January 2017.

Amar, Paul, 'Turning the gendered politics of the security state inside out? Charging the police with sexual harassment in Egypt', *International Feminist Journal of Politics Issue*, 13(3) (2011): 299–328.

Anderlini, Jamil, 'The return of Mao', *Financial Times*, Weekend, Arts and Society, 1–2 October 2016.

Andreasen, Alan, *Marketing Social Change: Changing Behaviour to Promote Health, Social Development, and the Environment*, Jossey-Bass Publishers, San Francisco, 1995.

Arase, David, *The Geopolitics of Xi Jinping's Chinese Dream: Problems and Prospects*, ISEAS/Yusof Ishak Institute, Singapore, 2016.

Authers, John, 'Unnatural calm sparks visions of a "Minsky Moment"', *Financial Times* Weekend, 31 December/1 January 2017.

Axelrod, Robert, *The Evolution of Cooperation*, Basic Books, New York, 1984.

Bagehot, 'Tony Blair is right on Brexit. Now he should get into the trenches or back off', Bagehot's notebook, *The Economist*, 17 February 2017.

Ball, Philip, *Critical Mass: How One Thing Leads to Another*, Heinemann, London, 2004.

Bandura, Albert, *Social Foundation of Thought and Action*, Prentice Hall, Englewood Cliffs, NJ, 1986.

Barber, Lionel, 'The year of the demagogue', *Financial Times*, 17–18 December 2016.

Barber, Lionel, Sevastopulo, Demetri and Gett, Gillian, 'The imperious presidency', *Financial Times*, 3 April 2017.

Barber, Peter, 'In reshaping presidency, Trump has changed, too', *New York Times* international edn, 2 May 2017, p. 1.

Barker, Alex, 'EU negotiators steeled for Brexit crisis after UK election', *Financial Times*, 8 June 2017.

Bayuni, Endy, 'Jokowi turns to Islam-nationalism to preserve Indonesia's diversity', *The Jakarta Post*, Indonesia, reproduced in *Straits Times*, 15 April 2017.

Beaumont, Joan, 'History, conflict and contexts: remembering World War II in Asia', in Nicolas Farrelly, Amy King and Michael Wesley (eds), *Muddy Boots and Smart Suits: Researching Asia Pacific Affairs*, ISEAS Publishing, Singapore, 2017.

Beck, Ulrich, *The Reinvention of Politics: Rethinking Modernity in the Global Social Order*, Polity Press, Cambridge, 1997.

Berlo, David K., *The Process of Communication*, Holt, Rinehart and Winston, New York, 1960.

Berry, Jerry, 'Citizens groups and the changing nature of interests groups politics in America', *The Annals of the American Academy of Political and Social Sciences*, 528(1) (1993).

Bershidsky, Leonid, 'The West's biggest problem is dwindling trust', *Bloomberg View*, reproduced in *Straits Times*, Opinion, 13 January 2017.

Best, Joel (ed.), *Images of Issues; Typifying Contemporary Social Problems*, Aldine De Gruyter, New York, 1995.

Biao, Teng, '"A hole to bury you": a first-hand account of how China's police treat the citizens it's supposed to serve and protect', *Wall Street Journal*, Opinion Asia, 28 December 2010.

Blau, Rosie, 'Chinese society: the new class war', *The Economist*, 9 July 2016.

Blinken, Anthony J., 'A ban is our loss', *New York Times*, international edn, 7 June 2017.

Bond, David, 'Social media groups defend record on hate content', *Financial Times*, 5 June 2017.

Brader, Ted, *Campaigning for Hearts and Minds*, University of Chicago Press, Chicago, 2006.

Bromwich, Jonah Engel, 'The America right's new, young and vocal media star', *New York Times*, international edn, 6 December 2016.

Buchanan, James and Tullock, Gordon, *The Calculus of Consent*, University of Michigan Press, Ann Arbor, MI, 1962.

Bull, Hedley, *The Anarchical Society: A Study of Order in World Politics*, Macmillan Publishers Limited, London, 1977.

Cappella, Joseph N., 'Research methodology in communications: review and commentary', in Brent Rubin (ed.), *Communication Yearbook 1*, Transaction Books, New Brunswick, NJ, 1977, pp. 37–54.

Chassany, Anne-Sylvaine, 'Inside the French far-right's laboratory town', *Financial Times*, Big Read, 17 April 2017.

Chaturvedi, Swati, *I am a Troll: Inside the Secret World of the BJP's Digital Army*, Juggernaut Publications, New Delhi, 2017.

Cheng, Calvin, 'The Population White Paper: time to revisit an unpopular policy?', *Straits Times*, 9 January 2017.

Cheng, Rachel, 'Why 6.9m was too much information: major policy shifts eclipsed by uproar over population projection', *Straits Times*, 16 February 2013.

Chin, Yolanda, Pavlovska, Nadica and Vasu, Norman, 'An immigration bonus for Singaporeans? Making the foreigners more acceptable', Rajaratnam School of International Relations, No. 145/2012, 7 August 2012.

Clegg, Nick, *Politics: Between the Extremes*, The Bodley Head, London, 2016.

Cobb, R. W. and Elder, C. D., *Participation in American Politics: The Dynamics of Agenda Setting*, Johns Hopkins University Press, Baltimore, MD, 1972.

Cohen, Bernard, *The Press and Foreign Policy*, Princeton University Press, Princeton, NJ, 1963.

Cohen, Roger, 'Trump's Chinese foreign policy', *New York Times*, international edn, 17–18 December 2017, p. 13.

Conklin, Jeff, *Dialogue Mapping: Building Shared Understanding of Wicked Problems*, John Wiley & Sons Ltd, Chichester, 2005.

Conklin, Jeff, 'Paper on wicked problems and social complexity', available at: www. cognexus.org, 2010.

Considine, Mark, *Making Public Policy: Institutions, Actors, Strategies*, Polity Press, Cambridge, 2005.

Converse, Philip, 'The nature of belief systems in mass publics', in David E. Apter (ed.), *Ideology and Discontent*, Free Press, New York, 1964.

Cook, Clive, 'The Republican healthcare paradox', *Financial Times*, 3 August 2009.

Crawford, Craig, *Attack the Messenger: How Politicians Turn You Against the Media*, Rowman & Littlefield, Lanham, MD, 2006.

De Castro, Renato Cruz, 'Philippines' strategic culture: continuity in the face of changing regional dynamics', *Contemporary Security Policy*, 35(2) (2014): 246–249.

Dean, Peter J. and Raymond, Greg, 'Strategic culture in the Asia Pacific: putting policy in context', in Nicolas Farrelly, Amy King and Michael Wesley (eds), *Muddy Boots and Smart Suits: Researching Asia Pacific Affairs*, ISEAS Publishing, Singapore, 2017.

Delgado, Gary, *Beyond the Politics of Place*, Oakland, CA: Applied Research Center, 1997.

Dervin, Brenda and Foreman-Wernet, Lois, 'Sense-making methodology as an approach to understanding and designing for campaign audiences', in Roland E. Rice and Charles K. Atkin (eds), *Public Communication Campaigns*, 4th edn, SAGE, London, 2013.

Donnan, Shawn, 'A political trade-off', *Financial Times*, 23 September 2016.

Dorman, Lory and Wallack, Lawrence, 'Putting policy into health communication: the role of media advocacy', in Roland E. Rice and Charles K. Atkin (eds), *Public Communication Campaigns*, 4th edn, SAGE, London, 2013, pp. 335–348.

Dye, Thomas R., *Understanding Public Policy*, 11th edn, Pearson Prentice Hall, Englewood Cliffs, NJ, 2008.

Elliott, Euel and Kiel, L. Douglas, *Non-linear Dynamics: Complexity and Public Policy*, Nova Science Publishers, New York, 1999.

Erlanger, Steven and Kanter, James, 'Plan to distribute migrants strains limits of European unity', *New York Times*, international edn, 24 November 2015, p. 5.

Everett, Burgess, Haberkorn, Jennifer and Dawsy, Josh, 'Trump knocks House health care bill as too harsh', available at: Politico.com, 13 June 2017 www.politico.com/story/2017/06/01/trump-urge-gop-senate-repeal-obamacare-239504.

Eyal, Jonathan, 'Europe yet to realise how badly Brexit will hurt', *Straits Times*, 12 September 2016.

Farrelly, Nicolas, King, Amy and Wesley, Michael (eds), *Muddy Boots and Smart Suits: Researching Asia Pacific Affairs*, ISEAS Publishing, Singapore, 2017.

Fasman, Jon, 'Jokowi's moment', *The Economist*, Special Report on Indonesia, 27 February 2016.

Feldman, Noah, 'Rule of law: 1, president's immigration order: 0', *Bloomberg*, reproduced in *Straits Times*, Opinion, 31 January 2017. p. A22.

Ferguson Devereaux, Sherry, *Researching the Public Opinion Environment: Theories and Methods*, SAGE, Thousand Oaks, CA, 2000.

Festinger, Leon, 'The theory of cognitive dissonance', in Wilbur Schramm (ed.), *The Science of Human Communications*, Basic Books, New York, 1963.

Fiest, Sam, 'Foreword', in Robert Fine, *The Big Book of Social Media: Case Studies, Stories, Perspectives*, Yorkshire Publishing, Goole, 2010.

Fine, Gary Alan and Turner, Patricia A., *Whispers on the Color Line: Rumors and Race in America*, University of California Press, Berkeley, CA, 2001.

Finsterbusch, Kurt, *Taking Sides: Clashing Views on Social Issues*, 16th edn, McGraw-Hill, New York, 2011.

Friedman, Thomas, *Lexus and the Olive Tree*, Anchor Books, New York, 2000.

Frizell, Sam, 'President Trump's toughest sales pitch was to his own party', *Time*, 1 March 2017.

Fukuyama, Francis, 'The emergence of a post-fact world', Project Syndicate, reproduced in *Straits Times*, Opinion, 28 December 2017, p. A22.

Gapper, John, 'China's internet is flourishing inside the Wall', *Financial Times*, 24 November 2016.

Goodhart, David, *The Road to Somewhere: The Populist Revolts and the Future of Politics*, C. Hurst & Co, London, 2017.

Graeber, David, *Debt: The First 5,000 Years*, Melville House Publishing, New York, 2011.

Green, Joshua, 'Jim Messina has a president to sell', *Bloomberg BusinessWeek*, 18–24 June 2012.

Hart, Roderick P., 'Politics in the digital age: a scary prospect', in Travis N. Ridout (ed.), *New Directions in Media and Politics*, Routledge, New York, 2013.

Ho, Kwon Ping, 'The rise of China's new money elite', *Straits Times*, 25 August 2010.

Horn, James, *Human Research and Complexity Theory*, John Wiley & Sons, Chichester, 2008.

Hornik, Robert C., 'Why can't we sell human rights like we sell soap?', in Ronald E. Rice and Charles K. Atkin, *Public Communication Campaigns*, 4th edn, SAGE, London, 2013, pp. 35–52.

Hsiu-an, Anne and Cheng-yi Lin, 'Taiwan's evolving policy toward the South China Sea dispute, 1992–2016', in Ian Storey and Lin Cheng-yi, (eds), *The South China Sea Dispute: Navigating Diplomatic and Strategic Tensions*, ISEAS Publishing, Singapore, 2014.

Hui, Yew-Foong (ed.), *Encountering Islam: The Politics of Religious Identities in Southeast Asia*, ISEAS Publishing, Singapore, 2013.

Hunt, Albert R., 'Obama wins traction for health plan', *International Herald Tribune*, 17 August 2009.

Ingram, Helen M. and Mann, Dean E. (eds), *Why Policies Succeed or Fail*, SAGE Publications, Beverly Hills, CA, 1980,

Innes, Judith Eleanor, *Knowledge and Public Policy: The Search for Meaningful Indicators*, Transaction Publishers, New Brunswick, NJ, 1990.

Jencks, Christopher, 'Does inequality matter?', *Daedalus*, special issue on equality, 131(1) (2002).

John, Peter, *Making Public Policy*, Routledge, London, 2011.

Johnson, Hank, 'Social movements and old regional nationalists', in Enrique Larana, Hank Johnston and Joseph R Gusfield (eds), *New Social Movements: From Ideology to Identity*, Temple University Press, Philadelphia, PA, 1994.

Kahin, Audrey, 'Natsir and Sukarno: their clash over nationalism, religion and democracy, 1928–1958', in Hui Yew-Foong (ed.), *Encountering Islam: The Politics of Religious Identities in Southeast Asia*, ISEAS Publishing, Singapore, 2013.

Kampfner, John, 'Twitter joke trial: for Paul Chambers common sense has finally prevailed', *Guardian*, Opinion, 27 July 2012.

Kandall, Diana, *Framing Class: Media Representatives of Wealth and Poverty in America*, Rowman & Littlefield Publishers, Lanham, MD, 2005.

Kaseem, Maye, *Egyptian Politics: The Dynamics of Authoritarian Rule*, Lynne Rienner Publishers, Boulder, CO, 2004.

Kay, Adrian, *The Dynamics of Public Policy*, Edward Elgar, Cheltenham, 2006.

Kazmin, Amy, 'Cyberbullies shake Indian politics', *Financial Times*, 20 February 2017.

Kessler Andy, 'The markets tough love delivers', *Wall Street Journal*, 23 May 2017.

Kingdon, John, *Agendas, Alternatives and Public Policy*, Little Brown, Boston, 1984.

Klapper, Joseph T., *The Effects of Mass Communication*, Free Press, New York, 1960.

Klar, Samara, Robison, Joshua and Druckman, James, 'Political dynamics of framing', in Travis N. Ridout (ed.), *New Directions in Media and Politics*, Routledge, New York, 2013, pp. 183–192.

Klotz, Robert J., *The Politics of Internet Communication*, Rowman & Littlefield Publishers, Lanham, MD, 2004.

Koenig, Louis, *An Introduction to Public Policy*, Prentice Hall, Englewood Cliffs, NJ, 1986.

Kotler, Philip, *Marketing Management: Analysis, Planning, and Control*, Prentice Hall, Englewood Cliffs, NJ, 1967.

Kotler, Philip and Levy, S. J., 'Broadening the concept of marketing', *Journal of Marketing*, 33 (1969): 10–15.

Kotler, Philip and Zaltman, Gerald, 'Social marketing: an approach to planned social change', *Journal of Marketing*, 35 (1971): 3–12.

Krikorian, Mark, *The New Case Against Immigration: Both Legal and Illegal*, Sentinel, New York, 2008.

Krugman, Paul, 'The age of fake policy', *New York Times International*, Weekend, 7–8 January 2017.

Kuper, Simon, 'Poor, white and no longer forgotten', *Financial Times*, Life and Arts, 17–18 December 2016.

Kynge, James, Haddou, Leila and Peel, Michael, 'The pivot to Phnom Penh', *Financial Times*, 9 September 2016.

Ladd, Jonathan, 'The era of media distrust and its consequences for perceptions of political reality', in Travis N. Ridout (ed.), *New Directions in Media and Politics*, Routledge, New York, 2013.

Larana, Enrique, Johnston, Hank and Gusfield, Joseph (eds), *New Social Movements: From Ideology to Identity*, Temple University Press, Philadelphia, PA, 1994.

Lasswell, Harold D., 'The structure and function of communication in society', in Lyman Bryson (ed.), *The Communication of Ideas*, Harper & Row, New York, 1948.

Lee, Pearl and Yong, Charissa, 'New ways of reaching out: dialect for seniors and Facebook for young people', *Straits Times*, 27 November 2016.

Lieberman, Debra A., 'Designing digital games, social media, and mobile technologies to motivate and support health behavior change', in Ronald E. Rice and Charles K. Atkin, *Public Communication Campaigns*, 4th edn, SAGE Publications, Los Angeles, 2013.

Lilla, Mark, 'The end of identity liberalism', *New York Times*, international edn, 21 November 2016.

Lindblom, Charles E., 'The science of muddling through', *Public Administration Review*, 19 (Spring 1959).

Lindblom, Charles E., *Politics and Markets; The World's Political-Economic System*, Basic Books, New York, 1977.

Lippmann, Walter, *Public Opinion*, Free Press, New York, 1922.

Luce, Edward, 'On life support', *Financial Times*, FT Big Read: US Healthcare, 11 July 2017.

MacShane, Denis, *Brexit: How Britain Will Leave Europe*, I.B. Tauris & Co Ltd, London, 2015.

Mahbubani, Kishore and Sng, Jeffery, *The ASEAN Miracle: A Catalyst for Peace*, Ridge Books, Singapore, 2017.

Mahnken, Thomas, *Secrecy and Stratagem: Understanding Chinese Strategic Culture*, Lowy Institute for International Policy, Double Bay Sydney, 2011.

Mason, Mark (ed.), *Complexity Theory and Philosophy of Education*, Wiley-Blackwell, Chichester, 2008.

Mayer-Schonberger, Viktor, *Delete: The Virtue of Forgetting in the Digital Age*, Princeton University Press, Princeton, NJ, 2009.

McCombs, Maxwell, *Setting the Agenda: The Mass Media and Public Opinion*, Polity Press, Cambridge, 2004.

McGuire, William J., 'Persuasion, resistance, and attitude change', in Ithiel de Sola *et al.* (eds), *Handbook of Communications*, Rand McNally, Chicago, 1973.

McGuire, William J., 'Some internal psychological factors influencing consumer choice', *Journal of Consumer Research*, 2 (1976): 302–319.

McLuhan, Marshall, *Understanding Media: The Extension of Man*, 1964, available at: web.mit.edu/allanmc/www/mcluhan.mediummessage.pdf.

Mehta, Suketu, 'A Bombay strongman's lessons', *New York Times*, international edn, 7–8 January 2017.

Miller, Tom, *China's Asian Dream: Empire Building Along the Silk Road*, ZED Books, London, 2017.

Mills, C. Wright, *The Sociological Imagination*, 40th anniversary edn, Oxford University Press, Oxford, 2000.

Mingfu, Liu, *The China Dream: Great Power Thinking and Strategic Posture in the Post-American Era*, CN Times Books, New York, 2015.

Mitchell, Tom, 'The rise of party politics', FT Series: Xi's China, *Financial Times*, 26 July 2016.

Mitchell, Tom, 'Smothering dissent', *Financial Times*, FT Series: Xi's China, 28 July 2016.

Morris, Errol, 'The certainty of Donald Rumsfeld', available at: https://opinionator.blogs.nytimes.com/2014/03/25/the-certainty-of-donald-rumsfeld-part-1/?_r=0

Mozer, Paul and Scott, Mark, 'Friction over fiction on Facebook', *New York Times*, quoted in *Straits Times*, 20 November 2016, p. B9.

Naim, Moises, *The End of Power*, Basic Books, New York, 2013.

Nair, Basskaran, *A Primer on Public Relations Practice in Singapore*, Institute of Public Relations of Singapore/Print and Publish Pte Ltd, Singapore, 1986.

Nair, Basskaran, 'Transport lessons from Govt's housing policies', *Straits Times*, 19 May 2014.

Nair, Basskaran, 'Governance in wired world', *Business Times*, 12 July 2014.

Nayar, Pramod K. (ed.), *The New Media and Cybercultures Anthology*, Wiley-Blackwell, Oxford, 2010.

Neubeck, Kenneth J., Neubeck, Mary Alice and Glasberg, Davita Sifen, *Social Problems*, 5th edn, McGraw-Hill, New York, 2007.

Neustadt, Richard and May, Ernest, *Thinking in Time: The Uses of History for Decision-Makers*, Free Press, New York, 1986.

Newsom, Doug, Turk, Judy VanSlyke and Kruckeburg, Dean, *This Is PR: The Realities of Public Relations*, 7th edn, Wadsworth/Thomson Learning, Belmont, CA, 2000.

Nordenson, Jon, *Online Activism in the Middle East: Political Power and Authoritarian Governments from Egypt to Kuwait*, I.B. Tauris, London, 2017.

Obama, Barack, Address to Congress 9 September 2009, available at: https://web.archive.org/web/20100919222243/http://c-span.org/Transcripts/SOTU-2009-0909.aspx.

O'Brien, Elizabeth, 'ObamaCare repeal: what you need to know right now', *Time*, 17 January 2017.

Oliver, Richard L., 'A cognitive model of the antecedents and consequences of satisfaction decisions', *Journal of Marketing Research*, 17(4) (1980): 460–469.

Oskamp, Stuart, *Attitudes and Opinions*, Simon & Schuster, New York, 1977.

Page, Benjamin I. and Shapiro, Robert Y., *The Rational Public: Fifty Years of Trends in American's Policy Preferences*, University of Chicago Press, Chicago, 1992.

Paisley, William J., 'Public communications campaigns: the American experience', in Roland E. Rice and Charles K. Atkin (eds), *Public Communication Campaigns*, 4th edn, SAGE, London, 2013.

Pandjaitan, Luhut B., 'Indonesia may have a Trump card in the new America', *Straits Times*, Opinion, 18 January 2017.

Pasquier, Martial and Villeneuve, Jean-Patrick, *Marketing Management and Communications in the Public Sector*, Routledge, London, 2012.

Pesek, William, 'Beijing remaking Hong Kong in its image', *Straits Times*, Opinion, 4 July 2017, p. A25.

Peters, Guy, *Advanced Introduction to Public Policy*, Edward Elgar Publishing, Cheltenham, 2015.

Politi, James, 'Migration opens door to Italy's populists', *Financial Times*, 7 August 2016.

Politi, James, 'Italy antitrust chief urges EU to help beat fake news', *Financial Times*, 30 December 2016.

Poniewozik, James, 'The new TV reality: all Trump, all the time', *New York Times*, international edn, 15 December 2016.

Prochaska, J. O. and DiClemente, C. C., *The Transtheoretical Approach: Crossing Traditional Boundaries of Therapy*, Dow Jones-Irwin, Homewood, IL, 1984.

Rachman, Gideon, 'The unstoppable mass migration into Europe', *Financial Times*, 13 January 2016.

Rachman, Gideon, 'The crisis in Anglo-American democracy', *Financial Times*, reproduced in *Straits Times*, 24 August 2016.

Reuters, 'Hundreds protest at Chinese chemical factory', quoted in *Telegraph*, 4 April 2013.

Reuters, 'China's grip on online news, network providers tightens', reported in *Straits Times*, 3 May 2017.

Reuters, 'China toughens rules on private think-tanks in ongoing crackdown', quoted in *Straits Times*, 6 May 2017.

Ridout, Travis N., *New Directions in Media and Politics*, Routledge, New York, 2013.

Riley, Jason L., *Let Them In: The Case for Open Borders*, Gotham Books, New York, 2008.

Rittel, Horst W. and Webber, Melvin M., 'Dilemmas in a general theory of planning', *Policy Sciences*, 4 (1973): 155–169.

Robinson, Piers, *The CNN Effect: The Myth, Foreign Policy and Intervention*, Routledge, London, 2002.

Roe, Emery, *Narrative and Policy Analysis: Theory and Practice*, Duke University Press, Durham, NC, 1994.

Room, Graham, *Complexity, Institutions and Public Policy: Agile Decision-making in a Turbulent World*, Edward Elgar, Cheltenham, 2011.

Rose, Chris, *How to Win Campaigns: 100 Steps to Success*, Earthscan, London, 2008.

Roth, William and Peters, Susan J., *The Assault on Public Policy*, Columbia University Press, New York, 2014.

Roy, Denny, 'The United States and the South China Sea', in Ian Storey and Lin Cheng-yi (eds), *The South China Sea Dispute: Navigating Diplomatic and Strategic Tensions*, ISEAS Publishing, Singapore, 2014, pp. 228–246.

Salinas, Peter D., *Assimilation, American Style*, Basic Books, New York, 1997.

Sato, Yoichiro, 'Japan and the South China Sea dispute: a stakeholder's perspective', in Ian Storey and Lin Cheng-yi (eds), *The South China Sea Dispute: Navigating Diplomatic and Strategic Tensions*, ISEAS Publishing, Singapore, 2014, pp. 74–103.

Savirani, Amalinda and Tornquist, Olle (eds), *Reclaiming the State: Overcoming Problems of Democracy in Post-Soeharto Indonesia*, Penerbit PolGov, Yogyakarta, 2015.

Scanlon, Luke, 'Twitter and the law: 10 legal risks, out-law.com', *Guardian*, Network, 10 August 2012.

Schramm, Wilbur (ed.), *The Process and Effects of Mass Communication*, University of Illinois Press, Urbana, IL, 1955.

Sen, Krishna and Hill, Donald T. (eds), *Politics and the Media in Twenty-First-Century Indonesia: Decades of Democracy*, Routledge, London, 2011.

Setjadi, Charlotte, 'Big party politics and discontent of urban poor behind Jakarta unrest', *Straits Times*, 8 November 2016.

Sharma, Mihir, 'Indians need a nudge, not a shove, to go cashless', *Bloomberg View*, 18 February 2017.

Sharp, Steve, *Journalism and Conflict in Indonesia: From Reporting Violence to Promoting Peace*, Routledge, New York, 2013.

Shaw, Randy, *The Activist's Handbook: Winning Social Change in the 21st Century*, 2nd edn, University of California Press, Berkeley, CA, 2013.

Singapore Government White Paper, 'A sustainable population for a dynamic Singapore', available at: https://lkyspp.nus.edu.sg/wp-content/uploads/2013/12/LKYSPP-Case-Study_-Landuse-Case.pdf.

Skinner, B. F., *Beyond Freedom and Dignity*, Knopf, New York, 1971.

Smith, Harold J., 'Warped US political system run by big money', *Financial Times*, 5 July 2017.

So, Clement Y. K. and Chen, Joseph Man, *Press and Politics in Hong Kong: Cases from 1967 to 1997*, Hong Kong Institute of Asia-Pacific studies, The Chinese University of Hong Kong Press, Hong Kong, 1999.

Song, Jung-a, 'South Korean President Park Guen-hye offers to step down', *Financial Times*, 29 November 2016.

Spitzer, Robert J., *Media and Public Policy*, Praeger Publishers, New York, 1993.

Srinivasan, Ramesh, *Whose Global Village? Rethinking How Technology Shapes Our World*, New York University Press, New York, 2017.

Staples, Les, *Roots to Power: A Manual for Grassroots Organizing*, Praeger Publishers, New York, 2004.

Stone, Deborah, *Policy Paradox: The Art of Political Decision Making*, W. W. Norton & Company, New York, 2002.

Storey, Ian, 'Rising tensions in the South China Sea: Southeast Asian responses', in Ian Storey and Lin Cheng-yi (eds), *The South China Sea Dispute: Navigating Diplomatic and Strategic Tensions*, ISEAS Publishing, Singapore, 2014, pp. 134–160.

Storey, Ian and Cheng-yi, Lin (eds), *The South China Sea Dispute: Navigating Diplomatic and Strategic Tensions*, ISEAS Publishing, Singapore, 2014.

Straits Times, 'Worrying risk as Modi waves surges on', Editorial, 25 March 2017.

Straits Times, 'Balancing pragmatism and principle', Editorial, 7 July 2017.

Strangio, Sebastian, *Hun Sen's Cambodia*, Yale University Press, New Haven, CT, 2014.

Stroud Jomini, Natalie and Muddiman, Ashley, 'The system today: is the public fragmenting?', in Travis N. Ridout (ed.), *New Directions in Media and Politics*, Routledge, New York, 2013.

Sullivan, Margaret, 'It's time to retire the tainted term "fake news"', *Washington Post*, quoted in *Straits Times*, Opinion, 10 January 2017.

Suryadinata, Leo, 'Indonesia's ideological war', *Straits Times*, 2 December 2016, pA31.

Tan, Jeanette, 'Population White Paper triggers nationwide debate', Yahoo News, Year in Review, 27 November 2013, available at: https://sg.news.yahoo.com/-yir2013-population-white-paper-triggers-nationwide-debate-101840966.html.

Tan, Shin Bin and Low, Donald, 'Long-term land use and planning in Singapore', Lee Kuan Yew School of Public Policy case study, 2013 LKYSPP-Case-Study_-Landuse-Case.pdf.

Teo, Chee Hean, 'Opening speech at the parliamentary debate on Population White Paper', *Straits Times*, 4 February 2013.

Tepperman, Jonathan, 'Canada's ruthlessly smart immigration policy', *New York Times* international edn, 29 June 2017.

Tett, Gillian, 'Emerging markets offer clues for investors in 2017', *Financial Times*, 1 January 2017.

Tett, Gillian, 'Politics and the power of the personal', *Financial Times*, 1–2 July 2017.

Thaler, Richard H. and Sunstein, Cass R., *Nudge: Improving Decisions about Health, Wealth and Happiness*, Penguin Books, London, 2009.

The Economist, 'Special report, artificial intelligence', 25 June 2016.

The Economist, 'The upper Han: who is Chinese?', 19 November 2016.

Timothy, Nick, 'Why I have resigned as the Prime Minister's adviser', conservativehome, 6 June 2017, available at: www.conservativehome.com.

Tomlinson, John, *The Culture of Speed: The Coming of Immediacy*, SAGE Publications, London, 2007.

Truman, David B., *The Government Process*, Knopf, New York, 1954.

Tuan, Hoang Anh, 'A Vietnamese perspective on the South China Sea dispute', in Ian Storey and Lin Cheng-yi (eds), *The South China Sea Dispute: Navigating Diplomatic and Strategic Tensions*, ISEAS Publishing, Singapore, 2014, pp. 186–204.

Velloor, Ravi, 'Pied Piper of India's politics', *Straits Times*, Opinion, 17 March 2017.

Vinson, Danielle, C. 'Congress and the media: who has the upper hand?', in Travis N. Ridout (ed.), *New Directions in Media and Politics*, Routledge, New York, 2013.

Waldman, Katy, 'Trump's Tower of Babble: it may sound like gibberish, but there's an accidental brilliance to Trump's style of speech', *Slate Magazine*, 2 November 2016.

Webber, Edward P. and Khademian, Anne M., 'Wicked problems, knowledge challenges and collaborative capacity builders in network settings', *Public Administration Review*, 68(2), 2008.

Webster, Frank, *Theories of the Information Society*, Routledge, London, 2002.

Weinstein, N. D., 'The precaution adoption process', *Health Psychology*, 7 (1988): 255–386.

White, Hugh, 'War and order: thinking about military force in international affairs', in Nicolas Farrelly, Amy King and Michael Wesley (eds), *Muddy Boots and Smart Suits: Researching Asia Pacific Affairs*, ISEAS Publishing, Singapore, 2017.

Wiebe, G. D., 'Merchandising commodities and citizenship on television', *Public Opinion Quarterly*, 15(4) (1951): 670–691.

Wolf, Martin, 'The march to world disorder', *Financial Times*, 6 January 2017.

Wolf, Martin, 'Donald Trump and the surrendering of US leadership', *Financial Times*, reproduced in *Straits Times*, 1 June 2017.

World Bank Report 2016, 'China and Tibet', available at: www.hrww.org/world-report/2016/country-chapters/china-and-tibet.

Xuecan, Murong, 'Scaling China's firewall', *New York Times*, international edn, 18 August 2015.

Yeo, Denyse, 'Dr Liu Thai Ker: Singapore needs to plan for 10 million population', *The Peak*, 7 October 2014.

Zohlnhofer, Reimut and Rub, Friedbert W. (eds), *Decision-Making under Ambiguity and Time-Constraints: Assessing the Multiple Streams Framework*, ECPR Press, Colchester, 2016.

Zuckerman, Ethan, 'Cute cats to the rescue? Participatory media and political expression', 2013, available at: ethanzuckerman.com/papers/cutecats2013.pdf.

INDEX

0 1341 1716139 5